OWEN DUDLEY EDWARDS, FRS⅃, was

born in Dublin on 27 July 1938. His father Robert was a founder of modern Irish professional historiography, his mother Sheila a Gaelic scholar and social historian. He was a pupil at national schools, and then at Belvedere College and University College Dublin. He studied and taught History at the Johns Hopkins University in Baltimore, Maryland, USA, and subsequently taught at the University of Oregon, the University of Aberdeen, California State University at San Francisco, and the University of South Carolina, and from 1968 to 2005 at the University of Edinburgh where he is now an Honorary Fellow. He broadcasted for Radio Telefis Eireann, the BBC and various US and Canadian networks, and wrote for the *Irish Times*, the *Scotsman*, *Tribune*, the *New York Times*, the *Radio Times* etc. He married Barbara ('Bonnie') Lee in 1966. They have three Scottish children, and four grandchildren. He is a Fellow of the Royal Society of Edinburgh, a member of the Scottish National Party, and of Plaid Cymru. He is currently writing a book on Sir Walter Scott's relations with Ireland. He worked in the Yes campaign in 2014 and found it like the Civil Rights movements he knew in the USA and in Northern Ireland, the protest movements against the war in Vietnam in the USA, Ireland and Scotland, and the anti-Apartheid movement in Ireland.

By the same author:

Celtic Nationalism (with Gwynfor Evans, Ioan Rhys and Hugh MacDiarmid Routledge and Kegan Paul, 1968)

The Mind of an Activist: James Connolly, (Gill & Macmillan, 1971)

The Sins of Our Fathers: Roots of Conflict in Northern Ireland, (Gill & Macmillan, 1970)

Burke & Hare, (Birlinn, 2014)

The Quest for Sherlock Holmes: A Biographical Study of Arthur Conan Doyle, (Penguin, 1984)

P. G. Wodehouse, (Marting. Brian & O'Keeffe, 1977)

Macaulay ('Historians on Historians' Series, Weidenfeld & Nicolson, 1988

Eamon De Valera, (University of Wales Press, 1987)

City of a Thousand Worlds: Edinburgh in Festival, (Mainstream publishing, 1991)

The Edinburgh Festival (with Robbie Jack, Canongate, 1990)

Hare and Burke (Play, Diehard, 1994)

British Children's Fiction in The Second World War, (Edinburgh University Press, 2007)

How David Cameron Saved Scotland, (Luath 2015)

Scotland's Waterloo, (Luath, 2015)

Saint Johnny, (Grace Note, 2015)

Our Nations and Nationalisms

Glimpses and Soundings

OWEN DUDLEY EDWARDS

Luath Press Limited

EDINBURGH

www.luath.co.uk

To two great creators
my wife Bonnie Dudley Edwards
and my leader Alex Salmond

First published 2022

ISBN: 978-1-910745-55-7

The paper used in this book is recyclable. It is made from low chlorine pulps produced in a low energy, low emission manner from renewable forests.

Printed and bound by Severnprint Ltd., Gloucester

Typeset in 11 point Sabon by Lapiz

Contents

History is Philosophy from examples.

Dionysius of Halicarnassus (attrib, c 330BCE)

'I'm beginning to understand the game scientifically. What a noble
    game it is, too!'
'Isn't it? But it's more than a game. It's an institution', said Tom.
'Yes', said Arthur, 'the birthright of British boys old and young, as
    habeas corpus and trial by jury are of British men.'
'The discipline and reliance on one another which it teaches are so
    valuable, I think', went on the master, 'it ought to be such an
    unselfish game. It merges the individual in the eleven, he doesn't
    play that he may win, but that his side may.'

Thomas Hughes, *Tom Brown's Schooldays* (1857)

I hear it was charged against me that I sought to
    destroy institutions;
But really I am neither for nor against institutions;
(What indeed have I in common with them? – Or
    what with the destruction of them?)
Only I will establish in the Mannahatta and in every
    city of these States inland and seaboard,
And in the fields and woods, and above every keel
    little or large that dents the water,
Without edifices or rules or trustees or any argu-
    ment,
The institution of the dear love of comrades.

Walt Whitman, 'I Hear it was Charged Against Me', *Leaves
of Grass* (1891–92)

A Final Note

Vladimir Putin's despicable invasion of Ukraine in 2022 began after this book had been completed and revised by me, and the Foreword had been written by my friend Alex Salmond, under whose leadership my party, the Scottish National Party, was elected to government of Scotland in 2007, and in 2011 was elected majority Government. I was greatly honoured when Alex interviewed me on the Russian TV show he chaired at that time, and whence he resigned when Putin began his mass-murder in Ukraine. Our work does not endorse the crimes of Putin, similarly Agatha Christie did not endorse the crimes of Stalin when at the request of the UK Foreign Office she wrote 'Detective Stories in England' (1945) for a Soviet journal.

Putin's conduct is a ruthless expression of his Russian nationalism. It no more indicts nationalism than does the brave resistance of the Ukrainians against him. You can no more outlaw nationalism for the behaviour of nationalists than you can outlaw humanity for the conduct of humans. As a Russian nationalist, Putin invokes the traditions of Ivan the Terrible, Peter the Great, Catherine the Great, the Romanov Czars in general, and Stalin whose Russian nationalist priorities gave him a hold on power lacked by the internationalist Bolsheviks Lenin and Trotsky. Putin is not a Communist even by the lip-service accorded by officials of the Union of Soviet Socialist Republics in its last days, but he is happy for a Union akin to Oliver Cromwell's as imposed on Scotland and Ireland however lacking in personal Puritanism. His readiness to accuse his Ukrainian victims of Nazism expresses his actual realisation that in this war he is the heir of Hitler, both in attacking Ukraine, and in his slaughter of civilians.

We should study conflicting nationalisms in the present war (as everyone except Putin calls it) on a comparative basis. Putin's denial of the existence of Ukraine recalls Ireland between 1925 and

1965 when the 26 Irish counties forming the Irish Free State (later Eire, later still the Republic of Ireland) insisted that Northern Ireland did not exist, while the Unionist Protestants controlling Northern Ireland practically took a similar view of the 26. Simultaneously Dublin governments and their publicists denounced the actual reduction of Roman Catholics in Northern Ireland to second-class citizenship, and Belfast governments continued to enforce the second-class citizenship while denying its existence save for security needs. The regimes declared that Irish unification or Northern Ireland preservation prevented reforms, without admitting that any were necessary. Frontier territories in Ukraine bordering on Russia show some divided loyalties, and the same is probably true of Russian territories whose Ukrainian inhabitants dare not question the violence Putin practises in Russia's name. During the thirty years' war in Northern Ireland from 1970, crimes of Putinesque barbarity were committed by insurgent Catholics and Protestants in the names of coreligionists and fellow-nationals, most of whom abominated them however secretly. On their side UK governments whatever their policies continued to treat nationalism as a social disease from which they themselves were immune, and to deny the constitutional integrity of non-violent nationalism in Wales and Scotland.

We humans are all nationalists, which means that potentially we may be Putins or Daniel O'Connells. If we realise that, we may behave better.

April 2022   ODE

Foreword

PENNING THIS FOREWORD gives me an opportunity to recount a story about the folly of youth.

Back in the mid '70s I was editing a student newspaper and asked a flamboyant young Edinburgh University historian to contribute an article or two. When speaking to him he asked if I would like to join him in a visit to Hugh MacDiarmid, then residing in his final home in Biggar.

The problem was I had a ticket that very day for the Edinburgh derby at Easter Road and that is where I duly ended up. So I was young and foolish enough to choose a game of fitba between two poorish sides, rather than a once in a lifetime chance to meet Scotland's towering 20th century poet!

Owen Dudley Edwards was the young academic and his own connection with MacDiarmid was that they had co-authored a book called *Celtic Nationalism* some time before. In some ways this volume reprises many of the themes set out in that book all of these years ago.

There is a major difference though. This new volume includes the elephant in the room, or at least the elephant which the Celtic nations have been placed in bed with - English and British nationalism.

I did not accept the invitation to write this foreword by way of a belated apology to Owen. I did it because more understanding of the conflicting nations and nationalisms of these islands has never been more timely and more required.

Britain is out of Europe and has yet to find a role or even any rationale for the damage that has been done. In the sense there was any logic to Brexit at all, it was driven jointly by the demons of English exceptionalism and the scarring social and regional disparities of English society.

A full century after partition, Ireland has never been closer to reunification but still remains a distance from full reconciliation. However, in the meantime, the Republic has emerged as a modern, prosperous democratic society shedding all semblance of theocratic backwater. Would that redoubtable Dubliner, Sir Edward Carson, still be upholding Ulster provincialism in these circumstances? That, of course, is one of these daft historical questions but one no doubt that Owen Dudley Edwards would take a decent stab at answering.

In Wales, Labour clings on to supremacy but largely because it has increasingly adopted the clothes of Welsh nationalism. Is that a viable long-term position or will Welsh Labour go the same way as the Scottish comrades, caught in a vice of being out-nationalist by the SNP and out-unionist by the Tories?

All of which makes Labour's English leader Sir Keir Starmer's recent denunciation of the 'the multi-headed hydra of nationalism' all the more unconvincing, as is his attempt to conflate Johnson's Conservatives with Sturgeon's SNP.

In Scotland the SNP is now electorally dominant but politically becalmed, apparently incapable of answering the obvious strategic question of what to do when England says no. Relying on the profound decency and sense of fair play of the plain people of England seems a doomed strategy when they are under the thumb of Albion's current perfidious leadership.

With all of that happening, or about to happen, there is no-one in these islands better schooled to write this necessary book than Owen Dudley Edwards. His family are steeped in the history of Ireland in all its terrible beauty and thus no-one respects more the steady constitutionalism of Scottish nationalism.

As a happy immigrant to Scotland for more than half a century Owen holds her dedicated civic and community-based pursuit of independence in high regard. Indeed his own attachment to the national cause is based on a nationalism which is more internationalist, more egalitarian and more peaceful than its British competitor.

In that period Owen Dudley Edwards has been on friendly terms not only with many of the substantial nationalist figures of the restless Celtic nations but also with Gordon Brown, the former Prime

Minister whose personal mission it has been to protect the survival of the British state.

It is a familiarity which gives context and authority to his learned insights of the politics of identity through British history. Long before the current crop of Westminster political pygmies thought of more muscular unionism James (VI) and (I) ascended to the throne of England as the best taught king in Christendom. He enlisted the greatest literary genius of the day in his plan to forge a single nation out of the disparate and oft warring tribes of Britain.

Four hundred years and more later Scottish nationalists can comfort ourselves with the thought that if the task of eliminating Scottish identity for the supposed greater good eluded James (I) and William Shakespeare it will probably be beyond Boris Johnson and the BBC.

Does that make an eventual nationalist triumph in Scotland inevitable? No just highly probable. Still less does it assist with timescale. But then Owen Dudley Edwards is a historian. It is not his job to tell you what will happen or even when.

But this book will help you enormously with the why.

Alex Salmond
Strichen
October 2021

Introduction: Defining Nations and Nationalism

IF YOU LISTENED to Gioachino Rossini's Overture to *William Tell* you would probably understand nations and nationalism better than you will by reading this or any other book, but you would not be able to say or write what you have learned: music criticism is no substitute for music.

So... why another work on nations and nationalism?

HAMLET: Examples gross as earth exhort me.

Shakespeare, *Hamlet* (1600) IV.IV.46.

The current UK Prime Minister, the Rt Hon Alexander Boris de Pfeffel Johnson, PC, MP, MA (Oxon), Hon LL.D. (Brunel), Hon FRIBA – and the endless swarm of politicians and communications media who regurgitate him – speak of the United Kingdom of Great Britain and Northern Ireland as a 'nation', but when forced to mention Scotland, Wales, Northern Ireland or even England will call each one a 'nation', and when alluding to them in total 'four nations', sometimes as the 'awesome foursome' (we are living in a Peter Pandemic probably staffed by Lost Boys). Two and two make four, but how can four be one, especially as one of the four is at least two (Northern Ireland having existed since 1920 because of its mutually hostile Catholic and Protestant nationalisms)? To educate Mr Johnson seems to have been beyond the powers of Eton and Oxford, whatever the official certificates say, but for all of our sakes a fresh attempt should be made. Is he unduly influenced by his fellow-Etonian Eric Blair – more commonly George Orwell – whose *1984* ends with his hero under torture saying two and two *do* make five? Mr Johnson is now said to have reversed himself on this, as on so much else, and his underlings now tell civil servants to refer to one entity, not four, as though the USA's President were to give orders to refer only to the USA, and not to individual states. The Prime Minister's almost invariable use of 'Britain' or 'Great Britain' where the United Kingdom was meant resulted in some delegates of the G7 Conference in Cornwall (11–13 June 2021) saying Northern Ireland was not in the UK.

Nations may define themselves by language as Welsh nationalism did, and Irish nationalism tried, and Scottish nationalism confronted in several differing forms. Latin is our best common root whether imposed by the Romans as in Britain or imported from them as in Ireland, being the language of medieval western Christendom. The Douai Bible translates the Apocalypse (Revelation 5:9):

> And they sang a new canticle, saying: Thou art worthy,
> O Lord to take the book and to open the seals thereof:
> because thou wast slain and hast redeemed us to God,
> in thy blood, out of every tribe and tongue and people
> and nation.

Repetition of synonyms may seem tautologous to us, but our ancestors used it for emphasis. If we pursue tribe, tongue, people, and nation into Latin and back, we often find the words interchangeable. The Version of the Bible Authorised by King James I (and VI) offers kindred in place of tribe, and most tribes probably began from families, as each tribe descended from one of the 12 sons of Jacob. *Ethnos* in ancient Greek gives us yet another synonym meaning tribe, people or nation with or without the linguistic factor declared by tongue. 'Ethnic minority' is frequently shortened to 'ethnic', but everyone is ethnic in one form or another eg:

> Did the native Scots find the English or the Irish to be
> Scotland's least assimilable ethnic group? And when?

'Tribe' may be most sublime in Revelations 7:3–8 when 1,200 of each of the 12 tribes descended from Jacob are 'sealed the servants of our God on their foreheads'. Lucy Maud Montgomery, Canadian author,

Presbyterian minister's wife, and creator of *Anne of Green Gables* and its seven sequels, devoted the two opening chapters of *Magic for Marigold* to a magnificently serious argument amongst almost all of the Scots-descended Lesleys of Prince Edward Island as to what the new baby is to be called. Ultimately the baby's life, threatened by a sudden illness, is saved by a woman doctor (despite prejudices against such a being) who then marries the bachelor uncle and the infant is given her name 'Marigold', and so the second chapter is entitled 'Sealed of the Tribe'. Montgomery's stories ripple with clerical comedy but the Lesleys, however individually absurd, almost in spite of themselves convey a grandeur in their tribalism consciously, if sometimes artificially, Scottish in thinking of themselves as a clan (Gaelic for family), headed by an engagingly ribald nonagenarian great-grandmother. And the choice of name also means establishing the child's claim to be one of God's elect, the sealed, the saved, but the chapter-title implies that Dr Marigold Woodruff Richards becoming a Lesley is thus also assured of salvation.

'Tongue' also has sacred implications, recognised by Elizabeth I in 1563 when (contrary to the orders by her foolish father the late Henry VIII) she authorised the translation of the Bible and associated scripture into Welsh (one of her grandfathers was Welsh, the other Irish). The 20th century Gaelic Revival in Ireland liked religiose slogans, pre-eminently *Gan Teanga Gan Tír* (without a language, without a country). This linked linguistic nationalism to the confiscation of Catholics' land for 175 years after the Ulster Plantation of 1607 until native Catholics owned about eight per cent, and *Tír-grádh* could mean love of country or love of land, patriotism or nationalism.

'People' appears usefully in the slogan of Glasgow Rangers Football Club 'We are the People', meaning the Protestant people of Ulster migrated to multi-ethnic Glasgow but still mourning the spiritual wounds of departure from their birthplaces with Psalm 94:14: 'For the LORD will not cast off his people, neither will he forsake his inheritance.'

The idea of the sanctity of the people against its ruling class was in tune with the rise of Labour across our archipelago and the emergence in the USA of the People's Party or Populists in 1890. The word 'populist' is slung around by every pompous ignoramus today. The realities of populism were ably asserted in Scotland as pressure rose for a Scottish Parliament, and on 30 March 1989 in the Hall of the General Assembly of the Church of Scotland before representatives of all religious faiths and none, the Wesleyan Canon Kenyon Wright foretold opposition from Prime Minister Margaret Thatcher (who had started referring to herself in public as 'we'):

> What if that other single voice we all know so well responds, saying 'We say No, and we are the State'. Well, we say Yes and we are the People.

What is a Nation?

Shakespeare (save perhaps in his sonnets) generally keeps his opinions to himself but equips his characters with theirs (public and private). His *Henry V* set in 1415 has captains from England, Wales, Scotland and Ireland among Henry's invading army before taking Harfleur. It was an obvious crowd-pleaser for a people still shaken by their own mortal danger from Spanish invasion in 1588. But the England of Elizabeth I was drained of troops through constant warfare against native Irish for the last nine years of her reign. When Henry v reigned, Scotland was independent and Ireland had little permanent control by England outside Dublin, so that in the play the Scots and Irish captains might be regarded as mercenaries. But Shakespeare's audience would also have thought of the rebellious Irish of their own day. The Irish Captain Macmorris bridles when Captain Fluellen from Wales remarks (III.II.122–27):

> FLUELLEN: Captain Macmorris, I think, look you, under
>   your correction, there is not many of your nation –
> MACMORRIS: Of my nation! What is my nation? Ish a
>   villain, and a bastard, and a knave, and a rascal.
>   What ish my nation? Who talks of my nation?

On the face of it, this is a joke for all seasons, characterising the Irish as permanently obsessed by their identity as a nation, not necessarily knowing what they meant by a nation, but ready to fight anyone and everyone who tried to defame or even define it. Henry v leads followers from all parts of the archipelago, but the superiority of the English is asserted, with the Welsh second (Shakespeare had Welsh antecedents, used Welsh legend in *King Lear* and *Cymbeline*, and included prose and verse in Welsh (now lost) in *Henry IV Part One*), Captain Jamy of Scotland third (handled respectfully enough, since by 1600 the next English monarch was pretty certain to be King Jamy of Scotland), and Macmorris fourth.

'Macmorris' mixes two Irish Nations, the Gaelic clans of Munster, and the Norman descendants of the Fitzmaurice and Fitzgerald invaders of Ireland in 1169. Elizabeth faced a formidable enemy in James Fitzmaurice Fitzgerald known as 'Fitzmaurice', nephew and cousin of Fitzgerald Earls of Desmond, maternal descendant of Gaelic families, Papal crusader killed leading an invasion against her in 1579, 'Macmorris' reminding the audience that he is partly of Gaelic descent. Elizabeth's enforcement of Anglicanism on Ireland diminished mutual hostility between Gaelic and Norman (or 'old English') Catholics so that Irish nationalism developed around the defence of Catholicism, its support in invasions from European Catholic potentates including the Pope, and evangelical missions in Ireland from Catholic friars. Macmorris's dualism was prophetic: the two leading 18th century Irish nationalisms were Jacobite, Catholic, Gaelic, peasant, smuggling; and Hanoverian, Protestant, Anglophone, squirearchical, Anglocentric; in 19th century Ireland they mingled, Protestant ideologues influencing growing Catholic bourgeoisie. From the 16th century nationalism increased in England against Catholic enemies in Europe, and in Scotland against Catholic French domination. Religion also enriched Welsh nationalism, in late 18th century high episcopalianism, and in late 19th century nonconformist revolt against Protestant episcopalian privilege. They are subtle stage nationals, more so than ethnicity elsewhere on the London stage from Shakespeare's day to Victoria's.

Tongue means language though its primacy in national options varies greatly. *Tribe* means an earlier stage in evolution surviving as one tribe declares that other tribes are at an earlier phase of history than itself and therefore merely disposable aborigines. *People* assumes equality between its component individuals, rapidly becoming paper-thin as snobbery permeates. *Nation* may demand recognition as a status earned, or capable of being earned. Irish, Scots and Welsh showed themselves original and compelling wordsmiths experimenting in English, becoming journalists and dominating the popularisation of intellect. Dublin's *Nation* (1842–1900) became the best-selling weekly in the archipelago, its title simultaneously claiming that Ireland was a nation, that it had formerly been one, and that it would become one. In theory these were the same identity; in practice they were very different. Charles Gavan Duffy a founding editor of the *Nation* was frequently, if unsuccessfully, prosecuted for treason, never repudiated his Irish nationalism, became Prime Minister of Victoria (Australia), and was duly knighted. His fellow-Irishman Edwin Lawrence Godkin emigrated to the USA where in 1865 he founded the New York *Nation*, a strong liberal reformist weekly whose title proclaimed it the paper of all the individual US states, and still flourishes. Charles Stewart Parnell the future Home Rule party leader who dominated UK politics in the 1880s during his rise in the late 1870s declared Ireland's right to be taken seriously instead of parochially by the Commons: 'she is a Nation'. Gladstone ended his career leading the Irish demand for Home Rule in 1893 whence the Socialist JL Hammond called his massive history *Gladstone and the Irish Nation*. To be a *nation* was an entitlement to some form of national status, whether being taken seriously by the House of Commons, being accorded devolved parliamentary government, or being accepted as an independent power. The Allied powers in World War II called themselves the United Nations and founded the post-war United Nations Organization, whose membership implies that a nation has won international recognition as such. It had almost a sacred implication. The Scottish National Party asserted as much in making membership of the UN its goal.

What is Nationalism?

A nation has been defined as shared memories, though to call it shared memories of shared memories may be nearer the truth. Nationalism is the awareness of at least some of these shared memories in the idea of that nation. This means that nationalism is a religion. Some great scholars have confronted that question – the historian of nationalism Carlton JH Hayes whose last book was *Nationalism: A Religion*, Conor Cruise O'Brien in his Massey lectures at Harvard *God Land – Reflections on Religion and Nationalism*, Adrian Hastings in his Wiles Lectures in Queen's University Belfast *The Construction of Nationhood: Ethnicity, Religion and Nationalism*, the prolific Professor Anthony D Smith in his more recent work. How can a rational scholar deny religion and nationalism in the public life of Joan of Arc, symbol of French identity asserted against English conquest, burnt by orders of the Inquisition in 1431 and canonised by the Vatican in 1920? Even Communism's official rejection of religion and nationalism demanded and required a religiose piety for its own doctrines and decisions, and divided itself on national lines.

Nationalism, like its parent, the nation, lived before written history and gave an ethic to ethnicity. It was needed to explain to its youth who their people were, whence they had come and why, what divine demands and crowd responses were entailed and, however deplorably, its vendettas against other nations. It was inseparable from history even when (as in the French Revolution) its votaries proclaimed the death of history and created a new calendar. Nationalism has had its numerous expositors, evangelists and educators, writing anonymously, pseudonymously, or otherwise. The Old Testament is an excellent example, much originating in oral transmission long before it was written, as acts of piety but also of policy: the future had to be guided by the past. National or clan bards played such parts, and historians openly or otherwise created or edited history to further their own politics.

Historians are nationalists in this sense, but what they mean by a 'nation' is not necessarily a country, merely that the history they teach and write is self-vindication, sometimes well masked. George

Orwell's *Notes on Nationalism*, inspirational but not infallible, revealed the author's English nationalism (which he sometimes peppered with Scotophobia). It categorised nationalism within broad contours, listing as nationalisms Neo-Toryism, Celtic Nationalism, Zionism, Communism, Political Catholicism, Colour Feeling, Class Feeling, Pacifism, Anglophobia, Antisemitism, Trotskyism and appropriate sub-categories such as 'Irish Nationalism' classifiable under 'Celtic Nationalism'. In 1945 there was little sign of common cause between Irish nationalism and Scots or Welsh, the Irish prominently political, Scottish cultural, Welsh linguistic. Irish nationalism in Eire (since 1949 the Republic of Ireland) was a useful doctrine requiring popular deference to ensure political stability, while in Northern Ireland it was an incentive to deny the legitimacy of the substate one way or another, opposing the Unionist majority's Anglocentric nationalism. Mid-20th century Dublin governments demanded the unification of Ireland and would have been appalled to get it, since it would have shattered the delicate balance of Irish politics, and weakened the political power of Roman Catholicism by including a vociferous Protestant minority.

Orwell also showed that nationalism can breed generalisation:

> No modern Irish writer, even of the stature of Yeats or
> Joyce, is completely free from traces of nationalism.

The logical conclusion is that everyone is a nationalist – which they are, often worshipping two or three different nations at the same time, eg Scotland and the UK (with varying priorities) – but countries house different nationalisms. If we admit Orwell's categories of 'Political Catholicism' or 'Zionism' (as we should) multi-icon nationalisms become easier to understand. Orwell's reduction of nationalism to a unitary faith may not be true, but then his own English nationalism was a little old-fashioned in its monotheism. A nation discovers its nationalism when under attack and particularly when it faces the danger of political, economic, or cultural obliteration. It may not entail a defensive response. A nation finds itself a storehouse for what it values, and its nationalism guards and celebrates of those values. The Scots, threatened with annexation by

Edward I, produced at Arbroath in 1320 the first formal declaration of nationalism known to us, expressed in the letter of its leading nobles to Pope John XXII repudiating English rule, swearing allegiance to King Robert Bruce, and promising to dismiss him should he ever accept subordination to England. That promise marks the document as nationalism.

Nationalism in Scotland today defines itself as love for its community; constantly seeking peace among nations; repudiating hate; welcoming those claiming identity with it whether as inhabitants of Scotland or refugees and immigrants; rejecting the manufacture, custody and sale of weapons of mass destruction; retention and expansion of National Health and rejecting its breakup, privatisation, and adulteration by inferior standards; subordinating legalistic chauvinism to international rule of law; using its own independence to aid victims across the world suffering medical, economic and environmental poverty: absolutely committed to non-violence. This is no mere shopping-list: all these beliefs are interdependent. As Pope Francis said of our sister and mother, Earth in his second encyclical *Laudato si'*:

> We have come to see ourselves as her lords and masters,
> entitled to plunder her at will. The violence present in our
> hearts, wounded by sin, is also reflected in the symptoms
> of sickness evident in the soil, in the water, in the air, and
> in all forms of life.

The English connection brought many benefits to the Scottish people, but today it is shackled to cults of conquest, of competition, of conceit. Scottish nationalism demands liberating Scotland from the mass murder weapons such as TRIDENT forced upon her soil and seas, from alliance with antihuman policies under irrational leaders like former President Donald Trump, from foreign policies shaped by self-imagined up-to-date Machiavellis. The United Kingdom of Great Britain and Northern Ireland perpetually endangers itself by imagining that it is still a great power, like a senile grandfather still trying to play rugby.

Ernst Friedrich Schumacher's philosophy *Small is Beautiful* animates Scottish nationalism. The UK is now unfit for purpose as an agent for Scotland's needs and wishes in foreign economic policy and international legal necessities. Sixty-two per cent of Scots rejected BREXIT in the 2016 referendum and saw the European Union as a common association among the powers with each seeking to further common benefits for themselves and the world, whereas the English majority imagined the EU as a chaffering of hucksters in Anglophobe conspiracy. As regards BREXIT, the Scots knew their own minds far more decisively than the English knew theirs. UK opponents of Scottish nationalism expressed surprise that the Scottish National Party should favour EU membership for Scotland while wanting to leave the UK: Scottish nationalism seeks EU membership as it seeks UN membership – to further international peace, prosperity and environmental responsibility, rejecting the 'top nation' mirage significantly relished by Prime Minister Johnson as 'incredible' and 'fantastic'. Scottish nationalism today repudiates a UK racist and imperial past formerly enriching many Scots, but seeks to conserve Scotland's portion of the endangered UK welfare state. The UK has stopped believing in itself despite politicians' desperate assertions of its superiority, while Scottish nationalism encourages the Scots to believe in themselves and increase their value for the rest of humanity.

The late great Gwyn Alf Williams questioned history, nationalism, and God knows how much else in his *When Was Wales?*. He could have written *Where Was Wales?* The earliest known date in Welsh poetry is roughly 600AD for Aneirin's Y Gododdin and a larger crop by Taliesin, but Aneirin flourished in or around what is now Edinburgh, while Taliesin flourished between the Clyde and Cumbria. Taliesin declared that he (and thus the Wales of his poems) had been with Noah in the Ark and would be present at the crack of doom, and Aneirin described an invasion of eastern England from Lothian down to defeat in Catterick and the loss of its heroes. Wales mingled a remote past with those of Cornwall and Brittany. Welsh may have travelled more successfully to the USA than did Gaelic, putting out its newspapers in new landscapes such as Racine, Wisconsin. Wales gave its conquerors heroic legends whence to claim profitable antecedents, notably in the 12th century through the legends of King Arthur initially preserved in the *Mabinogion*, through

Geoffrey of Monmouth's *History of the Kings of Britain* inventing a past for the island down from mythology into theology, and
through those of Gerald of Wales on the topography, exploits and
characters of the Norman plunderers of Wales, England and Ireland:
their perpetuation served Edward I as prospectus for his fraudulent
claims of ancient English sovereignty over Scotland, and the Eng-
lish-Welsh frontiersman William Shakespeare for the basis for King
Lear. Wales gave England a Tudor dynasty whose heir fought his
way to become Henry VII naming his first-born son Arthur as fitting
for the first Tudor Prince of Wales, thus charming the English poet
Thomas Gray into triumphant celebrations of Tudors and condemnations of Edward I and his heirs in *The Bard*. Wales produced rich
impassioned linguistic nationalism around the defence of the Welsh
language, but it also bred a different nationalism, one fulfilled by
reconquest of its lost land of Britain, whether through Henry VII in
1485 or David Lloyd George in 1916.

A false nationalism transfers responsibility for our actions to
the state or the governing body. To love a nation requires integrity, not idolatry. Critics (denying their own nationalism) insist that
nationalism demands blind obedience and may cite endless self-styled
nationalists in history whose messages stifled conscience. In such case,
the nationalism self-destructs and thought freezes. Correctly, nationalism involves knowing as well as loving the unit of identification, and
using that knowledge to benefit humankind for which the nation is a
vantage-point winning respect as well as love from its people. Nationalism is a useful unit for public self-identification: the next stop is the
world. If nationalism is to mean anything worthwhile, its believers
must realise how easily their pride may prove their shame. Imperial-
ism is not the extension but the negation of its parent nationalism.

A single person may subscribe to quite different and perhaps
conflicting nationalisms. A Scot in UK service, civil or military, officially affirms loyalty to the UK but in mind may believe in Scottish
Independence. Alternatively, a civil servant in Holyrood may secretly
abominate the idea of Scottish independence. Such things may realise themselves in priorities: yesterday a Scot might tell themselves,
and everyone else, that they are British, today that Scot may tell

themselves that they are Scottish but tell everyone else that they are British, tomorrow they may tell themselves and everyone else that they are Scottish. UK nationalism sometimes liked to rationalise this, or freeze the process, by encouraging the Scot to think of themselves as Scottish by all means, but with its UK identity ultimately superior in speech and thought.

The earliest nations were frequently nomadic. So it proved necessary to claim, repeat, define or imagine where that nation had come from, and what lessons had to be learned from such history, in lists of laws, in bardic verses, or in craft skills. History needs to record losers as well as winners, so Tacitus tried to make his fellow-Romans understand the probable nationalism of the Caledonians defeated by his father-in-law Julius Agricola. The metropolis produces its history, and condemns nationalism in the peripheries for distorting it, but the increase in peripheral nationalism means writing more and more peripheral history whether anti-nationalist, pro-nationalist, or as neutral as could be reached. The rise of Scottish nationalism in the last 50 years has made Scotland an enormously exhilarating historiographical battleground.

Perhaps Scottish nationalism will be finally vindicated when the Scots declare the Union as an investment outliving its value. Scottish Independence seems most likely to be achieved because of the blunders of UK government while wielding non-devolved power, notably war and peace. Scottish nationalism finds Westminster and Whitehall too inefficient to answer Scottish needs, and too perverse to represent them. London Tory intellectuals tell themselves that each of the three devolved governments are 'an abject failure', presumably to soften the ground for Boris Johnson should he decide – or be told – to cancel or destroy the Scottish Parliament and Welsh or Northern Ireland Assemblies, which at least in theory he can do whatever his incapacity in practice. The abolition of the devolved governments would probably ensure the suicide of the Union. The choice in Scotland is now between UK nationalism clutching destruction, and Scottish nationalism working to save people and planet at home and across the world.

CHAPTER ONE

Talking about Nationalism

And, behold, the LORD passed by, and a great and strong wind rent the mountains, and brake in pieces the rocks before the LORD; but the LORD was not in the wind: and after the wind an earthquake; but the LORD was not in the earthquake:

And after the earthquake a fire; but the LORD was not in the fire: and after the fire a still small voice.

1 Kings 19: 11–12

NATIONALISM IS OLDER than recorded History, and in fact invented it. Nationalism has always existed among groups of people however small. Their creation of history initially derived from their anxiety to win the fidelity of the future by telling their children about themselves, their families or clans, their doings, their dangers, their disasters, their debts and credits, successes, technology, identity, and their values, and was in full flow long before people knew how to write.

Probably most of the first historians were women. They wanted to keep the children quiet, they would answer their questions as best they could, and may have found they got better obedience by making their children proud of who they were. Some of them would have illustrated their discourses in cave drawings. As GK Chesterton remarked in *The Everlasting Man* our chief knowledge about cave-dwellers is their love of art. The usual subjects of history-telling were probably about their immediate locality, and about the world or the universe. If the children had been evacuated, their mother, grandmother, elder sister, cousin, aunt, great-aunt might tell them about where they came from, varying between whether the children remembered it or not, loved it or hated it, and judged the forces or persons who caused their migration. Local poets or bards might formalise or mythologise the stories and memories in verse or music. They might not become conscious of coming from a specific nation or country until a stranger told them they were English, Irish, Scots, or Welsh, particularly when they had left their homeland. If discovering identity by receiving contemptuous labels docketing their homelands, the travellers learned to justify their migration by declaring their own superior qualities whether moral or military, and their misfortune at the hands of some petty tyrant. Natives despising immigrants might also find common cause with them in abominating the homeland's supposed oppressor: Americans admitting no Irish ancestry might join the American-Irish in Anglophobia, and the American-Irish themselves might therefore cling more to Anglophobia than to Hibernophilia as the years continued. The deepest and most abiding impact on migrants might be that of music, quite possibly songs without words. Historians frequently reprove nationalism's existence, while unable to recognise that it in fact founded our profession.

Nationalism is Everybody Except me

Nationalism is also value-free. There is good nationalism and there is bad nationalism, and there is nationalism that is simultaneously both good and bad. Coarse modern rhetoric likes to classify by praise or blame, but to declare that nationalism by itself is good or bad is to define a blank page by colourings it does not have. Nationalism has also complicated its own issue by frequently sending itself up rotten so that the unwary student may find it impossible to tell whether it is being self-adoring or self-mocking, as in the English national anthem ('A Song of Patriotic Prejudice') invented by Michael Flanders and Donald Swann with chorus:

> The English, the English, the English are best,
> I wouldn't give tuppence for all of the rest!

The song is openly ridiculous, and its absurd libels on other peoples are obviously intended to be recognised as nonsense, mocking the English themselves insofar as any of them still believe that the Scots are mean or that the Welsh sing flat. (Anyone on the upper deck of a bus in a town where international rugby has just been played will confirm that drunken Scots, English and Irish sing horribly, but no matter how drunk a Welsh crowd, their singing will be glorious.) But the little joke about the Irishman grazes nearer the bone:

> He blows up policemen, or so I have heard
> And blames it on Cromwell and William the Third!

Flanders retained the ambiguities when introducing that song roughly like this:

> In the old days, when I was a boy [in the 1920s], we didn't bother in England about nationalism, I mean nationalism was on its way out. We got pretty well everything we wanted. And we didn't go around saying how wonderful we were: everybody knew that!... nowadays, nationalism is on the up and up...

Flanders may have known the words of Arnold J Toynbee in his *The Prospects of Western Civilization*, re-employed in the 12th volume (*Reconsiderations* (1961)) of his *A Study of History* (1934–61):

> I remember watching the Diamond Jubilee procession myself as a small [eight-year-old] boy. I remember the atmosphere. It was: well, here we are on the top of the world, and we have arrived at this peak to stay there – forever! There is, of course, a thing called history, but history is something unpleasant that happens to other people. We are comfortably outside all that. I am sure, if I had been a small boy in New York in 1897 I should have felt the same. Of course, if I had been a small boy in 1897 in the Southern part of the United States, I should not have felt the same; I should then have known from my parents that history had happened to my people in my part of the world.

C Vann Woodward used those words as epigraph to his *Origins of the New South 1877–1913* in 1951, which transformed the historiography of the Southern United States, partly by dissecting nationalism's manufacture of history. When nationalism is aware of itself, whether it admits it or not, history asks better questions. The most practical question to ask of a nationalism – or of a religion – is whether it is homicidal or not, or, to be subjective, will it kill me if I do not accept it? It depends on who controls it, and when. The Christian may say that Christianity was founded as non-homicidal by its Founder, Jesus Christ. Persons claiming to be His heirs have been exceedingly homicidal in their use of that inheritance. That indicts them, not Him. Similarly, what people have done with nationalism is the people's responsibility, not nationalism's. Modern Scottish nationalism, as expressed in the Scottish National Party, is non-homicidal. A case for SNP begins there, and defines it thereafter. At the heart of its nationalism is the commandment: 'Thou Shalt Not Kill'. Nor may the party accept the codicil, mockingly expressed in Arthur Hugh Clough's satire 'The Latest Decalogue' (as relevant as when it was written 160 years ago):

> Thou shalt not kill, but needst not strive
> Officiously to keep alive.

As Clough intended us to realise, those who let others die without trying to help them (and those who make and sell weapons of death with indifference to the human effects) join the killer category, alongside the preachers of killing however artistic their preachments.

Children may not play with trident

Nationalism is usually defined in relation to the nation, and to the nation-state. Nationalisms are categorised as either existing before the nation finds its state, or else existing when upholding and upheld by its nation-state. This has been convenient when nation-states can be packaged into modern history. But, if we admit the nationalism of Unionists, the packaging crumbles. We have only to look at 20th century Irish nationalism since Easter 1916 (born of the world-wide slaughterhouse) and at 20th century Ulster Unionism (born of the UK imperial and military traditions), to see the similarities. They have evolved while secretly or even publicly copying one another, including what were the mutually hostile forms of joyless warped Christianity, closest to one another in the eternal damnation each anticipated for the other. They derived from different military establishments, but when nationalisms are violent their other contrasts shrivel.

Non-violent nationalism must repudiate violent, whether a violent unionism seeking to obliterate its enemies, or a violent anti-imperialism seeking to ape Unionist militarism. One of the most dangerous infections corrupting non-violent nationalism has been patriotic songs of courage and suffering, sung merely as an additional community celebration of nationalism but all too quickly justifying violence. Naturally circumstances make for alterations, and evolutions. Unionist political parties are by nature fitted to discard old policies, but SNP by definition cannot discard the aim of self-rule, and by its nature cannot accept Scotland's housing, marketing, and potential using of, nuclear arms. Amongst its many common roots with the UK Labour Party are its hatred of war, of the arms trade, and of weapons of mass destruction. But Labour in its yearnings for power outgrew its anti-war antecedents. Its last leader, Mr Jeremy Corbyn, had to promise he would abandon his own anti-nuclear attitudes for practical purposes should he ever become Prime Minister. The sole surviving Labour MP in Westminster from Scotland, the industrious Mr Ian Murray of Edinburgh South (now restored under Sir Keir Starmer to Shadow Secretary of State for Scotland), rejected Mr Corbyn's capitulation and like his own SNP opponents abominates nuclear weapons in thought, word and vote. (It is a staggering indictment of Mr Corbyn's leadership of the Labour Party that commandos sworn to Corbynism tried before Election 2019 to have Mr Murray deselected, a clear proof that neither Scotland nor the Labour Party could have any real meaning for them: had they succeeded, Labour would probably have been wiped off the Scottish political map.)

The whole nuclear debate in the UK is in fact a meaningless posturing among shadows since the alleged 'independent deterrent' for nuclear warfare, TRIDENT, could not be used without US permission and enablement for use, and yet all Unionist parties are doctrinally bound to debate it as though it could. Today all Unionists – Tory, Labour (with honourable exceptions), Liberal Democrat, brexiteer, UKIP – apparently consider themselves bound to accept US leadership into or out of war, including hiring US weapons of mass destruction, and silence about US restrictions on their use. Recently it was rumoured that if nominally defied on some policy, the USA might stop sharing secrets of intelligence with the UK. In fact, the USA would never share intelligence secrets capable of injuring the USA, and will never stop sharing commercials or propaganda. Tories such as former Secretary of State for Defence Sir Michael Fallon have declared it 'unpatriotic' (inflatable to 'treasonable') to vote against the UK's right to hold, sell and use weapons of mass destruction: that certainly is UK nationalism. Nevertheless a few MPs – not always Tory – may find their bank accounts flourish thanks to the unwitting US taxpayer, so that they may help keep UK subservience that bit more subservient.

Volunteers become conscripts

The Scottish National Party was founded in 1928–34, partly in positive pride at having a song (auld and new) to sing around and about Scotland, partly in disillusion after the false promises of World War I for which the United Kingdom had demanded and devoured the lives of so many Scots apparently because UK and European politics had broken down in 1914. The warlords knew their Great War needed to inspire volunteers when it began, with a newly enfranchised (male) electorate – since Gladstone's Reform Act of 1884 – whence conscripts would be demanded 18 months later. The fundamental faith on which the warlords relied was UK nationalism, sometimes incorporating within itself such portions of English, Welsh, Scots and Irish nationalisms as still accepted the primacy of UK World War interests. August 1914 led many Irish to seek enlistment in the

UK armed forces as a logical consequence of their own local nationalisms. The few who took up arms to found an Irish Republic on Easter Monday 1916 were partly impelled to fight against the UK by infection from UK nationalism's war spirit. Irishmen, called cowards for not enlisting in the UK forces, fought against the UK to show they weren't cowards.

The most successful, or at any rate the noisiest, nationalism conceived in defiance of Great Britain was the United States of America, born in the Declaration of Independence of 4 July 1776 in which 13 British colonies individually rejected their colonial status, and a split second later united. US nationalism defined itself in the Constitution of 1787 recognising that split-second origin with consequent deference to what were still the original 13 states. US nationalism has been blessed by some of the greatest minds in world history, but it feared serious comprehensive definition, and therefore fought a Civil War in 1861–65, having divided itself in two.

The Anglo-Scottish union a desert island disc

Varieties of nationalism can and frequently do coexist within the same person, one nationalism perhaps holding priority now, another overtaking it, one a palimpsest dominating others, another ousting and replacing that palimpsest. *Robinson Crusoe* is the obvious reduction. Based on Alexander Selkirk, an actual Scot and sole inhabitant of a desert island, rescued in 1709 after four years of isolation, to be written up in literature by a scribbler of genius formerly an undercover midwife to the birth of the Anglo-Scottish Union of 1707 Daniel Defoe. So, the most famous solitary in English literature derived from a human experience whose future novelist was making a union which would transform the political identity of the isolated maroon, himself ignorant of its making and unknown to his future re-creator.

A country may lose its identity so that its nationalism is subsumed or incorporated into a larger entity. For instance, once upon a time there was England. It was threatened with obliteration in 1603 when the King of Scotland inherited the English kingship. But the two countries retained separate constitutional identities until in 1707 the

Scottish Parliament dissolved itself and was united, or, more accurately, enfolded within the English Parliament so that the English Parliament greatly outnumbered its new Scottish members: and in reality there was now a new country, Great Britain, which had existed only on paper since 1604 when James VI and I had proclaimed himself its king (not simply King of Scotland and England as he had been from 1603).

Scotland, as the poorer and weaker country, retained institutions (law, religion, education) now marks of identity, classifications and emphases supposedly – and sometimes actually – superior to existing counterparts among the more numerous, stronger and wealthier English. To be English after 1707 was real, to carry other identities prompted questionable complications. The English continued to call themselves English, but shared a British identity with the Scots. That is to say, the unionist Scots moved Heaven and Earth to declare Britishness, and the English sang along when they liked. The Scot James Thomson swelled the wild war-notes of critics of Prime Minister Sir Robert Walpole who had been forced against his will to take Britain to war in 1739 against Spain in the War of Jenkins's Ear, Captain Robert Jenkins having given evidence before the House of Commons in 1738 that Spanish naval officials had cut off his ear in 1731 when he was under suspicion of smuggling. Frederick Prince of Wales commissioned a patriotic masque, *Alfred*, for performance before his Court at his summer residence at Cliveden on 1 August 1740, music by Thomas Augustine Arne, script by Thomson and his fellow-Scot David Mallet, Thomson sole author of the only memorable song (Act II, Scene the Last):

> When Britain first, at Heaven's command,
> Arose from out the azure main,
> This was the Charter of the land,
> And guardian angels sang this strain:
> 'Rule, Britannia, rule the waves;
> Britons never will be slaves.'

In plainer words, if Jenkins wanted to violate Spanish waters he himself would be inviolate. Mallet revised *Alfred* for 1755 notwithstanding the intervening deaths of Thomson, Jenkins and Frederick. The original song was a Scottish morality: it implied that Britannia needed to be reminded of her duty to rule the waves, in which she had failed in 1731 whence Jenkins lost his ear. The triumphant revival in 1755 swelled the *Zeitgeist* inaugurating the Seven Years' War in 1756, and the execution of the innocent Admiral John Byng 'for failing to do his utmost' in 1757. This was nationalism as divine instruction and reprimand: Britannia's inadequate naval vigilance became a default as blameworthy as Adam's and Eve's, inspiring Voltaire's conclusion that the English shot an admiral from time to time '*pour encourager les autres*'.

The 19th century did not allow British fulfilment of divine orders to appear inadequate, and the world was told that Britannia did indeed rule the waves whether in 1805 with Horatio Nelson's fatal victory on the *Victory* or in 1878 with WS Gilbert's HMS *Pinafore*, so much so that Woodrow Wilson's war aims – as expressed in the Fourteen Points in January 1918 – seriously annoyed the UK by including 'Freedom of the Seas': it might have risked conflict had the USA not brilliantly spiked UK guns in the Washington Conference of 1921. 'Rule, Britannia!' was a wonderful proof of the ability of the Scots to invent British nationalism when more patronage was needed by a Scottish poet. But from 1801 Britannia had lost any legal existence on sea or land, having become the United Kingdom of Great Britain and Ireland, which in 1922 was dwindled into the United Kingdom of Great Britain and Northern Ireland. The individual countries retained some form, or forms, of nationalism painfully primitive by contrast with the up-to-date all-devouring union. Today it is the union whose rhetoric demands allegiance by banality: Prime Minister David Cameron celebrated the triumph of unionism in the 2014 referendum by stating that his infant son had worn tartan underpants in expectation and honour of the victory, Prime Minister Theresa May's 'precious, precious union' sounded increasingly like Gollum yearning for the Ring in Tolkien's *The Hobbit* and *The Lord of the Rings*, Prime Minister Boris Johnson defended the union by normally limiting himself to the one enacted in 1707. We can easily recognise these phenomena as 'tourist nationalism', destined for display as national treasures a century hence – underpants, preciosity, the Irish border in the Irish Sea.

When on the threshold of his premiership, Mr Boris Johnson sought a rhetorical brand-name acknowledging the continued geographical existence of England, Northern Ireland, Scotland, Wales, with individual legislatures in various degrees of devolution. He brightly waved 'the fantastic four' or 'the fabulous four' in the public's face (threadbare compared to the original Famous Five in Frank Richards' Greyfriars School, their title appropriated for the works of Enid Blyton). Even more revealing was his summation – 'this incredible United Kingdom' – which literally means that he does not believe in it and believes that nobody else could believe in it either, a veritable cloud-cuckoo-land indeed. Someone may have shown him Benedict Anderson's justly influential treatise on nationalism *Imagined Communities* for which he has been dutifully seeking to qualify ever since. The unreality persists even at the gravest of crises. Prime Minister Johnson, when addressing the UK on television on 23 March 2020 (and subsequently) on the pandemic and the requirements it necessitated, kept calling himself and his audience 'British', and telling them they were a nation, strictly British nationalism, as though Northern Ireland could wallow *in extremis* until all were slain, for what he cared. It is legally part of the same country despite not being on the island of Britain, and the UK spilled great reservoirs of blood and treasure over the last half-century so that it could remain in the UK while a majority of its people wished it.

Nationalism a protestant unionist creation

The first usage of 'nationalism' in English print seems to have been in the title *Nationalism in Religion*, a 16-page pamphlet preserving a speech delivered on 8 May 1839 before the Annual Meeting of the Protestant Association at Exeter Hall in London by the Reverend Hugh Boyd McNeile, an Ulster-born silver-haired 43-year-old Anglican clergyman, very tall and strong, whose eloquent pastoral life in his prime enlivened the spiritual welfare of his congregation in St Jude's Liverpool, thence in 1848 to St Paul's Princes Park, Liverpool, finally crowned at 73 by the Deanship of Ripon at the insistence of Prime Minister Benjamin Disraeli in 1868, despite the misgivings of Queen Victoria. McNeile made an excellent symbolic sponsor at the baptism of nationalism, casting shadows of religion from the past and democracy from the future around it. The religion was a passionately rejuvenated state Protestantism and the democracy anticipated future proletarian pressure to keep the United Kingdom Protestant.

Nationalism (unbaptised) had brooded over his early years. He was born near Ballycastle, a seacoast small town in the Catholic Northeast of Ireland within the predominantly Protestant county of Antrim. Ballycastle was the embarkation point for Rathlin Island, King Robert Bruce's legendary hiding-place from the troops of Edward I of England, where he supposedly saw the patient spider inspiring him to keep trying in spite of setbacks and defeats. He returned to Scotland, and began to win victories in 1307 when Edward I died. 500 years later, young McNeile was smuggled over to Scotland when French Revolutionaries invaded Ireland in 1798 and their local sympathisers, both Protestant and Catholic, won brief successes. The infant McNeile survived Francophile Irish outbreaks and found himself in a new country when, chiefly for reasons of military security, Prime Minister William Pitt the Younger carried the Act of Union of Great Britain and Ireland in 1800. Ireland had been under English rule since 1172 but from 1801 the Irish were part of the same country as the British. To Welsh, Scots, and Irish, the various unions opened up England as a potential happy hunting-ground for jobs, wealth and status. This included the Westminster Parliament at each of its unions. Pitt intended the Union to be taken literally: the Roman Catholics were to be included not only among voters (as they had been since 1793) but amongst MPs. George III vetoed this, Pitt resigned, and did not raise the matter when he supplanted the stop-gap Addington by becoming premier once more in 1804 and dying two years later.

Pitt wanted to make the Catholics stakeholders in the new United Kingdom of Great Britain and Ireland. Having been converted by Edmund Burke to recognise that Britain, Ireland and Roman Catholicism had a common enemy in the French Revolution, and the UK refusal of the promised potential places in Parliament for almost 30 years meant that when Catholic emancipation was extorted by the force of Irish mass public opinion mobilised by Daniel O'Connell, what Pitt had intended for reform had become a revolution. Had Pitt prevailed in 1801, a few grateful rich Papists might have filled a few seats in the Commons. Now all the world was to stare at the UK legislature: visibly no longer strictly Protestant, and the greatest subject in Christendom, Arthur Wellesley, Duke of Wellington, conqueror of Napoleon, now as Prime Minister 14 years after Waterloo forced to accept a constitutional transformation he had formed his government to oppose.

Irish Catholics of all classes had invented a new politics under O'Connell, the first Catholic to be admitted to Parliament since the exclusion of the Roman Catholic James VII/II and his Catholic heirs from the throne. The abolition of the Irish Parliament in 1800 impelled a search for new combat arenas, and the law courts became a popular spectator sport. As a Catholic O'Connell could not practise as a 'silk' or King's Counsel, but ordinary Catholics could not afford silks and O'Connell rapidly won fame as a tribune in criminal trials, turning proficiency into a forensic and political weapon in which he rapidly won fame as Catholic champion. Public attendance at assizes created heroes and villains for the crowd, whether volcanic advocates, masterly perjurers, or vituperative justices. Catholics having few legal rights before 1793, the law was generally enjoyed as a foreign game with hardly any sense of its being part of the Catholic public's nationalism. Trials carried the thrills of a favourite prisoner's life or liberty in danger, and to that extent fed Irish Catholic nationalist sentiments. If a Catholic or national issue were at stake, it heightened the fascination. Hearts might yearn for the victory of the man in the dock, but the lawyer who could dominate proceedings by vocation or by vocabulary made his way into popular folklore, being substituted for wizard or trickster in fireside repetitions of ancient tales. What added particular charm was his post-Gaelic Kerry voice skilled in bilingual oration, winning victories through mastery of the intricate technicalities imported from English courts. He won his admiring crowds from the courtrooms to the meeting-halls and ultimately to the great out-of-doors assemblies.

His illegal successful candidacy for Parliament in 1828 was in fact grounded in absolute hostility to violence. O'Connell declared Irish freedom was not worth the expenditure of a drop of Irish blood, but Wellington understood war, not peace, passed Catholic emancipation in fear of a bloody insurrection, and accepted O'Connell into the Commons where he proved the foremost orator of the day. After Wellington fell in 1830, the Whigs came to power. Prime Minister Charles, Earl Grey, disdained O'Connell and encouraged legal proceedings against him initiated by his Chief Secretary for Ireland Edward Lord Stanley for arousing the populace. However, 1833 saw O'Connell survive their departures from office followed by his own and his followers' maintenance of Grey's former Government underlings in a Commons majority until 1841. Stanley, Sir James Graham, the Duke of Richmond, and Viscount Ripon broke with the Whigs in 1833 on their proposed reallocation of funds hitherto bestowed on the established Protestant Episcopalian Church of Ireland whose wealth seemed in inverse proportion to its adherents. Here the Reverend Hugh McNeile found the makings of his nationalism.

He had seen with horror the supposedly inflexible anti-Catholic government of Wellington in 1829 admit a Papist to what God had intended to be the legislature of a Protestant state. In McNeile's eyes, his true church in the 1830s was being pillaged and dispossessed to enrich Popery in wealth, status and power. He knew the bitter Irish 'Tithe War' where Catholics (and everyone else) were legally obliged to pay tithes to the Church of Ireland resulting in ugly confrontations. To do him justice he, as a really hardworking Anglican cleric in England, had relatively little in common with the reverend absentees in (or rather out of) Ireland draining what they could from Irish people whom they seldom served and in some cases never saw. By now there were also evangelical Anglicans in Ireland inflamed with a new romantic yearning to convert the Irish Papists, thus developing an Irish nationalism of their own determined to save the masses from the Devil, and from his apparent agent, Daniel O'Connell.

The evangelicals allied with McNeile knew that O'Connell's political machine (financed chiefly by pennies from peasants and paupers) was frequently administered financially by Catholic priests, and sometimes oratorically reinforced in their Sunday homilies, and that Whig publicists sometimes thought of putting Irish Roman Catholic clergy on government salaries. Some British architects of the Union, some of Lord John Russell's Whigs and even a few of Sir Robert Peel's Tories might welcome such an idea, but parliamentarians largely steered away from it, representatives of every twig of militant Protestantism would have condemned it, and the Irish Catholic clergy and laity were almost all whole-heartedly against it, since the tremendous moral authority of Catholicism among the Irish peasantry and bourgeoisie stemmed from its days as a persecuted, outlawed church in 18th century Ireland.

The nationalism which McNeile invented was intended to suffuse all the British Isles, to mobilise the resources of Protestant church, the Tory Party, the law, the landed gentry, the evangelical press, the military, the aristocracy, the Universities of Oxford, Cambridge and Dublin, and (he hoped) the monarchy, to resist Daniel O'Connell: to denounce his popular crusades to Repeal the Union of 1800 and to extirpate his influence in UK Government (and perhaps even to repeal Catholic emancipation?). While Peel and the Tories were out of power in the later 1830s, McNeile drew much public support from them, particularly from the brilliant young MP William Ewart Gladstone. McNeile's Liverpool apostleship put his voice among the Protestant proletariat, themselves whether natives of Merseyside or migrants from Ulster faced with hardening competition for the lowest jobs from the migrant Irish Catholics. The migrants, all now from within the UK, grew more intense in their religious beliefs and practices having made the psychological rupture from country to city, evolving into specific mini-nationalisms bestowing righteousness the better to bear the misery of their living conditions with the assurance of eternal salvation. As pastor to working-class Liverpool Protestants McNeile developed a free flow of vituperation, for which Macaulay reproached Sir Robert Peel in Parliament on 18 February 1844:

It was pleasant to hear your opponents called by every nickname that is to be found in the foul vocabulary of the Reverend Hugh McNeile. It was pleasant to hear that they were the allies of Antichrist, that they were the servants of the man of sin, that they were branded with the mark of the Beast.

So nationalism in our islands was initially defined as a Unionist agenda.

Nationalism's patron saints

McNeile's nationalism centred around England and Ireland, having formed its cutting teeth in Ireland, and deriving from the union of the Church of Ireland and Church of England embodied in the Union of 1800, though unparalleled in that of 1707. It worked up elite support in both churches, as well as earning proletarian Protestant followers in Dublin, Belfast, and urbanising industrial Britain. McNeile explained Ireland's Great Famine in his sermon on 28 February 1847 as being the vengeance of God on the Irish for remaining Roman Catholic or for tolerating Roman Catholicism. McNeile's nationalism cultivated Scotland with hefty Tory dinners, but was weaker there since the state Church of Scotland was Presbyterian. Nineteenth-century evangelical romantic Anglicans, sworn to save the souls of the Irish Catholics by conversion, were revolutionary figures. They had the priorities of the frontier fighter, skilled at sermons in society but able to win the respect of vehement urban Protestant mobs. Their nationalism was UK nationalism.

O'Connell might claim to be the stimulus that drove them forward by antipathy, but his nationalisms were twofold: he wanted to advance freedom throughout the UK (and the USA), and he wanted to keep Irish Catholics' sense of identity in the forefront of their minds. His finesse knew how to draw them together: in 1843 he gave Dublin's great new Catholic church of St Andrew in Westland Row a painting of the assassination of St Thomas Becket by King Henry II's four knights, merging the different histories of the archipelago in a common Catholicism lying at back of present-day differences. O'Connell's UK nationalism wanted to create a better UK, healed of its religious and social injustices, and sworn to eradicate slavery and to repeal civil disabilities of the Jews now that the Catholics were emancipated. His Irish Catholic nationalism was bilingual, self-emancipating from latter-day Jacobite pieties, anxious to curb agrarian outrages against brutal landlords or Anglican clerics' agents, very much aware that long-despised Ireland produced in 1828 the UK Prime Minister Wellington, and US President Andrew Jackson.

Nationalism thrives on heroic leaders and symbols. Moses, Jesus Christ, and Muhammad, are the most obvious instances, enlarged by the vast body of ethical beliefs left either by them or by their commentators. In all three cases their cults commemorate and evangelise: we are strengthened by thinking of their lives, we progress by doing what we think they would want us to do. Translated into modern political terms, nationalisms – however atheist – rededicate themselves by their patron saints. Winston Churchill is an obvious example, admirably summed up in the last sentence of the biographical footnote given him in the great Socialist historian AJP Taylor's masterpiece, *English History 1914–1945*: 'The saviour of his country'. Churchill and Taylor had few theological pretensions, but the logic is sound. A patron saint has to take on a hint of the deity, a quality of martyrdom, a voice capable of the sublime. Which country Taylor actually meant is constructively ambiguous. Taylor justified his book's title on the ground that it meant what it said: 'Where the Welsh, the Scotch [*sic*], the Irish, or the British overseas have the same history as the English, my book includes them also; where they have a different history, it does not.' For some, but not all, of the English-speaking peoples, Churchill is a patron saint. He was denounced as a political traitor by innumerable Tories for much of his life. He was held in considerable affection by his Labour colleagues who forced the Tories to accept him as Prime Minister in 1940. Liberals liked to dwell on the cabinet posts he filled as a Liberal. In posthumous retrospect, for many, he might be an unspoken third revered after God and the Queen. As a figure in nationalism – English? British? UK? – his grandeur, his contradictions, his iconoclasm, his dedication, his internationalism, his rhetoric, his authorship, and his sense of humour still keep him under permanent contemplation. In England, forgetting Churchill seems as improbably blasphemous as Scotland forgetting Burns. Being folk-heroes and literary creators they invite wonder, but also laughter, and their laughter is shared with their wisest commemorative audiences. Neither seek adulation, both enlarge perception. And their truest worshippers make their most fervent prayers to them in silence and solitude.

Nationalism's ancient cargo

Patron saints began as local deities transfigured into suitable Christians, and their heaviest work must have been invocation by their worshippers to bring victory in war, as had been expected of the original little gods. Christianity's takeover of pre-Christian worship, most noticeably when the Winter Solstice became Christmas, might seem to show cracks through which the original pagan preoccupations were still faintly visible, which explains why Christmas was outlawed by Scots Calvinists. Catholic saints ought to function in complete harmony with God for He can do no wrong. Yet ancient local deities had duties in local nationalism, and so great Christian countries prayed to St George for England and St Andrew for Scotland while battling one another in the name of God. John Buchan put the theism of recent converts to Christianity into the mouth of an imaginary 9th century hunter in 'Wood Magic', ending:

> Wherefore to God the Father, the Son, and the Holy Ghost,
> Mary the Blessed Mother, and the kindly Saints as well,
> I will give glory and praise, and them I cherish the most,
> For they have the keys of Heaven, and save the soul from Hell.
> But likewise I will spare for the lord Apollo a grace,
> And a bow for the lady Venus – as a friend but not as a thrall.

'Tis true they are out of Heaven, but some day they may
win the place;
For gods are kittle cattle, and a wise man honours them all.

Buchan published the poem in his collection *The Moon Endureth*
where it follows 'The Grove of Ashtaroth', a tale told by a wooden,
moronic, no-nonsense administrator who discovers that a sensitive
friend is being enchanted by a surviving shrine of the Phoenician
goddess Ashtaroth, which the narrator destroys, and then in a final
sentence suddenly reveals unknown depths in himself:

And then my heartache returned, and I knew that I had
driven something lovely and adorable from its last refuge
on earth.

That capitulation from what had seemed an irredeemably pedestrian
mind highlights the hold imagination could lock on the modern
mind far more destructively than the deductions of the poetic pragmatic hunter a millennium earlier. Early 20th century nationalism
proved to have stocked ancient legacies whose revival helped induce
an Easter insurrection in 1916. Buchan's deliberate contrast of 'Ashtaroth' and 'Wood Magic' had a sensible moral: country folk have
lived for centuries with their conflicting cultures but the new sophistication of today is hopelessly vulnerable to unexpected resurrections.
We assume nationalism to be a custody and a presentation of familiar household gods and oft-remembered tales. But its strongest hold
may grip when the votary encounters the alien.

How English is English nationalism?

Folk-heroes may not be confined to a single nation. French peoples
tell tales of their great emperor Charlemagne and German peoples
of their Kaiser Karl der Grosse: the same man though not always the
same stories. The English with the aid of cunning Welsh story-tellers
such as the 12th century Geoffrey of Monmouth adopted the ancient
Welsh, and Cornish, hero King Arthur and had him 'Normanised'
by the 15th century Sir Thomas Malory and Anglicised by the 19th

century Alfred Tennyson. Folk tales about the ancient Gaelic hero Finn MacCool – or Fingal – might be found, sometimes in near-identical versions, in Argyll and Donegal, with Scotland or Ireland assigned as the locale according to where the story was retold. Robin Hood was an English ballad-hero, leading his 14th century outlaws in Sherwood Forest in Nottinghamshire, or in Barnsdale Forest in Yorkshire, against the enforcers of brutal Norman laws mutilating locals for killing the local deer put there by God and claimed by robber barons. The founder of modern social history, Walter Scott, trying his hand at the English 1190s for *Ivanhoe* (1819), made Robin a secondary Saxon hero known as Locksley peripherally involved in the rivalry between the Angevin brothers, King Richard 1 and his successor John, thus marooning him at least a century before his time in the subsequent Victorian fictionalisation of the old ballads. The children reading such stories often found Robin presented as a dispossessed Norman at odds with relatives or rivals, and thus ultimately a suitable authority figure claimable for English nationalism. Gilbert's *The Pirates of Penzance* satirised such snobbery forced on outlaws when its eponymous pirates are pardoned since they prove to be 'noblemen who have gone wrong'.

Christendom was founded on the deification of a victim of hideous imperial punishment, as the original Robin Hood ballads sometimes recalled (Robin's lieutenant Little John very appropriately swears by 'Him that died on tree'). Popular English nationalism at its deepest derived from folk memories of enemies of authority, hostile to tyrannical local officials such as the bloodthirsty Sheriff of Nottingham or prominent magnates such as the questionably wealthy Bishop of Hereford. Robin in the ballads is friendly to impoverished figures whether knights, craftsmen or clerics, notably Friar Tuck whom Scott includes in *Ivanhoe*. John Ball, the priest hanged, drawn and quartered in 1380 for inspiring the peasants' revolt, had asked 'when Adam delved and Eve span, Who was then the gentleman?' Contemporary with Ball, William Langland's *Piers Plowman* also linked piety to poverty, and to the ploughman. The tradition persisted when puritanism returned to allegory particularly in the tinker John Bunyan's *The Pilgrim's Progress*. English nationalism has so often been linked by its alleged inheritors to aggressive, rapacious greed that the moral strength and social truth of its Robin, its ploughman, and its pilgrim are missed, and yet we may find them at its heart of its unpretentious courage in 1940–41.

The alien as father of nationalism

Nationalism may find its sharpest symbols in foreign heroes, partly because being outsiders they can see nationalism's nation with a totality lost to the insider. We are all familiar with the nationalist leader from elsewhere, such as Georgian Stalin's rule of Russia, Austrian Hitler's rule of Germany, Corsican Napoleon's rule of France, half-American Parnell's rule of Ireland, American de Valera's rule of Ireland, half-American Churchill's rule of the UK, and Dubliner Carson's rule of Protestant Ulster. Yet the most striking case may be a man never becoming President of the USA yet shaping country and office – Alexander Hamilton. What united the USA anyway apart from the victory over Britain preceded by a brilliant cascade of political theory discovering its identity, and a mingling of literature and technology in Benjamin Franklin, and a masterly tactician as commanding general in Washington who ruled a Parnassus of intellectuals by seeing what they had missed?

I once surveyed what the leading American Revolutionary theoreticians said about Ireland – and some of them such as Ben Franklin himself, John Adams, Sam Adams, Hamilton, and the Scotsman James Wilson were fascinating, but Washington was the only one to remark that there did seem to be a religious problem in that country. Hamilton is in some ways partly Washington since he acted as amanuensis, secretary, aide-de-camp, ghost-writer, sidekick, wordsmith, think-tank, and honorary son. The influence was two-way, Hamilton surviving his mentor by only five years. Washington himself was the great unifying symbol of American nationalism in his time, but so little known that he is still commemorated by the entirely mythical event of his infant refusal to lie about having cut down his father's cherry-tree, whence Americans eat cherry-pie on Washington's birthday. The thing was an appalling libel: Washington's genius as a general lay strongly in taking deceptive action, and to assert that he would never tell a lie was to deny his military capacity.

To give the USA peacetime unity in 1789 when Hamilton took office as the first Secretary of the Treasury might well have seemed impossible, notwithstanding the glories of the Declaration of Independence and the grandeur of the Constitution. When they revolted in 1776, the 13 states consisted of a ribbon of white settlements running down the Atlantic seaboard surrounded on all sides by British-controlled territory or sea. From independence to 1861 Americans were forever devouring books about their country in hope of reassurance that it would survive although all the European democratic revolutionary regimes born in the same years had been obliterated. They read with intellect as well as with anger, and discovered what their identity seemed to mean to visitors from beyond. The reading and the reaction were in themselves American nationalism. We might call it passive American nationalism when they did not burn the book or caricature its author.

For active American nationalism we return to Hamilton. Born in Nevis in 1757 or maybe 1755, farther south and farther east than anywhere in the present-day USA. From the beginning he viewed the future continental USA as a totality, while almost all of his colleagues thought in terms of the individual colonies where they were born or to which they voyaged. As a student in King's (later Columbia) College in New York City, the teenage Hamilton showed himself one of the deepest polemicists in the pre-Revolution of the intellectuals, firmly declaring the global superiority of Continental Congress economic nationalism in answering a loyalist pamphleteer who had the additional attraction of being a friend of the college President. Hamilton always retained the ribald iconoclasm of a true student revolutionary, retained while organising an artillery company from first blood whose exploits won his place in Washington's entourage.

Washington, having led his USA to victory and then astounding humanity by resigning the supreme military command in the land he had liberated, knew how easily the younger Pitt (Prime Minister since 1784) might find it to win a return match, so to speak, with the European powers now far less hostile to Britain than during the war.

So he met with a few friends and acquaintances to think about improvements, whence his prestige led the existing Continental Congress to homologate their wishes. Washington's moral power, like that of the Church of Scotland in 1989, gave the impetus to constitution-making. The debates leading to the new Constitution in 1787 had little difficulty in devising a Presidency around Washington, so perfectly that no President since his time has quite reached the standard, whatever a candidate's other merits. The document as a whole showed its nationalism by its derivations and departures from British practice, French theory, and classical authorities. It meant a more centralised government with a real separation of powers between the executive, legislative, and judicial, and doing so clearly if not always faultlessly. It improved existing British and European theory, however grand. To sell the Constitution to a sufficient number of state voters for ratification, Hamilton, James Madison and John Jay produced 85 numbers of *The Federalist Papers* beginning in the New York *Independent or General Advertiser* on 27 October 1787. Hamilton, foremost among the Constitutional Convention's advocates of stronger central government power, knew that most of the 13 states would ratify (or not) far from his literary influence, but his own state, New York, would be crucial. His foresight and bargaining skill, charm and judgment, allies and organisation managed to defer New York ratification until late July 1788 when personal as well as polemical persuasion might have accumulated to greatest effect. The *Federalist* essays were intellectually challenging, but today's scholars may undervalue how widely Americans read and understood them. They were talking of their readers' future, and since 1763 American readers were accustomed to highbrow disputation. Today we have been depraved by the Murdochs and *Daily Mail*s so far that we devalue the intellects of our ancestors. They kept in mental training with much use of their Bibles. The New York *Independent* may not have had a wide fan-club, but it briefed readers to argue about its *Federalist* contents and inform themselves in the process. In the event, its greatest influence would have been on New York, with marginal effects on Delaware (ratifying the Constitution on 7 December 1787), Pennsylvania (12 December), New Jersey (18 December), Connecticut

(6 February 1788) and Massachusetts (with amendments 24 March 1788). We must also remember that however profound, the *Federalist* papers all signed PUBLIUS supplied endless fuel to stoke oral arguments among the public even in its public houses. The Constitution had taken the somewhat risky step of declaring it would become law for the USA when ratified by two-thirds. Just before Virginia (25 June 1788) and New York (26 July 1788) voted, the serious danger existed that with the two-thirds already reached by New Hampshire's ratification (21 June 1788), rejection by Virginia and/or New York would put major seaborne states outside the Constitution, and from Hamilton's viewpoint the country would be far worse divided than ever. Hamilton began the first *Federalist* essay (first published on 27 October 1787):

> After an unequivocal experience of the inefficacy of the subsisting federal government, you are called upon to deliberate on a new Constitution for the United States of America.

The author's youth, immigrant haste, genius and lack of scruple shone from the start. He made it appear that the existing constitutional situation under the Articles of Confederation (adopted towards the end of the war with Britain in 1781) would not be continued whatever happened: the status quo was not an option. In fact, the 'deliberation' to which voters were called could result in straight rejection and hence the maintenance of the existing Articles. Tiny Rhode Island did that on 24 March 1788 (only reversing that decision on 19 May 1790 when the Constitution had been accepted by the other 12 states). Hamilton opened the nine-month *Federalist* campaign by implying the sole alternative to ratification was amendments – on which several states would insist, thereby endowing the Constitution with its first ten amendments, now known as the Bill of Rights. He thus embodied nationalism at full gallop.

Machiavelli has traditionally been credited for 'nationalism' by specialists unready to admit any other users until the French Revolution, and certainly nationalists in the forefront of the nationalist fight frequently avail themselves of Machiavellian ethics. Nationalist leaders from Daniel O'Connell in 19th century Ireland to Barry Goldwater in mid-20th century USA were readily accused of tempering their rhetoric to their metropolitan legislatures while letting themselves go in their 'wild wests'. Hamilton from the outset also emphasised the international obligations of his nationalism, as do many nationalists. In fact, the ideal nationalist cause knows it is the cause of humankind. The debate on the Constitution would decide 'the fate of an empire in many respects the most interesting in the world'. His criterion was truly American in its salesmanship: the USA needed to win the world's attention more than to hope for acceptance, making a wiser claim than future American self-proclamation as 'the greatest country in the world'. Did the world face a future dictated by war or peace?

> [W]hether societies of men are really capable or not of establishing good government from reflection and choice, or whether they are forever destined to depend for their political constitutions on accident and force ... the crisis at which we are arrived may with propriety be regarded as the era in which that decision is to be made; and a wrong election of the part we shall act may, in this view, deserve to be considered as the general misfortune of mankind.

Nine months later he wrote *The Federalist*'s last words with characteristic war-cry to his audience for the next battle rather than any complacency:

> I dread the more the consequences of new attempts because I know that POWERFUL INDIVIDUALS, in this and other States, are enemies to a general national government in every possible shape.

This put his nationalism firmly in the tradition of Aristotle's and St Thomas Aquinas's views on the common good. He looked back to them, and forward to the democratic socialism of our own time, whence his major mid-20th century historian, Professor Broadus Mitchell, acknowledged his own socialism in the decade of McCarthyism and the Great Fear it engendered amongst intellectuals.

Hamilton's readiness to rally his fellow-nationalists against their powerful adversaries implied that nationalism was the weaker cause. His opponents (shortly to include his fellow-scribe of the *Federalist Papers* James Madison) would caricature him as the advocate of the rich, but he was a passionate supporter of workers when individual wealth demeaned and impoverished them. As Treasury Secretary he built up structures for the common good, a national banking system, championed protective tariffs for infant industries, bounties for agriculture, and insisted on redemption at par for state, as well as federal, public debts incurred during the American Revolution. It was characteristically Hamiltonian to make the people of the states think nationally by the hard economic fact of having the states' debts taken up by the federal government, as well as winning the USA a reputation as respected and reliable in its economic transactions, essential for its international commerce and investments by foreigners, above all the British themselves. He won his way on these questions by sophisticated negotiation with defenders of individual states' powers, and by encouraging and sharing scurrilous journalism at the expense of his opponents with enough glee of literary expression to make him the Peter Pan of the American Revolution as well as its economic giant.

Nationalism as a legal watchword

Hamilton's most remarkable legatee was his fellow-Washingtonian in Revolutionary War service, the Virginia lawyer John Marshall: appointed Chief Justice of the United States Supreme Court on 20 January 1801 by President John Adams (himself defeated in the Presidential election of 1800–01). Marshall would preside over the Court until his death in 1834. He would also deliver and mastermind Supreme Court decisions which would protect the America's good name in contract, prevent individual states from eroding federal legislation by adversary statutes, and enable inter-state communications to be opened up without blockage by self-interested parties.

On 24 February 1803 Marshall delivered judgment in *Marbury v. Madison* which held that Section 13 of the Judiciary Act of 1789 was contrary to the US Constitution, and therefore invalid. Until now the Supreme Court had shown some independence from US Presidency and Congress, but was too obviously a stage in ongoing legal or political careers. Marshall's judgment in the *Marbury* case established the principle of judicial review testing congressional legislation for its fidelity to the US Constitution. In so doing it enlarged time as test in American nationalism. Under the Constitution, the House of Representatives as a whole is elected every two years, while one-third of the Senate is chosen every two years. Thus the national political mood of one election year may be partly offset by that of two years previously, which in its turn is partly offset by that of two years before that. If the Supreme Court was now to judge whether Congressional Acts of former years were repugnant to the Constitution, once more the past would be enabled to correct the present.

Nationalism nourishes itself on a nation's awareness of its past, and the USA achieved a mathematical means of constitutional judgment of the present from past vantage-points. It does not mean that judicial minds remain where they had been at their date of appointment: Harlan F Stone of New Hampshire, President Calvin Coolidge's Attorney-General, was appointed Associate Justice of the Supreme Court in 1925 by him, and was President Franklin D Roosevelt's nominee for Chief Justice in 1941, the Great Depression having liberalised him. In 1953 President Eisenhower's choice for Supreme Court Chief Justice was Governor Earl Warren of California, a rival for the Republican nomination for President in 1952 and the Republican candidate for Vice-President in 1948. The Warren Court was the most liberal in living memory, and its landmark unanimous decision *Brown v the Board of Education of Topeka, Kansas* made desegregation of schools the vital first step in establishing racial equality before the law, despite little enthusiasm from Eisenhower. The magnitude of this achievement was replicated in the UK on 24 September 2019 when Marjorie Brenda Lady Hale, President of the UK Supreme Court, delivered a unanimous judgment declaring that Prime Minister Boris Johnson had given unconstitutional advice to Queen Elizabeth II to prorogue the UK Parliament, and that the resultant Order in Council was also void. Up to this point the UK Supreme Court looked like a characteristically artificial instalment in the Blair government's shop-window reforms. The UK had previously claimed separation of powers, which was ridiculous, seeing that the head of the English legal system, the Lord Chancellor, sat in the Cabinet and was removable by the Prime Minister. President Lady Hale established the Court as Supreme, as ready to tower over questionable decisions by government and legislature, as was the US Supreme Court when Marshall made his. Her achievement was the greater since she had no written constitution against which to measure disputes. Like Marshall and Warren, she vindicated nationalism in ensuring that her Court's decisions would be recognised at home and abroad as good law and just judgment.

Lincoln on Old Derry's Walls

In conventional political life, Hamilton's nationalism would be reaffirmed in various crises and confrontations by John Quincy Adams, Henry Clay, Daniel Webster, William H Seward and, most notably of all, by Abraham Lincoln. Adams's loss of the Presidency in 1828–29 to General Andrew Jackson created a different nationalism: officially hostile to the power of central government, its national bank, and its initiatives to help finance the growth of roads, canals and ultimately railroads in practical unification of the USA. Jackson instead altered focus on central government power, making the Presidency a personality cult flourishing a heroic, or at least inflatable, military record where possible. Jackson himself readily supplied a glorification of war as an American ethos, whether against the native Americans, the UK, Spain, and – when President – threatening war against France. Successors that owe their election victories to war service include William Henry Harrison, Zachary Taylor, Ulysses Grant, James Garfield, Benjamin Harrison, William McKinley, Theodore Roosevelt, Dwight David Eisenhower, and John Fitzgerald Kennedy.

Lincoln, the President whose nationalism remade the USA, had merely been a captain of volunteers in 1832 without experiencing combat. As Karl Marx pointed out, as President he differed from almost all politicians in accomplishing far more than he promised. He made moderation the tool of extremism. He appeared more moderate than many of his fellow-Republicans but his central theory was that no state could secede from the USA, and that secession conventions and post-secession elections were perpetually invalid. He offered generous terms to rebels who might seek return to the USA, and he hoped that the several states in rebellion would split between pro-Union and secessionist forces. However, when those divergences failed to produce enough useful results he reduced several southern states to near-starvation by scorched earth policies, realising that goodwill and diplomacy would not bring the reunion he craved. His armies ruthlessly – if perhaps unnecessarily – intervened to ensure his re-election in 1864, he ignored civil liberties and adverse Supreme Court judgments. He transformed pro-Union sentiment from malicious backbiting and empty boasting to a crusade for the liberation of the enslaved African-Americans under secessionist control. Arthur Conan Doyle, listening to the reminiscences of the dying black antislavery leader Henry Highland Garnet when they met off the coast of Liberia in 1882, thought those African-American troops must have resembled the puritans at war under Cromwell and Monmouth. His Sherlock Holmes stories celebrated the inter-racial marriage of a white woman to a black man, and denounced the Ku Klux Klan and other murder societies so uniquely for their first publication in the 1890s. Lincoln's own gentle, economic, sinewy, implacable rhetoric guided his followers and posterity whether in the Gettysburg Address on 19 November 1863 or his Second Inaugural Address of 4 March 1865. The Address dedicated the burial-ground for US fallen soldiers in the Battle of Gettysburg won by the US coincidentally, but appropriately, on 4 July 1863. Lincoln ignored the obvious secular sanctity of the day and instead took the great ground for nationalism by declaring its inspiration for humankind:

> ... from these honoured dead we take increased devotion
> to that cause for which they gave the last full measure

of devotion; that we here highly resolve that these dead shall not have died in vain; that this nation, under God, shall have a new birth of freedom; and that government of the people, by the people, for the people, shall not perish from the earth.

Using the dead sacrificed for nationalism to reaffirm, or to amend, nationalism's agenda was old. The French soldiers who would conquer at the Battle of Hastings in 1066 began their advance to a troubadour's song of the battle of Roncevaux where Charlemagne's men Roland, Olivier and their troops had been massacred by the Moors – in reality the Basques – in 778. Patrick Pearse's oration at the burial of the old Fenian Diarmuid O'Donovan Rossa in 1915 found his legacy in Irish commitment to independence thus foreshadowing Dublin's Easter Rising over which Pearse would preside the following year. The Canadian soldier John McRae used the same principle in his 'In Flanders Fields' where he pledged eternal belligerence in honour of the dead soldiers of the British Empire. But Lincoln made his nationalism's ideals universal. Promising to 'this nation, under God' 'a new birth of freedom' would automatically make most Americans identify the remade USA with God's own new birth as Jesus Christ, using the emancipation of slaves as a sign. The final words were sweeping but roughly accurate.

Where else on earth was this people-made government? The UK still lacked the serious beginnings of such a thing in law until the Reform Act of 1867. The French had dissolved their revolution-made democracies in the Empires of Napoleon I and Napoleon III. Having won his war in 1865, Lincoln's Second Inaugural made it clear in his penultimate sentences that whatever his earlier misgivings this newly-born USA would have to integrate black and white at whatever cost:

Fondly do we hope, fervently do we pray, that this mighty scourge of war may speedily pass away. Yet, if God wills that it continue until all the wealth piled by the bondsman's two hundred and fifty years of unrequited toil shall be sunk, and until every drop of blood drawn with the lash shall be repaid by another drawn with the sword, as was said three thousand years ago, so still it must be said, the judgments of the Lord are true and righteous altogether.

Lincoln, by his death a month later, became the martyr whose murder reaffirmed that new nationalism. Walt Whitman, poet of America and of humankind, drew patriotic symbolism from 1689, the relief of Derry whose Protestant British settlers had been besieged by French and Irish Catholic soldiers for 105 days, as told in Thomas Babington Macaulay's second instalment of his *History of England*. Macaulay's account appeared when huge floods of Irish Catholics fleeing the Great Famine led Americans, like Whitman, to fear that their freedom would be undermined by proslavery Irish Catholic politicians. Whitman particularly detested the militant sectarian Ulster-born Catholic Bishop of New York, John Joseph Hughes, who denounced Daniel O'Connell for telling the Irish emigrants to the USA to oppose Negro slavery. The starvation of the Derry Protestants in 1689 had been ensured by guns firing from the banks of the River Foyle but ultimately the ship *Mountjoy*, captained by the Derry-born Micaiah Browning, appeared, followed by two others:

At length the little squadron came to the place of peril. Then the *Mountjoy* took the lead, and went right at the boom. The huge barricade cracked and gave way: but the shock was such that the *Mountjoy* rebounded, and stuck in the mud. A yell of triumph rose from the banks: the Irish rushed to their boats, and were preparing to board; but the *Dartmouth* poured on them a well-directed broadside, which threw them into disorder. Just then the *Phoenix* dashed at the breach which the *Mountjoy* had made, and was in a moment within the fence. Meanwhile the tide was rising fast. The *Mountjoy* began to move, and soon passed safe through the broken stakes and floating spars. But her brave master was no more. A shot from one of the batteries had struck him; and he died by the most enviable of all deaths, in sight of the city which was his birthplace, which was his home, and which had been saved by his courage and self-devotion from the most frightful form of destruction.

These lines were placed on Derry's walls as an act of Ulster Protestant nationalism. They were placed within the Irish Free State's first major history for schoolchildren to admire in *A Class-Book of Irish History* by Irish Catholic republican scholar James Carty, fostering ecumenism in Irish nationalism. Whitman evidently read one of the thousands of American pirated printings of Macaulay's *History*, and mourned for Lincoln's death in lines also appropriate for that of Micaiah Browning, as by an imaginary Derry cabin-boy:

O Captain! my Captain! Our fearful trip is done.
The ship has weathered every rack, the prize we sought
is won,
The port is near, the bells I hear, the people all exulting,
While follow eyes the steady keel, the vessel grim and daring;
But O heart! heart! heart!
O the bleeding drops of red,
Where on the deck my Captain lies,
Fallen cold and dead.

O Captain! my Captain! rise up and hear the bells;
Rise up – for you the flag is flung – – for you the bugle
trills,
For you bouquets and ribbon'd wreaths – for you the
shores a-crowding,
For you they call, the swaying mass, their eager faces
turning;
Here Captain! dear father!
This arm beneath your head!
It is some dream that on the deck,
You've fallen cold and dead.

My Captain does not answer, his lips are pale and still,
My father does not feel my arm, he has no pulse nor will,

The ship is anchor'd safe and sound, its voyage closed
and done,
From fearful trip the victor ship comes in with object
won;
Exult O shores, and ring O bells!
But I with mournful tread,
Walk the deck my Captain lies,
Fallen cold and dead.

Whitman would have recognised Micaiah Browning's people as kin to the Scots-Irish who in frontier America had repeated the role they had sustained on the Anglo-Scottish borders and in Ulster, at odds with the natives, with local law enforcement, and with central government. The young Lincoln grew up in frontier Kentucky and frontier Indiana and settled in post-frontier Illinois. His ancestry both Welsh and English including the 9th century Welsh King Rhodri Mawr, the 13th century English King Edward 1, and the 15th century Welsh leader and hero Owain Glyn Dwr: all three of them exemplars in nationalism, Rhodri to unite Wales, Edward to unite the archipelago, Owain to resurrect Wales. Whitman did no violence to historical probability in the likeness he drew and the source whence he drew it. Both Bible-nurtured frontiersmen, Micaiah and Abraham, died for a Union whose central government was far from their own origins in manners, in morals and in nationalism, and for them the Union cause whether in the British Isles or in the United States had to be vindicated at whatever cost in bloodshed and in self-sacrifice, let courtiers in the capital vacillate as they might.

Nationalism and nationalisation

The ancestors of Lincoln's nationalism were classic enough, being the enactments of Hamilton, the judgments of Marshall, the programme of Clay. Yet as the doctrine was identified with what had proved itself the sacred cause of Union, the label of nationalism might seem forgotten while the actuality of nationalism has taken the supreme command. The label was commissioned by extraordinary hands. Edward Bellamy was a hardworking journalist and shy novelist who was born, and died, in Chicopee Falls, Massachusetts. In 1888 he produced *Looking Backward 2000–1887* which became the USA's best-selling novel to date other than Harriet Beecher Stowe's *Uncle Tom's Cabin* and General Lew Wallace's *Ben-Hur*. Its success as story and sermon was founded on structure. The protagonist, Julian West, falls asleep in Boston in the year 1887 and wakes up in 2000 to discover himself in an ideal society, where the nation controls the means of production and distribution, poverty and class conflict have been eliminated, the revolution has been achieved by non-violent means, all the inhabitants co-operate. They have found a true 'nationalism' in which the people of the nation vindicate their love of country by ensuring the best for all of its inhabitants. The principle is socialism, but Bellamy disliked the word and thought it likely that it would repel readers from acceptance of his ideas.

Nationalism, if somewhat outdated as an American word, still held a respectable, even a revered status. 'National' had proved a useful catch-all with which to describe the sentiments of all the USA's states, such as each political party naming its quadrennial meeting its 'National Convention' whose delegates from every state convened for nomination of their Presidential candidate. The USA sold 400,000 copies of *Looking Backward* by 1897; significantly the UK edition was subtitled *If Socialism Comes* and sold 235,000 from 1890 to 1935. The dynamic of the book lies in the final chapter where Julian West finds himself awake and back in the year 1887, realising as he never has previously its horrors of cruelties, hypocrisies, social injustice, class hatred, as the wealthy cling to what they have amassed and vilify honest social critics. The inferno suddenly ends as West wakes once again to discover that the return to 1887 has been the dream. All is well: he's in the year 2000 and will live happily ever after. We close the book – and realise that while West is safe, we are trapped in our own time. What are we going to do to save our contemporaries from the society in which they have imprisoned themselves?

The book had a terrific impact on both sides of the Atlantic, with vast numbers of nationalist clubs founded in America. Herbert

Croly preached the idea of a New Nationalism in his *The Promise of American Life* (1909) with Hamiltonian central government to eradicate social evils. In 1912 ex-President Theodore Roosevelt campaigned for re-election under a new Progressive Party making the New Nationalism its platform and winning over 4 million votes: easily beating the Republicans, but defeated by the Democrat Woodrow Wilson, who called his own ideological programme 'The New Freedom'. Once in office Wilson enacted much of the New Nationalism. Its ideas were revived, deepened, and made much more effective by, Roosevelt's Democrat cousin Franklin D Roosevelt's New Deal from 1933. It was based, at its most enduring, in the realities learned and taught by social workers but *Looking Backward* was revived and helped to fire the fuel to fight the Great Depression. Bellamy's biographer, Arthur Morgan, became the head of the new Tennessee Valley Authority utilising natural resources for public benefit rather than private profit. Meanwhile it was taken up in the UK by the young Labour Party. When the Welfare State emerged from the wartime UK in 1945, Clement Attlee's Labour Government called its programme 'nationalisation', of which the most famous creation would be the National Health Service.

CHAPTER TWO

Unionism is Nationalism – from Colin Kidd to Gordon Brown

To every thing there is a season, and a time to every purpose under the heaven:
A time to be born, and a time to die; a time to plant, and
a time to pluck up that which is planted;
A time to kill, and a time to heal; a time to break down,
and a time to build up;
A time to weep, and a time to laugh; a time to mourn, and
a time to dance.

Ecclesiastes 3:1–4

1707 *And All That*

I HAD ALMOST finished writing this book when my attention was
drawn to a speech by Professor Colin Kidd of St Andrews. He had
made the speech before a symposium (apparently held in Birming-
ham) called to discuss 'The Union and Unionism' on 21 May 2018.
It had been hosted by Policy Exchange, an institution claiming
independence for itself if not for anyone else, but which seems as
inseparable from the Tory Party as Ganymede from Jupiter (I speak
astronomically, of course). '1707', he told them, 'is not a significant date in Scottish popular culture, whether to Unionists or to
nationalists'.

Professor Kidd is one of the wisest, most entertaining and most
likeable historians amongst us. Like many other of his aphorisms,
his judgment on the year of the Anglo-Scottish Union is more
thought-provoking than clearly right or wrong. How many dates

are remembered in popular culture? The authority for that, as for so much else, is the invaluable satirical work of Anglo-Scottish scholarship, *1066 and All That* by WC Sellar and RJ Yeatman which held that there were only two memorable dates, 55BCE, when Julius Caesar arrived albeit briefly, and 1066AD. 1066 was 'a significant date' in English popular culture, but who remembers why (save that it included battles at Fulford Gate, Stamford Bridge and Hastings, three successive kings, a fourth (Edgar Aetheling) chosen but not crowned, and a fifth (King Harald Hardrada of Norway) killed in battle shortly after arrival)? Well, General Charles de Gaulle remembered why. In 1965 Prime Minister Harold Wilson asked him for a loan of the French Army for a pageant re-enacting the Battle of Waterloo, and the French President replied that he was unable to provide it since it would be needed for a re-enactment of the Battle of Hastings in 1966.

Charles de Gaulle was a profound nationalist whose fervour saved France in World War II by drawing on the strong historical French nationalist traditions of right and left. Above all on St Joan of Arc, recently canonised – her cult called on French Christianity, the Army, feminism and revolution. De Gaulle also relied on UK nationalism in 1940 – its finest hour – defying eminent French and British persons who were ready to settle for subordination under Hitler. The alliance between Churchill's UK and de Gaulle's Free French in London – with fervent but unknown support in occupied and neutralised France – was an alliance between two nationalisms at their bravest. It drew on histories and myths of their former glories, which inevitably meant drawing on memories of their countries' battles against one another: John Churchill (first Duke of Marlborough) defeats the French in the War of the Spanish Succession (1704–09); Joan of Arc defeats the English and is made a martyr by fire at their hands and those of their reverend stooges (1429–31); and Henry V invades France (1415) – immortalised by Shakespeare and brought to UK cinemas as moral (if somewhat self-centred) support for the actual UK and US liberation of France (1944–45). After the fall of France in 1940, Churchill and de Gaulle proposed a union between the exiled France and the UK, but like many other unions it was led by a fantasy.

Yet the spirit of this proposed union endured in the faith in a future where both countries would be free.

Does a union have nationalism?

Professor Kidd implies that a union perhaps ought to have a reverence towards its date of enactment. The festival the US honours above all others is the Fourth of July: the official birthday of the Declaration of Independence in 1776. Its 50th anniversary was marked by the deaths of the Declaration's two principal creators, Thomas Jefferson aged 83 and John Adams aged 90. Thereafter the Fourth wallowed even deeper in patriotic discourse from aspiring politicians in what seemed every township across the US, perpetually seeking to inflame US nationalism beyond all previous heat although somewhat anachronistically climaxing in defiance of George III. Communications media conventionally refer to the US as 'the nation', distinct from its 50 component states. The American Revolution had certainly created its nationalism, expressed in the Declaration itself and anticipated in some of the deeply learned polemics with which the most learned of the rebels anticipated it, as well as in the rude songs. We could even say that the British created American nationalism, let's give them their due.

Each nationalism wraps around its nationhood. US nationalism formally originates in the two documents – one declaring, and one defining, the existence of the US – on display in the US National Archives in Washington, DC and to be buried in the bowels of the earth by the pressure of a button in the event of a nuclear attack (as close as possible to the moment the President of the US presses a nuclear button). The Declaration of Independence remains as it was when enacted in 1776, absorbing the independence declared by each of the 13 former British colonies immediately united together and followed by admission of 37 more states to date. The Constitution of 1787 has continuously been enlarged by amendments since its ratification onward.

UK nationalism formally originates in the reigning sovereign king or queen (save for the interregnum period of 1649–60) and its national anthem instructs God to save the king or queen as the case may be. Each US and UK national anthem originated when each regime was in mortal danger, which both 'nations' have taken pains to forget, dropping awkward verses in the process. 'God Save the King' was first performed at Drury Lane and Covent Garden Theatre in the most perilous moment for Great Britain between 1707 and 1801. The Jacobite army, headed by Bonnie Prince Charlie having won the battle of Prestonpans on 21 September 1745, were heading southward. English suspicions were increasing that that George II might flee back to his native Hanover and doubts were whispered as to whether this or that Tory squire might not revert to his family's Jacobite sympathies 30 years since. Was God being told subliminally that it was up to Him rather than anyone else? The Hanoverians were not beautiful, and were expensive, their best politician being George's dead wife Caroline, as hilariously described in Walter Scott's *The Heart of Midlothian*. On 11 May 1745, in the War of the Austrian Succession the King's younger son, William Duke of Cumberland led his troops to defeat at Fontenoy (chiefly by Irish Catholic soldiers exiled under the Hanoverian regime) which gave some fire to the ensuing Jacobite insurrection under Prince Charlie in Scotland, who landed at Eriskay on 23 July 1745. Cumberland back from the European battlefields was made commander-in-chief but had not yet displaced the experienced Marshal George Wade saluted by the new national anthem in the verse:

> Lord, grant that Marshal Wade
> May by thy mighty aid,
> Victory bring.
> May he sedition hush,
> And like a torrent rush
> Rebellious Scots to crush,
> God save the King.

English nationalism might have doubts about its kings, but clearly knew its enemies. In any event, Cumberland superseded Wade and confronted Charlie back in Scotland at Culloden, where he crowned his victory with treatment of the defeated soldiers immortalising him as 'the Butcher Cumberland': the English remembered him in the flower 'Sweet William'. A marching song was recast in his in his honour. 'The British Grenadier(s)' now ran:

> Some talk of Alexander,
> And some of Hercules,
> Of Hector and Lysander,
> And such great men as these;
> But of all the world's great heroes
> There's none that can compare
> To the gallant Duke of Cumberland,
> And the British Grenadier!

But when some Scottish soldiers had been recruited and begun to win battles for Hanoverian England, the Butcher's name was replaced by the anodyne: 'With a tow row-row-row row-row-row row-row-row/ To the British Grenadier(s)!'. Similarly, the national anthem elided the verse requiring the crushing of rebellious Scots, now that they were expected to do the crushing.

The US took over a century to name Francis Scott Key's 'Star-Spangled Banner' as its national anthem, but it too was supremely symbolic. The War of 1812 had gone badly on land for the Americans, and on the night of 24 August 1814 the UK captured and burnt the US's capital city Washington, DC. After this they attempted to capture the world's port of Baltimore, Maryland, and thus divide the US between north and south and decisively demoralise its citizens, particularly those in New England who were contemplating abandonment of the union. Everything turned on the defence of the US Fort McHenry, whose bombardment the Maryland lawyer Scott Key witnessed. Agonising through the night of 13 September as to the fate of the fort, and that of the country, Key wrote the first verse: so confidently sung today but created with searing doubts as he waited. Then he sees the American flag still flying over the fort and all is well. His third verse turned his fear and anger against the ruthless UK troops, but even more against the doubters and potential traitors:

Oh, where is that band
Who so vauntingly swore
That the havoc of war
And the battle's confusion
A home and a country
Should leave us no more?
Their blood has washed out
Their foul footsteps' pollution.
 No refuge could save
The hireling and slave
From the terror of flight
And the gloom of the grave.
But the Star-spangled banner
In triumph doth wave
O'er the land of the free
And the home of the brave!

This verse was duly disappeared in the reaffirmation of the union
when New England had returned to its allegiance and – 103 years
later – the Union Jack and the Star-Spangled Banner flew alongside
one another in the Great War. The strength of the national anthems
partly derives from the concealed terror in which they were written.
They have their darker side, the UK's as expressed in Byron's 'The
Vision of Judgment' verse 13:

God Save the King!
It is a large economy
In God to save the like.

He supplied a context (this time on George IV rather than George
III the recently deceased subject of the 'Judgment'):

But still there is unto a patriot nation,
Which loves so well its country and its king,
A subject of sublimest exaltation.
Bear it, ye Muses, on your brightest wing.
Howe'er the mighty locust, Desolation,
Strip your green fields and to your harvests cling,

> Gaunt Famine never shall approach the throne!
> Though Ireland starve, great George weighs twenty stone!

Don Juan (1823), VIII. 126.

Byron, courtesy of his friend and future biographer Thomas Moore, had become an honorary Irish nationalist. Francis Scott Key deserves his fame, and the defenders of Fort McHenry deserve applause for saving their country, but Key's third verse carries a terrible – and presumably unintentional – irony. African Americans today sometimes sing that same third verse in memory of the American slaves who fled to British lines during the war of 1812. Key's use of the word 'slave' to express ultimate contempt was all too natural: he was a slaveholder in Maryland, a state still maintaining slavery half a century later. His 'land of the free' was also the home of the brave who, during the War of 1812, were throwing themselves on the mercy of the UK – the national enemy – in hope they would thereby become free. His song became the national anthem in 1931 in the same era that his namesake and collateral descendant F Scott Fitzgerald, with incomparable art, was exposing the self-destruction of the 'American Dream' in *The Great Gatsby*. What gave both of these songs their immortality and ghostly tension is the spectre of doubt hovering over both, however little their present-day singers and listeners recognise it.

They embody true nationalism, and perhaps nationalism can only reach truly heroic stature when in mortal danger. The Jews wrote down the sacred narratives they had recited down the generations when they had been defeated, massacred, and exiled in Assyria, Babylon, Persia. The Romans won themselves their immortal epic, Virgil's *Aeneid*, by narration of their alleged ancestors in a hellish defeat, the destruction of Troy, recited by Aeneas with such agony of memory in the second book. They are national anthems, but each was born of their Union in peril. 'God Save the King' was first sung with fear that Scotland was about to be lost from the United Kingdom; 'The Star-Spangled Banner' feared the loss of New England from the American Union.

Colin Kidd's implied question

Nationalism is usually damned for being created against someone or some people, but unions in our British archipelago are far more directly children of hostilities – against the Pope in 1536, against Louis XIV in 1707, against Napoleon in 1801, against Irish Catholics in 1922. If the US and UK are both unions, why doesn't the UK celebrate 1707 as Americans celebrate the creation of their union? Perhaps on the date of its first operation after enactment, 1 May? May Day is certainly celebrated for other reasons, notably socialism, and perhaps revolution, and certainly ancient pagan rites of spring, but none seem very relevant to the Lords Queensberry, Godolphin and Marlborough. Indeed, in February 2011 Parliament, under the Cameron Tories, contemplated the creation of a United Kingdom Day, perhaps 21 October to coincide with celebration of the Battle of Trafalgar, but at least downgrading the month of May known for associations with workers. No doubt the idea won applause from resurrected Tories, but its rapid disappearance reinforces Professor Kidd's perception.

How far did the extension of the union of 1707 into the Union of Great Britain and Ireland in 1800 and its retraction into the Union of Great Britain and Northern Ireland in 1922 produce different nationalisms? Why is the Union of England and Wales in 1536–42 overlooked in most talk of unions? (The Welsh have been the most successful among the weaker partners of unions of the British Isles in maintaining their own visible linguistic identity, but with little encouragement from prominent unionists – apart from David Lloyd George, who waged war for the Union in Ireland in 1920–21 until manoeuvred towards diplomacy by George v.) How unique is the Union of England and Scotland in 1707 in being between two independent countries with one monarch, while Wales in 1536–42 and Ireland in 1800 had both been conquered by England long ago? There is the problem, that mobilisers of the Union seem perpetually doomed never to get its name right.

The Union from 1707 to 1801 was 'Britain', indeed in its makers' minds 'Great Britain'. However, as pointed out by Nancy Mitford, it was vulgar ('or non-U') to say 'Britain': to be 'U' or upper-class one had instinctively to say 'England' (her grandfather had been married to Winston Churchill's wife's aunt). We could perhaps trace it back to St Bede the Venerable, father of English history, who wrote in the early 8th century very much aware of Britons, Picts, Scots and English but primarily concerned with the English whom he defined as mingling Angles, Saxons and Jutes. The problem continues to the later 20th century when the slightly desperate use of 'English' for 'British' by latter-day snobs has trickled away, since when 'Britain' is omnipresent with adverse results for the Union and its scholarship. Professor Steven Grosby in *Nationalism: A Very Short Introduction* mused, 'what is one to make of Great Britain, which contains England, Scotland, Wales, and Northern Ireland?'

One is to make nothing of it, since it doesn't. Great Britain has been no more than a geographical expression since New Year's Day 1801 when the Union of Great Britain and Ireland came into legal effect. The Union of Great Britain and Northern Ireland has been the state's legal title since 1922. From the point of view of simple arithmetic, Great Britain hardly deserves its usurpation, having been the shortest-lived union on record. The Union of England and Wales from 1536–42 to 1707 ran for 165–171 years, the Union of Great Britain for 93 years, the Hiberno-British Union for 122 years, the Union of Great Britain and Northern Ireland for 100 years, so far. The indolent failure of British politicians and their media camp-followers to give Northern Ireland its due (despite 50 years' expenditure of blood and treasure) is having its effect. Northern Ireland in the 20th century has been easily considered as Protestant Unionist nationalism embedded (in perpetual virginity) with Irish Catholic nationalism. At least some observers recognised that each category was divided into the violent and the non-violent, allowing for sympathies for the violent, rising and falling among some of the non-violent. Today Northern Ireland is becoming a nation in the eyes of many of its citizens, the Catholics aware of their emotional exploitation by Dublin, the Protestants of chief valuation as parliamentary lobby-fodder by London. The wretched device of 'Team GB' excluded Northern Ireland from the UK Olympic Games in 2012, leaving its athletes to take refuge with the Republic of Ireland while the very great Olympic champions from the UK were venerated by the UK Government and Olympia officials only as far as the seashore. (For some of us its supreme moment was Andy Murray's tennis victory, foretelling Wimbledon 2013 when he would regain the Wimbledon Championship last won by Britain in 1936, a truly appropriate victory for a supporter of Scottish independence.)

During its first 50 years Northern Ireland reduced its Roman Catholics to second-class citizenship. Today many Northern Irelanders of any religion, or none, conclude that London regards the entire province as a second-class backwater. They signal a noteworthy birth of a new nationalism. In its own way it is the latest outbreak of a permanent London disease evident for diagnosis since the Middle Ages. It was a general maxim for London administrators that after five years in any place beyond their island but under English (and later, British) rule, English officials have probably gone native. The American Revolution, for instance, ended by winning independence, but the original quarrel often looked as though the Americans insisted on their Englishness, which the English denied. This was irrelevant to the Anglo-Scottish Union of 1707, our only union officially achieved without lengthy and vicious wars of conquest. They had their wars, but those were not precursors of the Union of Crowns under James VI/I in 1603 any more than for the Parliamentary Union of 1707. That last had its own elements of fraud, not simply those legislators who are now being proved to have believed in what they took money and status for doing. But as the late, great John Davies wrote in his *Hanes Cymru*, translated as *A History of Wales*:

> Deception and trickery were necessary in order to induce the members of the parliaments of Scotland and Ireland to acquiesce in their abolition, but at least there was acquiescence; the Welsh Act of 'Union' was passed solely by the parliament of England, a body lacking members from Wales.
>
> Furthermore, 27 Henry VIII c 26 claimed that union between Wales and England already existed. The

> preamble states: 'Wales… is and ever hath bene incor-
> porated, annexed, united and subjecte to and under the
> imperial Crown of the Realme as a verrye member…
> of the same.'

The 'ever hath bene' (probably the work of Thomas Cromwell) is a nice touch. Firstly, it removes its argument from sanity (or should we imagine Adam telling Eve how Wales was always part of England?), and secondly, it brings itself smartly down to George Orwell's *Nineteen Eighty-Four* where Oceania is at war with Eurasia and has always been at war with Eurasia until, in mid-speech, the eternal war becomes against Eastasia with Eurasia as our glorious ally. The control of eternity is the ultimate of nationalism when it rots into totalitarianism. Henry VIII had stronger 20th century links than mere Brexit. That Thomas Cromwell was executed half-way through his making of the union with Wales is picturesque proto-Stalinism.

With all due disrespects to Cromwell (whose recent cult seems a somewhat sinister fashion), the union's meaning for Henry himself may be even more interesting. Henry VIII's father Henry VII was born in Wales, son of a legitimised Edmund Tudor and of Margaret Beaufort, granddaughter of a legitimised son of John of Gaunt, son of Edward III. Various, usually legitimate, Plantagenet cousins were executed by every Tudor monarch. In strict terms of genealogical descent Henry VIII's claim to England's throne was through his mother, Elizabeth of York, daughter of Edward IV. This was also matter of concern to Tudor civil servants. When James VI of Scotland was proclaimed James I of England in 1603 the official English statement of his eligibility wasted little time in proving his obvious cousinhood to his late predecessor Elizabeth I. Instead it took pains to argue that Margaret Tudor, wife of James IV of Scotland (James VI's great-grandmother from whom he inherited his claim to the English throne), was the legitimate granddaughter of Edward IV. Henry VIII may have owed his beautiful singing voice, and skill as musical performer and composer to his Welsh ancestry, but he wished to disavow any suggestion that he favoured Welsh rights: Wales being clearly associated with questionable genealogical Tudor claims other than his father Henry VII's claim by right of conquest having defeated Richard III, slain at the battle of Bosworth in 1485. Hence Henry VIII's demand for Welsh-speakers to be denied office in Wales, his insistence on English perpetual superiority, abolition of Welsh law, usages and customs.

Henry's bastardised daughter Elizabeth I had more sense and tied Protestant reform in Wales to the translation of the Bible and Prayer-Book into Welsh thus making Welsh Protestantism an affirmation of Welsh nationalism, which it revived. In the late 19th and early 20th centuries the disestablishment of the state Protestant Episcopalian Church of Wales was the foremost cry, seeking equal rights for the Calvinistic Methodists and Baptists.

Unions united parliaments; but did they unite countries? The Union of The Irish Parliament, dissolved by its own consent, had officially served a population four-fifths Roman Catholics forbidden to be elected to it. It bred a strange myth basic to Catholic nationalism that they had suffered a great wrong in the abolition of the Irish Parliament. The myth had its uses in leading Irish Catholicism to the forefront of pressure towards democracy, somewhat contrary to prevailing thought in the 19th century Vatican. Predominantly Catholic countries succumbed to early 20th century totalitarianism, notably Italy, Spain, Austria and Portugal. Ireland was infected with the ethos of military heroism, as was all of Europe, but Irish fascism hardly ascended beyond the ridiculous. The English were much credited by their rivals, enemies and restless subjects with dividing the territories they ruled amongst mutually hostile religions, lifestyles and economies. In fact, all four countries in the archipelago paid far too little attention to one another. Their nationalisms did enable some of them to study one another culturally as well as politically. Their internal divisions were organic, Lowland vs Highland, Gaelic vs English vs Scots, rural vs industrial.

Nationalism on the Fifth of November

When the Union of Great Britain and Ireland had been enacted with effect from 1 January 1801, the Edinburgh authorities issued public statements that all persons well-affected towards the UK would naturally welcome the new union. Hence there was no need to celebrate it, and anyone found celebrating it would be dealt with forcibly. Presumably the authorities would distinguish between people still continuing their celebration of Hogmanay beyond 31 December 1800, and those celebrating Union with Ireland. There may also have been suspicions of another form of union: in the 1790s the United Irishmen had evolved from Irish reformers to Francophile revolutionaries ending in rebellion, slaughter and executions in 1798. They had mysterious counterparts in the United Englishmen and the United Scotsmen, whose survivors might find celebrating the union useful disguises for reuniting the united. An event that means most to a posterity is remembered above all on its supreme day, *1066 and All That* reporting on the Gunpowder Plot that:

> [T]he day and month of it (though not, of course, the year) are well known to be *utterly* and even maddeningly MEMORABLE... Although the plan failed attempts are made every year on St Guyfawkes' Day to remind the Parliament that it would have been a *Good Thing*.

Sellar and Yeatman demonstrated how easily the supposed villain of the commemoration may become the hero. To many 17th century Roman Catholics, Guy Fawkes and his mates were the heroes, or at least the martyrs. What was intended to kindle anti-Catholic renewal might by its very bonfires venerate Protestant martyrdoms such as those of Hugh Latimer and other clerics in the reign of the Catholic Mary Tudor. The annual processions and final immolation of an image of Guy Fawkes show origin in processions bearing images of Jesus Christ and His mother Mary at Catholic festivals. Guy Fawkes and his memorialists bore two opposing nationalisms. Nationalisms continue to poach from one another's paraphernalia, all the more when they are mortal enemies. The annual ritual 'Remember, remember, the Fifth of November' may have been adopted within a year or so of the original plot and its detection, and echo Shakespeare's *Julius Caesar* when Brutus, having been driven from Rome after murdering Caesar, demands that his fellow-assassin Cassius reaffirm Brutus's own self-justification:

> Remember March, the Ides of March remember:
> Did not great Julius bleed for justice' sake?
> What villain toucht his body, that did stab,
> And not for justice?

Nationalism at its most vocal demands the purity of its knights, much as chivalry demanded that they suffer penance and win absolution for their sins before combat. The audience knows that Cassius, for one, was additionally motivated by jealousy. But Brutus and he stabbed Caesar to protect the republican integrity of Rome – in other words, for nationalism. Nationalism depends on memory, however imaginary. The play ironically shows the actions of Brutus and Cassius sealing the fate of the republic they are trying to save, and if their nationalism retains some of its hold on Roman political identity thereby it strengthens a new (Augustan) empire to come to fruition in *Antony and Cleopatra*.

It was a Welsh victory – that of the future Henry VII at Bosworth in 1485 – which cleared the way for an Anglo-Welsh constitutional Union. Common nationalist fears against France ensured the Union of England and Scotland in 1707, fleshed out by uneasy respect for Marlborough's armies. The rebellion of Irish Catholic and Protestant nationalists in 1798 led to the Union of 1800. UK wartime nationalism, Ulster Protestant Unionist nationalism, and Irish Catholic neo-nationalism in 1920–22 remodelled the 1800 Union into its present identity. All of them turned on remembering 'with advantages' – as Shakespeare's Henry V judges in the eponymous play (IV.III.50) – their particular versions of the past. *Henry V* is English poetic nationalism in the raw, but *Hamlet* equates nationalism with a dead father, commander, king – its most personally effective symbols. (It also shows nationalism theatrically devaluing diplomacy for all of its skill in maintaining an honourable peace – objectively, Claudius was a better king than old Hamlet, and killed far fewer people.)

The neo-jacobite unionists

The Union of 1707 has won little popularity among Scottish politicians or tourist-trappers, and was defended with dislike in its own time as well as later. Creativity in speech, song, poetry and prose kept a far more complex and sophisticated perception of the past alive than was evident in the works of those whom Thomas Carlyle labelled 'Dryasdust'. Romance was on the side of losers, whether Jacobites or Covenanters. Good Protestants from Queen Victoria down to mid-20th century readers of the *Adventure* comic (published by DC Thomson of Dundee) thrilled to latter-day Jacobite verse and swashbuckling prose. But there had been a good deal of 18th century realism in the old cause. Irish Jacobites, for instance, yearned for the return of the Royal Stuarts but thought it hopeless to recover Ireland or Scotland without conquering England, as had been shown by the failure of Scots and Irish Jacobites to hold their own kingdoms for the Stuarts once the English and (even more) the Dutch consolidated their counter-attack in 1689–92. Sir Walter Scott was a unionist in cultural rebellion against unionism past and present. The long-term effect of the Union was to discourage British interest in Scotland as an historical entity. Scott poured his life into the preservation of the past, whether from folklore, from his publication of ancient documents official or personal, from his creation of social history in his fiction or from his bardic ability to make the Scottish past in his prose and verse prove itself as enthralling as the wars of Greeks and Romans. History was his means of making contemporaries respect a living Scotland; Scott manipulated his contemporary King George IV as a tourist attraction, potentially lucrative for Scotland. He was in fact a classic cultural nationalist and formally a Tory Unionist for reasons indicated in his *Redgauntlet* where an insurrection in 1759 is planned but quietly abandoned at the end as hopeless by now. The two protagonists Darsie Latimer the folklorist and Alan Fairford the lawyer are both partly self-portraits, deeply moving in their mutual love, symbolising the generosity and the schizophrenia of Scott's nationalism nurtured by the past. Politically he was narrow-minded (with startling moments of rebellious polemic) protecting the nationalism on his historiographical agenda, and resembling a person looking through a keyhole through which they can see in many dimensions enchanted landscapes and people. His literary disciple Robert Louis Stevenson showed in *Kidnapped* how his fellow-unionists could be drawn into alliance with Jacobites, his youthful readers usurping the involuntary capitulation of the innocent boy Whig David Balfour decisively captured in Muriel Spark's *The Prime of Miss Jean Brodie*.

The uses of union in 1900

The centenary of the Union of 1707 was of little visible relevance in 1807. 'England expects that every man will do his duty' signalled Nelson leading the navy to victory at Trafalgar in 1805 and leaving Scotland, Ireland and Wales to fall in silently (although Prime Minister Pitt had formed a devoted partnership in politics with the Scot Henry Dundas, First Lord of the Admiralty up to the year of Trafalgar). In fact, Nelson had perfectly summed up what was demanded by English nationalism, which assumed any other nationalisms in the Union would know their places. Hence in 2011, the Cameron Tories' idea of a UK Day.

1900, the centenary of the Union of Great Britain and Ireland, occasioned mobilisation of the big battalion. The octogenarian Queen Victoria sailed for Ireland on 2 April, exact centenary of the Irish Parliament having voted its own extinction in 1800, although that latest union only became effective on 1 January 1801. Victoria had founded the Irish Guards on 1 April 1900 (with specific duties to guard the Royal Family) in recognition of Irish service in the Second Boer War which otherwise was proving tough going for the UK. The siege of Mafeking still continued after 170 days, another 47 still ahead: the wild celebrations in the UK at Mafeking's relief reflected the shock at such prolonged Boer resistance. Irish Catholics had been officially vetoed as military recruits during most of the 18th century, despite the success with which the recently rebellious Highland Scottish Jacobites had been turned into cannon-fodder during the Seven Years' War. God had been told 'Rebellious Scots to Crush', but the Seven Years' War and its sequels ensured they would die as recruits rather than rebels. Irish Catholic service in 18th century European armies had reinforced morale among the disarmed Catholics in Ireland. Their use by the UK in the wars against revolutionary France and Napoleon was a serious attempt to bring Irish nationalism into British military service, recalling the success in building up Scottish nationalism as a recruiting device.

Nationalism in Ireland was heavily split during the Boer War, the nationalism rallying behind the UK war effort being strongest among Protestants such as Captain James Craig who sailed for service in South Africa the month before Victoria's arrival in Dublin. (He would later become an MP, train armed volunteers against Home Rule for Ireland, and be made first Prime Minister of Northern Ireland.) Leading sympathisers with the Boers included the racist journalist Arthur Griffith founder of non-violent Sinn Féin seeking a dual monarchy, the father of the Irish agrarian Land League of 1879 Michael Davitt, Arthur Lynch sentenced to death for service as a Boer Colonel leading Irish troops against the UK and subsequently MP for West Clare, and John MacBride Major in the Boer service to be executed for being an Easter rebel leader in 1916. WB Yeats wrote several public letters from London denouncing the Queen's visit to the Irish constitutional nationalist *Freeman's Journal* declaring:

> She is the official head and symbol of an Empire that is robbing the South African Republics of their liberty, as it has robbed Ireland of hers. Whoever stands by the roadway cheering for Queen Victoria cheers for that Empire, dishonours Ireland, and condones a crime.

It echoed his most famous poem, 'The Lake Isle of Innisfree', written in 1888–90, where rural Ireland is the earthly paradise and his present dwelling in Bedford Park, London, at best a purgatory:

> I will arise and go now, for always night and day
> I hear lake waters lapping with low sounds by the shore;
> While I stand on the roadway, or on the pavements grey,
> I hear it in the deep heart's core.

The centenary of the Union and Victoria's visit polarised the self-assured, self-enriched metropolis against the virtuous simple impoverished Irish countryside. Dublin was in some ways closer to the metropolis which many of its citizens aped, than to Innisfree. James Joyce exhibited these conflicting nationalisms in 'The Dead', himself a case study in egocentric Irish nationalism. The Union of 1800 itself was more abhorrent to Yeats than to Joyce in 1900, as it was to Protestants more than to Catholics in 1800. The Irish legislature whose life the Union ended was an exclusively Protestant Parliament run by a cultivated, if considerably corrupt, Anglican oligarchy from whom Yeats descended. In Catholic retrospection it transubstantiated into a Paradise Lost, for whose restoration Daniel O'Connell and Charles Stewart Parnell had struggled in vain, in the process making the Irish the most sophisticated political playboys in the western world.

Whose parliament?

Irish Catholics in general favoured the proposal of Hiberno-British Union, in part, because of its architect the younger Pitt's promise of full Catholic civil rights. Although even in 1800, the most promising young Catholic leader Daniel O'Connell did not. In addition to his 29-year leadership of the Catholics' demand to be seated in the UK Parliament, O'Connell focussed on the ultimate ideal of a separate Irish Parliament which would eventually mean Catholic control of Ireland. Irish nationalism in the 18th century had meant many different things, frequently at odds with one another. For most of the century (as one judge on the Irish bench put it) the law did not recognise such a thing as an Irish Roman Catholic to exist, whilst comprising over 80 per cent of the population, and by that stage owning about ten per cent of Irish land. The Irish Catholics – like the Jews throughout Christendom – used their outlawry to build up wealth in commerce, skilled trades and manufacturing: the mid-century's greatest performance of Shakespeare's Shylock in *The Merchant of Venice* on the London stage was by the Irish Catholic actor Charles Macklin (born Cathal Mac Lochlainn).

Catholics kept up with Jacobite news and invasion prospects by smuggling potential recruits for European armies and prospective clerical students outward, and importing wines, silks, tobacco, priests and Bonnie Prince Charlie. Ireland's Jacobites might seem practitioners of dream nationalism, but smuggling was hard-headed work, massive organisation from Nantes and Bordeaux and ruthlessness to profit well from the slave-trade with little sense of identity of experience with their African victims. Even their beautiful Gaelic poems might be Jacobite intelligence sung under secret codes. The law was popularly identified as impoverishment of Catholics and hunting their priests, and its users gave it little respect. The real law was outlaw justice, killing and maiming informers, land agents, livestock, so well controlled that by 1881 it had developed community moral pressure as a fine art and given boycott its name.

Democracy emerged from nationalism as a tough baby. Nationalism one way or another invokes the past and either demands our fidelity to it, or our readiness to break with it: or both. It is often rural in its loyalties, or else urban of recent rural origin. For instance in Ireland O'Connell in Kerry, Parnell in Wicklow, Eamon de Valera in Limerick all grew up in the countryside. From Gladstone's first Home Rule Bill in 1886 Unionist Protestant nationalism mobilised an urban proletariat against it, a rebellion of the rich enabling rural aristocracy and squirearchy to retain power longer than anywhere else in our archipelago. The ruling Ulster Protestant Unionist elite drew heavily on their military connections with officers displaying their ranks reached in Boer War and Great War. This became standard practice during the inter-war years where Ulster Unionist candidates, where possible, flourished captaincies at the very least. While in England the title 'Captain' in popular fiction usually meant self-style by a crook irrespective of whether he really was a Captain. The Orange order in the 20th century naturally accommodated such militarism, as did local Freemasonry. However, like much else in the nationalisms of Ireland, militaristic brotherhoods also mushroomed among Irish Catholic nationalists such as the Ancient Order of Hibernians, the Knights of St Columbanus, the Friendly Sons of St Patrick. The national anthem of the Republic of Ireland *'Sinn na Fianna Fail'* ('The Soldiers' Song') reciprocates the killing ethos.

The 19th century had seen frequent Irish domination or paralysis of the Commons, particularly under O'Connell and Parnell who consciously played vital roles in the gradual liberalisation and democratisation of UK politics, thus showing themselves UK as well as Irish nationalists seeking to eradicate abuses disgracing the entire United Kingdom. The revolution in popular Irish attitudes to Parliament under the Union needs threefold assessment: what the people thought of the Irish Parliament while it existed, what they thought of it when it ceased to exist, what they thought of the Union Parliament from 1801–1922. The Irish nationalism, whence the Protestant Episcopalians in the Irish Parliament asserted its supposed rights against the claims of superiority by the Westminster Parliament, must have won some Catholic hitch-hikers. Until 1766 Catholic moral allegiance went to the true King James VII/II expelled in 1688–89 or to his son 'King James VIII/III' reigning but never ruling from 1701 to his death in 1766, except for the Pope allowing him to appoint Catholic bishops of Ireland. From a Catholic viewpoint the Irish Parliaments under Anne, George I, and George II, were all enemies of Jesus Christ enacting or maintaining laws under which almost all Christ's true priests were outlawed and His true believers impoverished. They were all notoriously corrupt as shown in George II's reign (1727–60) when the Irish Parliament was elected as constitutionally required after the new king was crowned and thereafter had no general elections. The Catholics officially believed that the Irish Parliamentarians were damned as Protestants anyway, but doubly damned for their anti-Catholic and anti-Papal legislation. The Presbyterians were also excluded from the Georges' Parliaments, partly from the ruling Anglicans' fear that just as the Scottish Presbyterians had seized control of the Church of Scotland in 1688–89, the Irish Presbyterians might one day capture the Church of Ireland. On this logic George II's sole Irish Parliament kept remained ruthlessly Anglican.

The Presbyterians did not officially damn the Anglicans on the automatic assumptions within which they damned Roman Catholics, but they damned most, if not all, of them on their merits. As Roman Catholics improved economically in George III's reign they developed wishes to vote in elections for the Irish Parliament as from 1793 they were permitted where qualified by wealth and property. Yet, they were still denied the right to be elected, so that the Irish Parliament remained reprehensibly an anti-Catholic fortress which some day might be captured and liberated. Pitt intended to prevent anything like a Catholic takeover of the Irish Parliament, but felt Catholics could be sunk without much trace in the Westminster Parliament as recreated under the new union. The 29-year denial of that Catholic membership of a London Parliament, resulted in O'Connell keeping the ideal of constitutional nationalism before the Catholics' eyes, while keeping in their minds the dream of a Parliament they would control either through votes or through pressure-groups. The 18th century Catholic hopes of redemption and salvation when James VIII/III came into his own again, translated from 1801 into hopes of a national parliament similarly to restore Catholic rule to a Catholic island. The dream of Repeal of the Union and the hard-bitten deployment of day-to-day bargains, favours and jobbery under its auspices began with O'Connell's nationalism, but often forgot his internationalism calling for the liberation of non-whites and non-Christians. O'Connell was never going to win Repeal of the Union, but his pressure won liberal Irish administration by alliance with the Whigs, and repeal of Catholic grievances from the Tories.

The Great Famine killed over a million Irish, drove O'Connell to his death, and discredited the Union Parliament which had come into existence in 1801 with the presumption that Ireland's needs would be met by Westminster. As a result of the Union of 1801 maintaining the colonial administration of Ireland in Dublin Castle while abolishing the Parliament with which it had worked, the Union Parliament never quite convinced its Irish constituents of its representative character. The Irish MPs would think of themselves as suppliants rather than equals alongside the British. Fanatical separatists transported to Australia or migrating to America might declare the Famine a British murder of the Irish Catholics, but Catholic reaction in Ireland was subtler and deeper. The Famine showed that the UK would not sufficiently prioritise Ireland. Irish nationalism had progressed from the dream of liberation to the reality of hard bargain. From a pragmatic standpoint the Union of 1800 ultimately appeared unfit for purpose.

Twentieth-century Scottish nationalism went the same way as 19th century Irish nationalism: ultimately concluding London was too self-absorbed and hence too inefficient to govern the periphery. Wales from the Tudors to Lloyd George had hopes of ruling London. Much was made of the corruption by which the Union of 1800 was passed, as much was also made of the corruption with which the makers of the Union of 1707 were credited. Gladstone ended his great parliamentary career not only as UK premier become English broker but as newly-born Irish leader to enable the creation of a new Irish Parliament. He had convinced himself that the Union of 1800 was fraudulent, but much more because the Union of 1800 was now inefficient. Similarly, Scottish nationalism sang Robert Burns to itself about a parcel of rogues in the nation, and worthy unionist late 20th century historians went to much trouble to prove many rogues had believed in the Union they made, quite apart from the money they made. What really swelled SNP support was that the Union of 1707 was beginning to look as inefficient as the Union of 1801. After all, in both cases, the real demand for the Union of 1707, as for the Union of 1800, had been to avert further French invasion: the warlords Marlborough under Queen Anne and Nelson and Wellington under George III had disposed of the French. The French had made nationalists of everyone, though not always in the same direction.

Uncivil politics or civil war?

'Scotland did once have a unionist party – between 1912 and 1965', reflected Professor Kidd:

> It was a capital 'U' Unionist party, which stood first of all for Britain's Union with Ireland, and then, after 1922, for its Union with Northern Ireland. Scottish unionism – 'small 'u' unionism – has been relatively inarticulate, and invisible by contrast.

The Scottish Unionist party was born in 1912 under the Canadian-born Glasgow ironmaster and new Tory leader Andrew Bonar Law. Fanatically devoted to Protestant Ulster, which in youth he would visit at weekends to hear his Presbyterian father preach, and committed to civil war if necessary, should Home Rule for Ireland be enacted and enforced. Scottish nationalism had only honorary constitutional or cultural existence at this point but Bonar Law was ready to recruit it for Ulster Unionism. At Comber, County Down on 8 April 1912 he publicly asked himself how Scotsmen would like to be treated as HH Asquith's Liberal Government 'was treating Protestant Ulster':

> I know Scotland well, and I believe that, rather than submit to such a fate, the Scottish people would face a second Flodden, or a second Bannockburn.

Scotland could read his shorthand: Flodden a massacre of a huge Scottish army by a small English one in 1513 and Bannockburn a massacre of a huge English army by a small Scottish one in 1314. Martyrdom was the most likely eventuality for Bonar Law's imaginary Scottish revolt, victory the more remote but glorious hope. The 'fate' meant being subjected to Roman Catholic rule: Law knew how to appeal to anti-Catholicism emotively but evasively. Arguably the entire Tory Party pledging itself to resist by force if necessary a Third Home Rule Act was chargeable with high treason. World War I intervened: and nobody can tell whether the relatively well-trained Protestant Ulster Volunteers under Law's Irish allies Sir Edward Carson and Captain James Craig would have been mobilised in their thousands for combat; but many of them were killed in the UK forces, most at the Somme in 1916 where many of their Home Ruler Irish Catholic countrymen also died. In 1920 Craig was made Prime Minister of the new substate of Northern Ireland, the enemies of Home Rule thus receiving Ireland's six most Protestant counties as their own home rule. Professor Kidd was accurate in his choice of 1965 as the end of the 'unionist' identity for Scottish Toryism. Northern Ireland's anti-Catholicism drew television attention after Labour's victories in the 1964 and 1966 UK elections. Irish Catholic migration to Scotland, vast in the 19th century, was scarcely a trickle from 1920. Scottish Tory bitterness at the Dublin Easter Rising, in the same year as the Somme, mined popular Scottish anti-Catholicism beyond previous depths over the next 40 years. The General Assembly of the Church of Scotland, regarded before 1997 by many Scots as Scotland's closest approximation to a national parliament, reiterated at each of its annual meetings from 1923 that Roman Catholicism was an alien faith. Therefore, the UK should stop all Irish immigration to Scotland, occasionally hinting that they should deport the Irish already there, inspiring mob action in 1935 against Roman Catholic infants processing to church in First Holy Communion finery.

Adrian Hastings, *The Construction of Nationhood: Ethnicity, Religion and Nationalism* (1997) pp. 69-70:

Language, law, literature, a sense of historic identity, a particular kind of culture sustained by the orders of bards, jurists and monks, that surely is sufficient to show that Wales and Ireland were by the mid-eleventh century well past the dividing line between ethnicity and nation, far as they were from achieving, or even seeking, a nation-state. When the Lord Rhys of Deheubarth held his famous assembly of poets and musicians at Cardigan in 1176, where the men of Gwynedd carried off all the poetry prizes, he was doing something very Welsh, but also something significantly national. It reminds one of that other great assembly of bards and scholars held at Christmas 1351 in Ui Mhaine, in Connaught – an exciting moment in the Irish Gaelic revival of the fourteenth century. This was to demonstrate a different way of imagining a nation. It was something which the English could not conceivably have done.

In almost all of this Scotland could not be more different and anyone wanting to define roads to nationhood and the role of ethnicity therein could hardly do better than ponder the contrast between Scotland and Wales. A Committee of the

---

Church of Scotland reporting in 1923 upon Irish Immigration, seen as a dangerous intrusion into Scottish life and tradition, concluded that 'God placed the people of this world in families, and history, which is the narrative of His providence, tells that when kingdoms are divided against themselves they cannot stand. Those nations which were the homogeneous in race were the most prosperous and were entrusted by the Almighty with the highest tasks.' The point of recalling here this particularly absurd statement is that of all the peoples of our islands the Scots have been by far the least 'homogeneous in race'.

Scottish anti-Catholicism suddenly declined after the advent of the ecumenical Pope St John XXIII, and of the Moderator of the General Assembly of the Church of Scotland, the Reverend Dr Archie Craig, who flew to Rome to greet him in 1961. The visit of Pope St John Paul II in 1981 was so generously received by many Scottish Protestants that many, perhaps most, Scottish Roman Catholics no longer felt second-class citizens. When the Heath Tory government in 1970 continued its Labour predecessor's reluctant British military intervention in Northern Ireland to quell sectarian hostilities, it was no longer as the ostensible partners the Tories had been in the days of Scottish Tory identification with Northern Ireland Unionism. The politics of conspiracy had been replaced by the politics of condescension. One effect of this transformation flourished in the Brexit rhetoric of 2016–19: all parties in Britain spoke of 'Britain' meaning the United Kingdom of Great Britain and Northern Ireland. Northern Ireland founded in 1920 had been the UK's first devolution, winning much local autonomy and metropolitan indifference in theory and, still more, in practice until 1969, but also eroding to unspoken second-class status for the devolved area. Wales might have liked the perpetual usage of 'Britain' and 'British' better, since the Welsh were the original Britons. UK unionism in 1912–14 was positive nationalism seeking to unite the Protestant classes in Ulster. Some of its theorists drew on Edmund Burke whose positive nationalism – both Irish and British – throughout his career had also inspired the Gladstonian Home Rule Liberalism of the late 1880s and 1890s. Mobilisation of urban and rural proletariat characterised Irish nationalism whether calling itself Repeal, Home Rule, or Ulster Unionist, all of them strengthening democratic impulses across the UK. Yet UK Unionism, while definitely a form or forms of nationalism, often lapsed into mere negative denial of nationalism particularly when reduced to bogus legal indictments against charismatic nationalist devolutionary leaders such as Daniel O'Connell, Charles Stewart Parnell, Mohandas K Gandhi and Alex Salmond.

Scot versus lot

Colin Kidd continued his gallant education of his Tory auditors:

> Whereas Northern Ireland has an articulate Unionism opposed to nationalism, in Scotland unionism is virtually dead. The union survives, but there is no ideology of unionism that supports it. In 2014, the leader of Scottish Labour, Jim Murphy – then in effect the leader of unionist forces north of the border – said 'I am not a unionist'. What he meant was, 'I'm not one of those Proddies, like Ian Paisley'. He was speaking to Labour's large Scottish Catholic constituency, saying it's OK for them to support the Union. Support for the Union, in other words, was not tantamount to unionism, which remains something of a dirty word in some quarters.

The foremost historian of modern Scotland, Professor Sir Thomas Devine, observed in 2014 that Scottish Catholics now favoured SNP, although their parents had voted Labour since the 1920s. Hence the blandishments of Jim Murphy, and hence in part his failure. Labour habitually kept its Catholic sheep from straying by well-chosen barks alleging SNP anti-Catholicism. Poor Jim Murphy sought vainly to keep the sheep quiescent by denying the unionism he was trying to preach, reminiscent of St Peter's denial of Christ. By 2016 the Scottish Parliament was controlled by an SNP majority. Jim Murphy as head of Scottish Labour was yesterday's man. He showed courage to be so, and Professor Kidd's calling him the unionist leader symbolises the fall of Scottish Tory unionism notwithstanding the UK's Tory government in 2016. The Independence Referendum of 2014 voted 'NO', but the 2015 Westminster elections reduced every unionist party in Scotland to a single MP apiece: and Labour's was not Jim Murphy.

Scottish nationalism ruled from london

SNP voter appeal in 2015 relied on the fact that SNP policies, good or bad, were made in Scotland. This situation was by no means inevitable, for SNP any more than for anyone else. The tragedy of the mere 11 SNP MPS 1974–79 was that for practical purposes they silently took policy out of the hands of the party Chair William Wolfe in Edinburgh, and made policy from Westminster. It infected them with Westminster fashions and conventions, and while defying unionism in parliament imitated its follies, political witch-hunting included. Alex Salmond, himself the victim of such lunacy, saw SNP must be ruled from Scotland, particularly after the Scottish Parliament was born (again) this time in Edinburgh's Holyrood. Donald Dewar, Holyrood's first First Minister, ruled, but his death in 2000 meant unionist Labour leaders in London competed in manipulating their rival vassals in Holyrood. In 2011 Tory Prime Minister David Cameron had Holyrood's Scottish Tory leader stand down and ordained her successor. The Liberal Democrat MPS' destruction of their most successful UK leader, Charles Kennedy, cost them dearly in Scotland which did not share Westminster enthusiasm for regicide. The new Scottish Tory leader in Holyrood, Ruth Davidson, discarded Tory pomp in dynamic campaigns such as endeared Theodore Roosevelt to the American public. In what was probably the best speech on the question she vindicated Scottish enactment of same-sex marriage, answering claims of its peril to family life. She was born into a happy family and now wanted a lesbian wedding so as to have a happy family in her turn. She led Scotland's anti-Brexit Tories during the 2016 Brexit Referendum, demolishing Boris Johnson in debate, but lost hope of keeping Scottish Toryism immune once Mr John-son won the Tory beauty contest to succeed Theresa May in 2019. Today's Scottish unionist parties denounce nationalism in a style as nationalist as possible, vainly denying they run Scottish 'branch offices' ruled by their London executives. In general, most Scots whatever their politics probably recognise that self-government is likely to be more efficient than long-distance manipulation. Tradi-tional assumptions might argue conservatives were cautious and nationalists revolutionary, but the coronavirus crisis has shown Lon-don Tories as more headstrong and SNP in Holyrood more measured. Prime minister Boris Johnson sounds like a schoolboy pretending to be a schoolteacher, whereas First Minister Nicola Sturgeon appears like the teacher in full command. SNP argued for efficiency, like early 20th century American Progressives Theodore Roosevelt, Woodrow Wilson, and Robert LaFollette. Scottishness certainly helps. The misfortunes of Mr Richard Leonard (Labour's previous Holyrood leader) began with his English origin and accent: on BBC 'Question Time' in Newcastle-upon-Tyne, he was a man transfigured, happily and attractively English, charming, quick, congenial – but for him Arthur's Seat and Castle Rock are not the hills of home.

Scratch players

Colin Kidd continued:

> The SNP has always supported some form of association with an entity larger than Scotland, whether it be domin-ion status within the British empire, independence within the European Union, or the Union of Crowns. Ultimately, the SNP favours a supra-national solution to Scotland's predicament, but something other than the existing Union of 1707, even as amended by the evolving devolution settlement.
>
> Alex Salmond, as well as being a nationalist, has also cleverly appropriated unionist arguments whenever convenient. In the referendum campaign he spoke of

the 'social union' – which hinted at the maintenance of cross-border welfare standards, he spoke of the union of crowns, he spoke of the European Union, he supported a currency union, and a shared British monarchy. In other words, yes, Alex Salmond is a nationalist, but he's also capable of spiking Unionist guns, by capturing so many unionist symbols and arguments for the nationalist camp.

Ultimately you can only get to grips with Scottish politics if you realise that when you scratch any unionist, you'll find a nationalist underneath...

When a first-rate intellect adjusts its operations to teach an audience of much less certain intellectual quality, the cannibal may devour the missionary. Yet despite the danger of the word 'always', we can applaud Dr Kidd's perception in concluding SNP seeks a larger entity. Winifred Ewing won the Hamilton by-election of 2 November 1967, and declared 'Stop the world! Scotland wants to get on!' For 70 years SNP have asserted that their ambition is to occupy a seat for Scotland at the United Nations. Hugh MacDiarmid's masterly introduction to the *Golden Treasury of Scottish Verse* is the starting-point for understanding 20th century Scottish nationalism and turns on a simple astronomical point: Scotland eclipsed in London's shadow can wither as it apes cultural parochialism, or it can seek inspiration and audience across the globe. Scottish nationalism wants Scotland attracting immigrants who realise they are in Scotland, demanding more while Prime Minister Boris Johnson decrees less. It's an economic as well as a cultural demand which Holyrood Opposition knows as well as Holyrood Government. Professor Kidd balances so beautifully on the tight-rope between unionist myths and nationalist realities, yet must realise that Alex Salmond and other Scottish Nationalists think Burns, and 'social union' is born from 'To a Mouse' as well as from larger entities:

I'm truly sorry Man's dominion
Has broken Nature's social union
An' justifies that ill opinion
Which makes thee startle

At me, thy poor earth-born companion,
An' fellow-mortal.

We may accept Kidd's brutal instruction to scratch a unionist, although today unionists scratch themselves. If UK Governments have difficulty knowing the limits of their control over the Scottish Government, and even greater difficulty in keeping their hands off their own party comrades in the Scottish Parliament, they must envy the successive SNP Scottish First Ministers who know themselves to command their Westminster party.

Saving scottish household gods from disintegrating union

We may agree with Professor Colin Kidd that Alex Salmond is 'clever'. To find his equivalent we must consider Daniel O'Connell, Benjamin Disraeli, Charles Stewart Parnell, or David Lloyd George. All five of them were apostles of nationalism with excellent senses of humour. They were all outsiders in conventional political eyes, transforming the politics they found, and pursued by exceptionally vicious political enemies. But Professor Kidd has singled out evidence of the nationalism of unionism even more than of the unionism of nationalism. The UK has its own nationalism. You can entertain yourself by deciding whether its first practitioner was the Roman General Julius Agricola, King Arthur, or King Edward I? Whatever triumphs each had were of brief duration. James VI/I is the UK's real father, uniting our archipelago in his own person although unable to unite its parliaments. UK nationalism was a palimpsest hanging over the many nationalisms beneath its own majesty, and never more formidable than when commanded by our archipelago's revolutionary head of state, Oliver Cromwell, who could claim the frankest form of union-making, namely to tell his military administrators in Scotland and Ireland to send their choice of delegates to his parliament. Whatever his merits, Cromwell induced extreme reaction against his methods after his death; his Union was renounced. Although, its ghost may sometimes be visible on dark nights. It was the ideal if unrepeatable form of UK nationalism, though today secretly venerated by his dearest enemies, the Tories.

Three centuries after Cromwell, UK nationalism as palimpsest still kept itself a priority over much else in Scotland and Wales. Many locals were unionists by priority, and nationalists far lower down, in their own agenda. Margaret Thatcher moved Scottish desire for parliaments from bare agreement in 1979 to 73 per cent in 1997. Similarly, Wales initially showed little enthusiasm even in the Welsh-speaking north-west for a Cardiff talking-shop. Eleven years of Thatcher produced a clear majority for a devolved assembly. Scots initially cold to independence began to think that the farther they could get away from Thatcher's Whitehall and Westminster the better. As a UK nationalist she was but a superficial tourist: her loyalties, not merely her priorities, were English. Her favoured Scottish servants were such devotees such as Michael Forsyth who assured her and the public that the more Westminster seats the Tories lost in Scotland, the more Scotland needed more Thatcherism, not less. Alex Salmond controversially suggested that she aroused even greater social than economic hostility, and he was probably correct. Thatcher performed in Scotland as a great county lady amusedly making friends with the backward child of one of her tenants. It was obviously artificial, inducing artificiality in those she met at the cost of their self-respect, or else it won honest antipathy. It persuaded some Scottish Tory officials to never vote Tory again. Professor Kidd's metaphor of Mr Salmond spiking unionist guns was shrewd but simplistic: to hold his audience the professor made the hero – and Alex Salmond is a hero – appear unique, when he was actually embodying widespread Scottish nationalist opinion as recorded by friends and foes. Certainly, Mr Salmond is a most courageous opponent of war. The spiking metaphor was relevant: one of the fundamental tenets of modern Scottish nationalism is its hatred of war, particularly of nuclear weapons. Some of its leaders having been imprisoned or sentenced to community service for pacifism, many more having marched in protest against the UK's ownership, or housing of, weapons of mass destruction especially in Scotland. But anti-war traditions are English, Welsh, and Irish as well as Scottish. In this, as in veneration for the welfare state and its National Health Service, SNP remains devoted to the traditions that self-deluding Labour pragmatists have discarded. Alex Salmond didn't capture these unionist symbols: he took back their control. He wants us – in Scotland, in the UK, and in the world – united against war.

Scotland nationalising the queen?

As to the Union of Crowns, Mr Salmond in 1981 was expelled from SNP – illegally, as it proved – by Gordon Wilson (whom Salmond would ultimately succeed as SNP Chair). Salmond was expelled for his membership of the ecumenical ''79 Group' which was nominally 'republican': the word is pretty toxic, embedding you simultaneously with the Provisional IRA and Donald Trump's party. Alex Salmond, Stephen Maxwell, Kenny MacAskill and the other expelled '79ers may never have realised it but the SNP old guard had been really frightened that the commitment to republicanism signalled sympathy for the Provisional IRA. Which apart from one misguided individual, it certainly did not. SNP has always been resolutely non-violent, but it had had occasional anxious moments in diagnosing potential advocates of violence in the 1950s, including attempted infiltrators on secret service payrolls such as MI5, CIA, and KGB to work as *agents provocateurs*. Anti-monarchism was an easy headline-grabber for secret agents anxious to discredit SNP, and in the late 1970s many – perhaps most – SNP members were in favour of abolishing the Scottish monarchy in the event of independence. Scotland's most profound theorist of modern nationalism, Tom Nairn, produced a first-class critique of monarchy's destructive impact on political society, *The Enchanted Glass: Britain and its Monarchy*, diagnosing the disease which leads so many institutions, companies, universities to turn themselves into monarchic entities headed by officials immunised from democracy and possible criticism of any kind.

Elizabeth Queen of Scots is probably much more popular than the monarchy. As the party prospered and ultimately came to power in devolved Scotland, SNP found that, now and then, the monarchy can be useful under its present incumbent. Present and future historians have to be careful here: the Queen can afford to pay her household and administrative servants such generous salaries and wages that no bribery from the communications media should tempt them. Thus, all journalistic claims of royal data discovered from 'sources', 'friends', or 'spokesmen' are evidently lies, unless an actual person is authorized and credited (and perhaps not even then). Misinformers have frequently included Prime Ministers, notably Mr David Cameron who has missed a vocation as a spiritualistic medium, judging by his disclosures. We have little or no actual knowledge of Queen Elizabeth's political opinions, save that in Ireland she won the applause of almost every Irish nationalist open or dormant by her personal decision to bow her head in honour of the insurgent leaders of Easter 1916, rebels and martyrs executed for high treason in alliance with the UK's German enemies during the worst war the United Kingdom of Great Britain and Ireland had ever known. She astounded and delighted her hosts at the state dinner by opening her speech in beautiful Irish-Gaelic. These were personal actions. Similarly, Daniel O'Connell and his followers happily, lengthily, and affectionately toasted Queen Victoria at dinners for the Repeal of the Union in 1844. It followed from his progress of the Catholics from latter-day Jacobitism that Victoria became the Stuarts' heir. Democratically, a country's nationalism needs the support of all its citizens, and some may see devotion to the existing monarch as integral.

Scotland a part of the continent

What of the European Union? We may acquit Professor Kidd of the moronic unionist insistence that it is inconsistent to want to remain in the EU while wanting to leave the UK. Many unionists may feel it inconsistent for SNP to yearn for Scotland's membership of the UN, yet many want UK out of UN, as their ally President Donald Trump wants US out of UN when his wind is in that direction. The crypto-unionist argument may be answered thus:

a) in June 1979 the EU and Winifred Ewing saved SNP
    when its morale was lowest,

b) SNP wants Scotland in the EU in the way the UK should
    have been, not the way it was. If SNP wants former
    unionist symbols, it wants them in good working
    order, and here Alex Salmond has been both repre-
    sentative and pioneer.

In any case, a nationalist Scotland must respect the previous UK
nationalism of its citizenry, and ease its evolution. The whole
history of Scottish nationalism is the history of a people pro-
gressing from unionism, and frequently UK nationalism was a
priority over Scottish nationalism, not an intransigent opposition.
Winifred Ewing had a special place in SNP hearts from her sensational by-election victory at Hamilton in November 1967, and
her warmth, congeniality, humour, kindness and courage kept her
in their affections. Defeated in the 1970 election, she was heart-
ened by the last result of the night, Donald Stewart, Provost of
Stornoway capturing the Western Isles, the first SNP seat won in
a general election, the direct result of Hebridean anger against
Whitehall's using the islands as location for nuclear weapons and
rocket-range, for activation when necessary. Donald Stewart held
the seat until he retired in 1987. In February 1974 Winnie Ewing
defeated the then Tory Secretary of State for Scotland, Gordon
Campbell, in Moray and Nairn which she held until defeated,
along with eight other SNP MPs, in 1979.

As SNP spokesperson on external affairs she had been chosen
Member of the European Parliament for the Highlands and Islands
in 1975 when the national parliaments sent delegates, and having lost her seat in Westminster on 3 May 1979 she was elected
to the European Parliament on 10 June. Suddenly Westminster, as
the centre of the party's electoral ambitions, diminished as a focal
point and she vociferously informed her party how she was now
carrying their banner into a more international establishment than
Westminster, where she was taken far more seriously. She also took
the European Parliament much more seriously than the UK's more
parochial politicians did, and made it obvious to her European

colleagues. Westminster's somewhat ludicrous conviction of its superiority to the European Parliament was well symbolised by the virtually permanent placeman of the BBC, David Dimbleby, chairing a report on results of a UK election to the European Parliament, and telling the BBC audience 'Now, if this were a real election... '.

Hugh MacDiarmid had preached the message that London was parochial, and Scottish nationalism must mean global horizons, and now Winnie Ewing was Scotland's chief symbol of that. She was simultaneously a child at a party and a shrewd criminal lawyer: so were Daniel O'Connell and Sir Edward Carson, both appropriate symbols as leaders of different nationalisms in Ireland. If Margaret Thatcher's victory in May 1979 had ended Ewing's Westminster days, she saw the Tory Prime Minister and her minions repelling their European colleagues by snobbish chauvinism. Ewing in the European Parliament watched the Irish delegations from Dublin and Belfast closely, saw that she had so much to gain and learn by working with them, and introduced the Reverend Dr Ian Paisley to Síle de Valera, granddaughter of the Irish national leader for a quarter of the 20th century. The Irish method was simple enough: read up on the EEC and EU quietly, keep eyes and ears active, show sound knowledge but don't bluff, and ask everyone have you heard the latest absurdity from Margaret Thatcher? Winnie Ewing convinced continental Europeans that Scotland existed, that it is not England, and that it thinks small is beautiful. When not strutting her stuff as grand panjandrum of an empire, Thatcher relaxed with Europeans by telling them ancient English chestnuts about silly foreigners: and hence Ewing was much in demand at the EU bar where serious negotiation is done. On the level of real (as opposed to professional) public relations, she probably did the UK better service in the EEC and EU than any unionist, by showing that the British could be human, after all. Their Scottish nationalism had a heart-warming iconoclasm about it: Scottish nationalism thought a stuffed shirt was a 'Toom Tabard', an empty suit of armour (the mocking title given to John Balliol before Robert Bruce became the Scottish people's choice). Ewing's laughter and sheer enjoyment of

Scotland in Europe bubbled back to Scotland while the grey greed of Thatcherism settled down over the UK.

Why did SNP decide on independence in Europe? Winnie Ewing told them to, and very few dared dissent. The party National Executive cowered beneath her reports, which were enthusiastic, exciting, and emphatic. If anyone seemed to question her evangelism, what followed would have made Moses smashing the Ten Commandments sound like a genteel cough. She also got first-class support from her family and from devoted aides from MacDiarmid's son, Michael Grieve, to Duncan MacLaren, the future head of world Roman Catholic charities. Whether or not she knew Dean Acheson's sneer that Britain had lost an empire without finding a role, she worked within its implications. Thatcher insisted on booming her own cheap edition of a great power and drove the UK in 'Europe' remorselessly into adversary snobbery. Winnie Ewing (and for that matter Ian Paisley and Síle de Valera) knew that it was essential to know that your people's highest and lowest status was being one of a number of partners, and abandoning pretence of being the Empire on which the sun, once upon a time, never set. But she became familiar with peripheries like Lapland, the Frisian Islands, Sicily, Corsica, or Catalonia, and made friends with truly representative politicians from capitalist to communist. And she could see Ian Paisley formally cursing the Pope, and then informally plotting with the Catholic Ulster MEP John Hume to increase benefits for Northern Ireland. Winnie Ewing herself achieved tremendous feats in gaining EEC munificence for the Highlands and Islands. Sociologists might note these achievements as proof of the peripheries occasionally outweighing the metropolis.

Irish unionism as Irish nationalism

Colin Kidd's unionist-scratching is accurate. Unionism *is* nationalism. Let us return to those Irish examples so instructive for Winnie Ewing and the Europhile Scotland she made: evident in the Scottish 62 per cent voting Remain in the 2016 Brexit Referendum, surpassing Northern Ireland's 56 per cent (which might have been a higher total had the late Reverend Dr Ian Paisley still led the Democratic Unionists). Ian Paisley really was a nationalist by any other name, modern in financial techniques, traditional in love of evangelical tradition and history. Sir Edward Carson was even more remarkable: as a Dubliner he was a passionate nationalist for a dying country: Ireland as part of the United Kingdom of Great Britain and Ireland. To get the best terms, he had to be 'Ulster's Sir Edward', and also be the head of the English bar. He was not even anti-Catholic: his last great case before his Ulster crusade vindicated a victimised Catholic naval cadet, George Archer-Shee. He proudly went to the funeral Mass for his leading Home Rule opponent John Redmond in 1918 and lamented him in Parliament. Even more than Redmond, he was the heir of Charles Stewart Parnell although himself the supreme opponent of Irish Home Rule which Parnell had made possible. Both of them despised the self-obsession of the House of Commons. Carson's effect on the Ulster Protestants was Parnell's on the Irish Catholics, and Salmond's on the Scots: thanks to them, their chosen people walked taller.

Nationalism's motes and beams

Colin Kidd, doubting whether 1707 is a memorable date, questions the contrasts of the UK unions (from England and Wales onward), their copycat quality, and their want of comparative study. Our Acts of Union (1536–42, 1707, 1800 and 1922) win devotion more or less in inverse proportion to the worshipper's knowledge: indeed, as Professor Kidd hinted to Policy Exchange, those who invoke them seem uneasy as to which Act they are revering. If we agree that these unionists are in fact nationalists as fully as any self-styled nationalist, we open up wider fields to plough and may close a few cul-de-sacs. The unionists' complaints about nationalists are brought within the limits which Jesus proclaimed: that we should recognise our own sins before we denounce the sins of others.

Jesus Christ in *ST MATTHEW, GOSPEL*, ch.VII.1–5:

Judge not, that ye be not judged.

For with what judgment ye judge, ye shall be judged: and with what measure ye mete, it shall be measured to you again.

And why beholdest thou the mote that is in thy brother's eye, but considerest not the beam that is in thine own eye?

Or how wilt thou say to thy brother, Let me pull out the mote out of thine eye; and, behold, a beam is in thine own eye?

Thou hypocrite, first cast out the beam out of thine own eye; and then shalt thou see clearly to cast out the mote out of thy brother's eye.

Jesus's parable deliberately entertains us by absurd exaggeration to make it memorable. The mote is a speck, so tiny as to be scarcely visible if not actually invisible; the beam is a great plank sustaining a ceiling or roof. So we are virtually contrasting nothing and infinity. I cannot see the mote; my eye could not house the beam. It is because it is ridiculous we remember it. I cannot possibly remove motes from anyone else's eye if my own vision is blocked by the plank from the roof. Psychologically, Jesus tells me, I have become a censorious busy-body to conceal from myself and everyone else my hideously impaired vision. The parable relates to our sins, my own bigger, yours far smaller. So the more we denounce nationalism, the more we prove that we are nationalists, and that our condition is far advanced, although there may be nothing wrong, or right, with nationalism *in itself*. It follows that everyone is a nationalist, just as everyone sees the sins of others as far more heinous than their own, and that these sins and nationalisms have existed before history was first recorded. Shakespeare's play-title in *Measure for Measure* is virtually a parable illustrating Jesus's instruction, the final act following justice without mercy, with mercy making justice more just.

John Wycliffe elected against Europe

Nationalism's beam-carriers might be SNP and Plaid Cymru, except that they loudly announce their nationalism, so much so that their critics denounce their honesty. The Tories, Labour and Liberal Democrats denounce Ms Nicola Sturgeon for saying SNP wants independence, and tell her she should stop mentioning it, as they have so often stopped talking about issues they once adored but now deem electorally unprofitable. The other suspects for beam-carrying are the brexiteers, from Mr Boris Johnson to certain intellectuals of high quality and integrity: some are self-admitted 'nationalists' especially when supporters of SNP or Plaid Cymru. English brexiteers may dislike being called English nationalists but have little defence against it. An early example of English nationalism out of the closet was Douglas Carswell who resigned from the Tories on their failure to leave the EU, and then resigned his seat in Clacton-on-Sea winning it back in a by-election on 9 October 2014. His victory speech quoted Abraham Lincoln's Gettysburg Address: 'Government of the people by the people for the people', and pointed out that Lincoln's source was probably the 14th century John Wycliffe, first known translator of the Bible into English and enemy of the Papacy. This neatly established his English nationalist credentials, since advocacy of the national language and defiance of international religious unity proclaimed an early antecedent for anti-EU England. The precursor previously cited by anti-EU crusaders was Henry VIII, the human Tyrannosaurus Brex. Wycliffe had risked his life for his beliefs; Henry risked everyone else's for his. Henry was an interesting test of English nationalism winning many admirers from mid-Victorian to early neo-Elizabethan England, but while recent feminism might sympathise with his break from Roman spiritual leadership, two executed wives damn him. Carswell played the intellectual card with a skill and relevance pleasurable to witness. As a delicate contrast to the wild and whirling words of the demagogic Nigel Farage, nominally Mr Carswell's new leader, his use of intellect in modern politics could not have been better managed. The promise of superiority would be well kept. A sense of superiority was one of the most obvious points of English nationalism, with which it alienated and then infected the various nationalisms throughout the archipelago.

English nationalism at its greatest

There was another English nationalism in the field, ultimately divided, betrayed, martyred. During the Brexit struggle several prominent Tories proved themselves heroes at the cost of their parliamentary careers – Rory Stewart, Amber Rudd, Dominic Grieve, Sam Gyimah, Kenneth Clarke, Sir Oliver Letwin, David Gauke, and Justine Greening. They believed their England would be diminished by Mr Boris Johnson's agenda, and their English nationalism demanded resistance to isolation and Trump-lickers. It would be 'unEnglish' to admit participation in so coarse and crude a thing as nationalism. English nationalism is the love that dare not speak its name. In that sublime anonymity it has been powerful and paternal. Its many seeds flowered in the less English parts of Britain, in the Irish nationalist fratricidal twins in north and south, across the Empire and in the USA. We can see how London initially linking clusters of villages built its own sense of identity, its own nationalism, from its settlers. Scotland may be nearer to London nationalism now than formerly. Witness the massive remain votes recorded in the 2016 Brexit Referendum, leaving London voters in their hundreds of thousands isolated above the vast foaming sea of English brexiteers. Hitherto the metropolis devoured its immigrants from elsewhere in the UK while their homelands resented its increase in power and parochialism. In World War II, London took pre-eminence as brave target in self-sacrifice for the entire archipelago notwithstanding the appalling human destruction throughout the UK.

A story of two Irishmen

As England's capital, London and its home counties drew in many nationalisms from other nations entering its life. Nearly half a century divided Edmund Burke and Daniel O'Connell but both in their common Catholic antecedents developed UK nationalism, drawing on their ideological inheritance to educate English Whigs into improvement of political life; they also played great parts in development of Irish nationalism by pushing for removal of anti-Catholic legislation. Their immediate ancestry was Roman Catholic, their youthful upbringing partly in heavily Catholic remote rural fastnesses, Burke in the Munster Blackwater Valley near Mallow in north Cork, O'Connell in Derrynane, Cahirsiveen on Kerry's wild Atlantic coast. They both deplored the 17th century destruction of Irish Catholicism, yet identified for much of their lives with the Whig heirs of the Glorious Revolution of 1688–89 despite it having finalised the confiscation of Irish Catholic land. Both won vital advancement through the law – the enemy of Irish Catholicism. Both deeply sympathised with aspects of the American Revolution, Burke defending it until it declared independence, O'Connell perpetually animated by its example. His major modern biographer Oliver MacDonagh finished his first volume *The Hereditary Bondsman* in 1988:

> Behind the apparent infinity of the directions which he might take lay the same simple dream that had driven him on since childhood. During the long vacation of 1814 he had held a grand picnic for a group of friends on an island in one of the Killarney lakes. On 22 May 1829 he recalled that day [to the American actor-playwright John Howard Payne composer of 'Home, Sweet Home!'] and 'the speech I made on giving the memory of Washington'. His conclusion had been much cheered. 'Did it not convey this idea? '"He found his native land a pitiful province of England. He left her – O Glorious destiny! – an independent and mighty nation."' Whether we move backwards or forwards in time, the frame was ever the same. ... There would never be escape from his own inherent ardour, or the hereditary bondage of his ancestry, time or place.

Burke and O'Connell both detested the French Revolution, in addition to their hatred of its civil and military carnage. As Conor Cruise O'Brien said of Burke when introducing his *Reflections on the Revolution in France*, their anger at the anti-Catholic cruelty and rapacity of the French Revolution released their concealed resentment at the impact on Irish Catholicism of the English Revolution a century earlier. They abominated mob rule which had endangered Burke's life during the Gordon Riots of 1780, while O'Connell had spent terrifying months receiving a Catholic education at St Omer and Douai amidst the revolution which guillotined Louis XVI on the day the 17-year-old Irish boy finally got out of France. Both of them mingled identities as native Irishmen and as Westminster statesmen. Ireland had shown them dehumanisation and degradation of Catholics, whence Burke and O'Connell would pressure governments under their influence to enact civil rights for the archipelago's ethnic minorities. Each of them was at the forefront of redressing cruelty to non-whites whether Burke indicting UK administrators in India or by O'Connell calling on American Irish to repudiate slavery and its marketeers in the USA.

The Gladstone of our times

The long-term influence of Edmund Burke and Daniel O'Connell was probably greatest on Prime Minister William Ewart Gladstone, whose UK statesmanship strengthened his own Irish nationalism from the defeat of his First Irish Home Rule Bill in 1886 when he was 77, to the victory of his Second in the Commons and its massive dismissal in the Lords in 1893 when he towered as thinker, orator, and campaigner over his contemporaries, British and Irish alike. We have learned a great deal more about old men in political leadership in the last 60 years. President Eisenhower, at 70, in his Farewell Address drew on his lifetime's military and political experience to warn his countrymen – vainly, as it turned out – about the dangers of military-industrial entrapment of government into endless weaponry build-up and increased proximity towards war, giving a lifetime's learning to the future of the tribe, a final public act of nationalism.

After Parnell's death in 1891 Gladstone became effective leader of Irish nationalism in speaking, writing, and campaigning to broaden UK nationalism by the eradication of its abuse of power. Our most instructive parallel for Gladstone beginning his fourth term as Prime Minister at 83 may be with Senator Bernie Sanders of Vermont campaigning for the US Presidency at 78. Rejuvenated by their nationalisms they staked their lives to purge the UK and US of their sins. Senator Sanders's anger at the victimisation of Latin-Americans inside and outwith the USA by President Trump won their passionate support. Gladstone's devotion to the Irish cause earned global Irish response, including the great American actor James O'Neill declaring in 1887 that his son the future playwright was to be named Eugene Gladstone O'Neill (an earlier son being Edmund Burke O'Neill) as a tribute to the only Englishman who ever did anything for the Irish. A self-discovering intellectual interest in the victimised people was present in both, Gladstone with his voracious reading, discussion and dissection of Irish history, Sanders flying to Rome mid-campaign in 2016 to consult with Pope Francis on his social teaching. Watching Sanders in an hour-long speech before an exultant crowd brings home the vigour of what Gladstone's monster meetings in Midlothian in 1879–94 must have been like. Both showed a Christ-like quality: Gladstone's preserved in his portrait reading the Lesson in Hawarden Church, Sanders in oratorically turning a slogan into a lesson from a Rabbi.

Nationalism often prided itself on heroes dying for their country in battle, which would usually include them killing. But for some of the most devout nationalists, acceptance of death did not mean taking any other lives although it might prompt bloody reprisals. Gwynfor Evans of Plaid Cymru prepared to die by hunger-strike so that Wales would get a Welsh-speaking television channel which he thought – probably rightly – would be essential for the survival of the Welsh language. Among self-sacrificial killers, several leaders of the 1916 Dublin Rising welcomed subsequent execution as following in the bloody footsteps of Christ's self-sacrifice, setting aside the fact that Christ killed nobody. The USA brutalises its armed forces as prelude for war, but many of its peacetime leaders ended in solitary self-sacrifice, the most visible point in their nationalism. Benjamin Franklin at 70 enjoyed telling his fellow-signatories of the Declaration of Independence that they must all hang together otherwise they would all hang separately. American Progressives followed the social gospel to do the most for the nation's people.

The most famous risked their own deaths against medical advice when in mid-crusade: Theodore Roosevelt finished a speech in his Presidential campaign of 1912 believing he had been mortally wounded when shot by an assassin, Woodrow Wilson dragged himself round the USA in 1919 campaigning for the League of Nations although warned of a disabling stroke which duly struck and impaired him for life, Robert LaFollette was told it would kill him to campaign as a Progressive party Presidential candidate in 1924 – and it did, Franklin D Roosevelt stayed in office in 1944 leading his country to the end of the World War II and died within weeks of his re-election. It was the principle of the Good Shepherd who would stay guarding His flock in all circumstances.

The supreme English conqueror

The most successful English nationalism of all time is the English language. It is a ruthless beautiful conqueror bitterly resented by cultural nationalists watching their own languages decline until they themselves can only resent it in English. Mid-twentieth-century Ireland walls sometimes carried chalkings calling '*Bás do'n Béarla*' ['Death to the English language']. Forty years ago I heard Dutch speakers of perfect English denounce the impact of Anglophone tourism in forcing the retreat of their native language. Welsh fought hardest against giving ground and, by the courage of Gwynfor Evans's determination, a Welsh-language television station was extorted from Thatcher – partly through Michael Foot and William Whitelaw manoeuvring skilfully to save Gwynfor's life.

The politics of linguistic nationalism were not always so straightforward. The Irish Free State from 1922 demanded proficiency in Irish-Gaelic for employment in government service, including the post and the police. The language won little popular revival, partly owing to the post-colonial maintenance of corporal punishment in education destroying its aesthetic appeal. The mandatory language qualification meant that the civil service personnel would not simply continue existing UK recruitment; the imperialist ethos must henceforth defer to the native peasant speech. Cultural nationalism had triumphed in an arid survival of Victorian bourgeois respectability grafted on to Christian puritanism. Creative use of English was set back by a Censorship Board particularly fond of banning books by young Irish authors. But ultimately the English language resumed its conquest of Ireland winning a freedom born of a cultural struggle which might seem anti-nationalist but, in reality, fought for the best varieties of national cultural expression. The abolition of Irish censorship also let loose on the Republic the vilest materialistic and semi-pornographic effluvia from the untaxed absentee press lords of London. The English language both diminished and expanded the Irish imagination as participation in the Gaelic vernacular declined. As with nationalism, neither language could be intelligently termed good or evil. Both foisted superlatives on the culture of their speakers, which made their nationalisms sound like empty boasting. English public figures will seriously and habitually call this or that English institution 'the best in the world' and would think it unpatriotic to substantiate the claim. Whereas the clichés of other nationalities retain a somewhat defensive sense of humour such as the Scots's 'here's tae us, wha's like us, nane but a few, an' they're a' deid', or the Irish response to some farcical disaster 'where else could this happen but in Ireland?'. Gaelic, Scots, and (most emphatically) Welsh speakers of English are more uneasy with the self-lauding superlative: you cannot be best when you don't talk in the native language. Nationalism has long shadows.

Union nationalism versus independent nationalism

The current UK struggle between UK nationalism and Scottish nationalism continues, complicated by the passionate insistence of the many forms of nationalism on the Union side that nationalism is an abomination of desolation. As I write, a UK government elected by extreme brexiteer Tory nationalism holds on by its 73-strong Parliamentary majority. The SNP remain in government in Scotland with the conditional support of the Greens, and opposed by unionist parties pretending that their unionism is nationalist enough to get by, or *vice versa*. Devolution has shown Scotland that nationalism

can govern. The UK Parliament can abolish the devolution legislatures of Scotland, Wales and Northern Ireland, and the Tory press
denounces or implies their 'abject failure', but the Scottish Parliament is used to that. When it began, the *Scotsman* could look back
on its quarter-century of advocacy for what had at last been won.
However, the paper fell into the hands of absentee landlords who
hired Mr Andrew Neil as their executive editor under whom the
paper's most notable policy was reversed, the Parliament was rub-
bished incessantly, and a succession of short-lived editors writhed
under the daily long-distance telephonic commands of Mr Neil. The
paper rapidly lost half its circulation, and eventually the owners grew
tired of failure and sold it. Mr Neil was inexplicably accommodated
by the BBC in self-indulgent minglings of cynicism, sadism, racism,
and peculiarly unctuous hypocrisy. Essentially he is a destroyer. His
general effect might sicken the public with all politics, and almost
certainly contributed to the demoralisation of the English electorate. Scotland, Northern Ireland, and Wales have been partly rescued
because nationalism gives idealism its opportunity whether for or
against independence, and whether the nationalism be good, bad, or
a mixture of both.

The innocence of Dr Brown

The last Scottish Prime Minister of the UK, Dr Gordon Brown, who
served from 2007 to 2010, is one of the most dedicated people in
modern UK politics. What was a career to the Wilsons, Callaghans,
Thatchers, Majors and Blairs, is a vocation to him. He is sworn to
save the UK from nationalism, and is thus a nationalist. He is also
one of the kindest and most likeable students with whom I have
worked: we were alternating Chairs at the Edinburgh University
Student Publications Board, he as student-elected Rector of the University, and I as a co-opted member of staff, coincidentally from the
History Department whence he won his first-class MA and his PhD.
I was not one of his teachers, but like many other students he taught
me a great deal. I became a Scottish Nationalist in those years partly
because Scottish Nationalists were so ready to make their Scotland

my Scotland and the Scotland of my fellow-immigrants, and because
the SNP was totally opposed to violence. In the Ireland where I had
grown up we did not go to war, we hadn't done so since the Irish
civil war of 1922–3, but the whole ethos of Irish nationalism in my
time glorified war. Gordon and I did not talk religion but I knew his
father, whom he loved, was a minister in the Church of Scotland. He
was a believer in the Labour Party to which Gordon was devoted,
however critical. Labour was truly a religious faith to him, and those
outside the faith were in danger of eternal damnation: I didn't equate
this with Church of Scotland theology so much as find it reminiscent
of Irish Catholic parish priests before the Second Vatican Council.
In 1974 he was editing the *Red Paper on Scotland* published by
the Board: it demanded a genuinely egalitarian Scotland, contained
many contributors who were socialists, some decidedly Left of Gordon. He generously included me arguing for socialism and Scottish
nationalism: we agreed that we disagreed, without much argument.

I knew Gordon for a person of terrific courage, in some ways
one of the most courageous people I have ever known. As student
Rector he had to defy the University Court which wrongfully tried to
prevent him from chairing its meetings as had been done by previous
Rectors, such as the future Prime Minister Lord Rosebery elected
in 1880. The Court included senior judges and tried to have him
unchaired by a High Court action which they lost. Neither side may
have fully realised it, but he intimidated them, justly penetrating the
more vulnerable parts of their consciences with a manner more theological than he knew. He exposed the University's secret investment
in South African shares which its executive had officially denied.
He once resigned a tutorship (whose income he needed) because
he thought it impossible to maintain it during his Rectorship when
his trade union required his observance of a strike demanding his
absence which might have disadvantaged students whom as Rector,
he represented. His politics were also unusual in having a very strong
historical dimension, and his doctorate was on Scottish Labour history whence came his *Maxton* biography. He was a fine historian
reflecting the necessity to seek objectivity of the history he wrote
and spoke to be as true as it could be. Nonetheless, he could no

more desert the Labour Party than I could desert the Roman Catholic Church.

As a student leader he won terrific admiration, but for all of us he was a beloved colleague, not a doctrinaire disciplinarian, and the work of the Board was carried out with conviction and laughter. The Board was a school of journalism run by self-training students: it chose what it thought the best people for various publishing enterprises as well as running student, literary, medical, and sociological periodicals. For instance, the editor of *Festival Times*, the constructively iconoclastic periodical we published in four numbers during the Edinburgh Festivals and Fringes in 1975–6 was a devout monarchist whom Gordon and I liked as well as respected very much. Gordon played a major part in acquiring, publicising and publishing the prison letters of Antonio Gramsci studying where Marxism could integrate with nationalism, being drawn to the work by the folklorist and poet Hamish Henderson who came to know it while serving in the UK army during World War II and edited and translated it for the Board. Among Gordon's many inadequate biographers one said that he went through the usual left-wing student cult of Gramsci: but it was Gordon who had created that cult among Scottish students. Gordon was a creator, which is probably the key to his political life. As it happened, so was Alex Salmond, with similar misreading by *his* biographer (on which Alex remarked 'I had no idea that my life was so dull'). These two were not Scots participating in normal political life: they created as part of what they taught and served. Obviously neither Gordon nor Alex was a messiah nor would they claim to be, but the word may help us to understand them. This probably lay at the heart of Gordon's difficulties with Tony Blair.

Mr Blair is a careerist who saw the Labour Party as a better bet: it was Gordon's heart and soul. Mr Blair went to war in Iraq when so instructed by President 'Dubya' Bush, having careerist reasons to know that he had no alternative. Gordon Brown followed him into that war because he believed Labour in power would destroy itself by an open split, the repression hardening his own growing anger against Mr Blair. Gordon continued to work with former colleagues from student journalism, among whom Bill Campbell founded

Mainstream Publishing, a very lively Edinburgh house, and they brought out important political studies including Gordon Brown's *Where There is Greed: Margaret Thatcher and the Betrayal of Britain's Future*. This would be cited against him 20 years later, when he received Baroness Thatcher at her former residence of 10 Downing Street now inhabited by him. In truth he was probably very sorry for her, now virtually witless and sunk by alcohol: she may not even have known who he was. He tried to jolly her up by stating she was a 'conviction politician' and so was he: that was kind packaging, but as a salutation from the author of *Where There is Greed* to its chief target the compliment had sharp edges. The lesson of his book-title summed up the case against her: she had made greed the ethos she preached, at one point announcing that she thought souls going to Heaven would find it provided a share in British Telecom which she had just privatised. Meanwhile her germ of greed infected UK politics far and wide, Gordon innocently preaching it when Chancellor of the Exchequer by extravagant plaudits to US financial 'statesmen' such as Alan Greenspan. During his all too brief premiership Gordon Brown performed Herculean feats in saving the UK from the worst effects of the banks' collapse: a direct consequence of their capitulation to Thatcherite greed. He also achieved some of the most socially beneficial items in the Labour agenda. For his pains he was accused for the next ten years of having landed the UK in bankruptcy, which is equivalent to blaming Prime Minister Boris Johnson for the Coronavirus.

Under which king, Bezonian?

Gordon as a true Labour devotee was always bound to see Scottish nationalism as an abominable heresy, if not actual infidelity, while realising it attracted Scots sometimes on progressive grounds. In the 1970s he had tried to come to terms with what seemed valid in its growing appeal, and incurred brutal bullying from Scottish Labour Party hardnoses. He worked to the point of exhaustion in 1979 trying to win a referendum victory for a Scottish legislature, saw his cause win by too narrow a majority and then denied to Scotland and himself by the wrecking amendment moved by George Cunningham who subsequently apostatized from Labour to the Social Democrats. In the general election two months later, Gordon had to fight the Tory stronghold Edinburgh South (impregnable since 1918) where he worked so well that it was captured in the 1987 election by his devoted follower Nigel Griffiths.

Before the 1979 referendum Labour and SNP party members had worked together shoulder to shoulder with cold co-operation in Westminster and much greater comradeship further down the ranks. Prime Minister James Callaghan had never been favourable to devolution, supporting it primarily to keep Labour in power. When, under the Cunningham amendment, the proposal was dropped Callaghan declined to guarantee a further attempt. SNP having held the balance of power in the Commons were now spiked on the horns of a dilemma: if they continued to support Labour with no further constitutional profit they could be dismissed as patsies incapable of justifying their continued Westminster identity as a separate party, and if they abandoned their alliance they would precipitate a general election with all too authoritative fears of a victory of the Tories under their new fundamentalist leader Margaret Thatcher. Westminster SNP withdrew support for Labour and Callaghan sneered that they were turkeys voting for Christmas. His sneer proved to be his last hurrah. The exhausted Gordon Brown fought Edinburgh South where I was editor of the local SNP propaganda and made much of the refusal of Labour to participate in a hustings of the five parties, the Greens being in the field now. Labour insisted that they were justified since the Tories would only debate against Labour, and we trumpeted that this was clear evidence of the big two unionist parties in a corrupt alliance mutually supporting one another in anti-democratic practices. My friend Gordon then telephoned me to inform me with irritation that Labour now agreed to a five-party event because the Church of Scotland minister who had agreed to chair a Tory–Labour debate now threatened public resignation from the role unless the big two also agreed to participate in a hustings including all parties. His telephone call to me was, I suppose, a kind of congratulations on my having been a successful nuisance ironically noting that I, as a Catholic, had mobilised a Church of Scotland clergyman against himself, the son of a Manse, but his news was ominous for SNP.

Our propaganda had been far too successful, as could be judged by its persuasive effect on the Presbyterian cleric, and now we had lost our vote-getting grievance and landed ourselves with very doubtful prospects for the ensuing fray. We had a worthy candidate, Bob Shirley, a professional economist, who would have been an excellent addition to Westminster, but who as a debater was unlikely to prove the greatest star. The five candidates duly convened, the best performer far and away was the Liberal Democrat Dr Bryan Lovell. Our man was authoritative but longwinded. The Tory candidate, new and vigorous, and concealing as best as he could his status as heir to the Marquisate of Lothian, nevertheless radiated his improvement over his indolent predecessor the Tory incumbent. Gordon was exhausted, worn out so thoroughly in the recently lost cause of his country that he bore little sign of being the likely alternative. The Green candidate stood up, held a number of index-cards, and nervously dropped them on the floor of the stage: I looked around with horror, and saw vote after vote clearly being transferred to him in the minds of the many kindly old ladies in the auditorium.

I attended the Labour–Tory debate the following day, to wreak what mayhem I could, choosing a double-pronged question about their election addresses in which I asked Gordon of the picture on his address showing him apparently about to punch James Callaghan in the solar plexus while Callaghan took what cover he could by holding his spectacles in front of him photo-captioned 'BEST FOR SCOTLAND'. Was it one of these election promises forgotten in the event of success, or, to put it another way, if Callaghan dropped Scottish devolution what would Gordon do? Gordon was laughing so hard that he couldn't reply initially. Then told me firmly that Labour had entered in the fight for devolution not as narrow chauvinists like SNP but to do what they thought best for Scotland and the UK. I assured him I never thought of him as a narrow chauvinist, merely a broad chauvinist, and then asked the second half of my question to 'the Earl of Ancram' which elicited a hiss of horror from the Tories present since the candidate perpetually referred to himself quite incorrectly as 'Mr Michael Ancram' – when not calling himself an Earl, he should have been 'Michael Kerr' – but he certainly established 'Earl' as a four-letter word. In fact, while the election was prelude to the Thatcher doom of Scotland, it was already a harbinger of revolution, set on foot by SNP but not at this time profiting them. The Earl of Ancram would prove a great improvement on his predecessor Michael Clark Hutchison who, like many MPs hitherto elected for Scotland in the 20th century, did not even live there. Ancram's vigour signalled Tory realisation that under SNP challenge, the unquestioning Scottish Deferential Vote was becoming extinct. In 1986, Ancram as MP went to our parent-teacher meeting in our children's school Liberton High (his predecessor probably did not know of its existence unless it became voting premises on election day). Thatcher had made her mark on Scotland, and the meeting's Chair, Headmaster Henry L Philip tore the MP's commercial to pieces by itemising the disastrous effects of Thatcherism on Scottish education. She had politicised him and he went on to become a most effective Chair of the Edinburgh South Labour Constituency Association still campaigning vigorously into his late 80s. Labour had similarly benefited from the Deferential Vote, and Harold Wilson in his memoirs *The Labour Government* took pride in Labour's Scottish MPs endlessly filing into the requisite division lobbies without question. Nine of 1974's 11 SNP MPs fell in 1979, but unionist MPs could no longer hope to survive as mere lobby-fodder. Gordon's candidacy in 1979 was unsuccessful in the election but his work for devolution and election meant the Scottish Labour Party realised it had to think Scotland. Few of them had thought as Scottish as Gordon.

The spiritual nationalism of Theresa May

As I write, he is still repeating his favoured adjective 'narrow' in captioning an article in the *Observer* for 18 January 2020. He writes: 'The United Kingdom is too precious to be lost to narrow nationalism'. He is still proving himself more Scottish than the unionist norm (including the *Observer* itself which has dropped its Scottish column since the last election), thus marking a stage in unionist abdication.

Was it the *Observer* or former Prime Minister Brown who headlined the union as 'precious'? It is former Prime Minister Theresa May's copyright, except that she doubled it: 'our precious, precious union'. Both Theresa May and Gordon Brown are children of pastors, and as the daughter of a High Anglican priest she may have instinctively derived 'precious' from Isaiah 28:16:

> Therefore thus saith the Lord GOD, Behold I lay in Zion
> for a foundation a stone, a tried stone, a precious cor-
> ner stone, a sure foundation: he that believeth shall not
> make haste.

As with many passages from Isaiah, a Christian would automatically take this for a prophecy of the advent of Jesus Christ, all the more when taken in conjunction with its citation in the first Epistle of Peter 2:6:

> Wherefore also it is contained in the scripture, Behold,
> I lay in Sion a chief corner stone, elect, precious: and he
> that believeth on him shall not be confounded.

And the Gospel according to St Matthew 21:42 gives Jesus's self-identification with the Lord's establishment of the corner stone:

> Jesus saith unto them, Did ye never read in the scriptures,
> The stone which the builders rejected, the same is become
> the head of the corner: this is the Lord's doing, and it is
> marvellous in our eyes.

St Paul told the Ephesians 2:19–20:

> Now therefore ye are no more strangers and foreigners,
> but fellow citizens with the saints, and of the household
> of God;
> And are built upon the foundation of the apostles and
> prophets, Jesus Christ himself being the chief corner stone.

With regards to religion, Prime Minister May is entitled to very serious consideration, holding what faith she does among memories of her parents, her upbringing and their family life. Theresa May's idea of the union is as sacred to her as to a genuinely religious man of the Orange Order. Unlike almost all of her party she did think of Northern Ireland when she thought of the union, she had even spoken there – against Brexit – on the eve of the referendum in 2016.

May was exceptional even amongst the cabinet-level Tories for her evident dislike of immigrants, and while St Paul was being ecumenical with the Ephesians the same quotation makes Theresa May's precious union look like an exclusion of strangers and foreigners, and the form of its equation with Jesus seals it off from those not currently citizens. There may also be an implication that 'precious' derives from Catholic reverence to 'the precious blood of Our Lord', the word itself meaning 'the price in blood shed by Christ that we might be saved'. This is the blood shed while He still lived, all the way from the scourging which tore out the flesh of its victims, the crown of thorns forced on His head, the imprints of where He fell, the nailing to the cross, until after death the body was finally drained by the soldier's spear. Gaelic pauper poets pictured His mother finding the way to Calvary from the 'streams of blood'. The identification of local nationalism's wars with the sacrifice of Christ is a nauseating trope of 'Christian' government pageant and propaganda to the present day. Perhaps Prime Minister May meant that the union had been achieved by bloodshed and thus was comparably sacred. Countless volunteers and conscripts died in the wars to make and sustain the varieties of union, many of them in genuine conviction of self-sacrifice, but the notion that such bloodshed sanctified the Union is to imply that Christ died in furtherance of the policies of Pontius Pilate. Theresa May's nationalism may merit intellectual respect but can hardly escape moral condemnation.

Orwell for beginners

Labour's defence of the Anglo-Scottish Union has to steal its adjectives from the Tories. Did any real contrasts between Scottish Labour and Tories survive their alliance against Scottish independence in the 2014 referendum? The Tory government in the 1990s livened up its post-Thatcher intellectual bankruptcy by deriding Labour as too inexperienced to govern, so that Labour belief in the Tories long survived the Tories' belief in themselves, and its shades were evident in 2014. Gordon Brown quoted George Orwell in his 2020 *Observer* piece: but the most relevant Orwell text seems to be *Animal Farm*: when the pigs and the men become indistinguishable. Gordon declared that 'Orwell made the distinction between patriots who love their country and nationalists who see life as a constant struggle between an "us" and a "them" and invent enemies – and grievances – where none exist'. Here he was also hanging Tory linguistic laundry on his clothes-line, Territorial Army Colonel Ruth Davidson MSP having understandably made what profit of Orwell she thought she could, when delivering the Orwell Lecture on 15 May 2017. Orwell actually wrote in his 'Notes on Nationalism' (October 1945):

> Nationalism is not to be confused with patriotism. Both words are normally used in so vague a way that any definition is liable to be challenged, but one must draw a distinction between them, since two different and even opposing ideas are involved. By 'patriotism' I mean devotion to a particular place and a particular way of life, which one believes to be the best in the world but has no wish to force upon other people. Patriotism is of its nature defensive, both militarily and culturally. Nationalism, on the other hand, is inseparable from the desire for power. The abiding purpose of every nationalist is to secure more power and more prestige, *not* for himself but for the nation or other unit in which he has to secure his own individuality.

On this definition patriotism virtually wallows in the extreme English nationalist boast of being 'the best in the world', and it is interesting that Orwell apparently saw little wrong with it. The Dutch historian Gustaaf Johannes Renier devoted the second chapter of his best-seller *The English: Are They Human?* to the endless reiteration in contemporary English newspapers that in any admirable quality, product, or asset, the English were 'the best in the world', culminating in one English claim that English weather was the best in the world, and another that 'we' are the most self-abnegating people 'on earth'. His examples were drawn from many offenders, above all from the *Daily Express*, which in those days was still a newspaper. Most English (or perhaps British) scholars and serious commentators take it as unquestionable that English (or occasionally British) is the best in the world when they say it is. Fewer English called themselves British in 1931.

Introduction to GJ Renier, *The English: Are They Human* (1931):

I am speaking about the English, not about the British. There is no question in this work of the Scots, proud, intelligent, religious and unfathomable. Nor the Welsh, minute, musical, clever, and temperamental. I am not writing about the charming, untruthful, bloodthirsty and unreliable Irish. I shall be exclusively concerned with the English, the unintellectual, restricted, stubborn, steady, pragmatic, silent and reliable English.

Orwell, contrasting patriotism and nationalism, may recall AP Herbert's 'By statesmen I mean the members of my party, by politicians I mean the members of yours'. We might agree that SNP members want more power and prestige for their party and country. Yet on the other hand, would either Ruth Davidson or Gordon Brown readily yield the monopoly in such ambitions to SNP and deny it to their own parties? If so, the Tory Party is not merely at prayer, it should retire to monastic orders, and the Labour Party follow the friars. Would either of them deny that Scotland is their country? If either would (which I doubt), would they think it wise to tell that to Scottish voters? Davidson and Brown are now retired from front-line party combat, however vehement their occasional resurrections, but present-day chieftains of their parties may be less sure. Mr Douglas Ross MP was chosen as leader of the Scottish Tories in preference to all Scottish Tory MSPs, obviously by decision in Downing Street, London: several of the superseded MSPs were clearly better qualified. But Scottish Labour chose Anas Sarwar whose Muslim faith and Pakistani paternal origin may mean a new Scottish identity for the party, broadening and enriching Scottish political culture.

The great value of Orwell's essay today is religious – as I would infuriate him by claiming. As a historical document it is fascinating but its main importance is to make all of us ask ourselves – honestly – how far we deny obvious truths in the cause of our loyalties, our nationalisms. It is probably Orwell's fault that, as his constant reader for the last 66 years, I find nationalism almost omnipresent, even in excess of the multiplicity he thrust on it. His essay says little about Scottish nationalism, on which his record was dubious, since he transferred against the Scots his anger as a public schoolboy at wealthy classmates whose English or Anglicised fathers owned Scottish grouse-moors. It lasted until after World War II when he went to the Isle of Jura and began to die there, and fell in love with it. This is instructive, since it was probably typical of less articulate English schoolboys of all ages, and partly accounts for the hardening of Scottish nationalism among Scots between the world wars. His 'Notes on Nationalism' tied in anti-Semitism with other nationalisms (but his own anti-Scottish-isms in his correspondence were from the same wholesale butcher-shop):

> Obviously there are considerable resemblance between political Catholicism as exemplified by Chesterton, and Communism. So there are between either of these and, for instance, Scottish Nationalism, Zionism, Anti-Semitism, or Trotskyism. It would be an over-simplification to say that all forms of nationalism are the same, even in their mental atmosphere, but there are certain rules that hold good in all cases.

It being 1945, Orwell naturally thought in military terms, and to him nationalism's obsession with increased power meant covet thy neighbour's country, specifically:

> Nationalism is power-hunger tempered by self-deception... as soon as fear, hatred, jealousy and power-worship are involved, the sense of reality becomes unhinged... the sense of right and wrong becomes unhinged also.... Loyalty is involved, and so pity ceases to function.

This is a timely warning to everyone at every time. But today this relates to the media moguls and the powers they dominate by calling great. Orwell's essay concluded that:

> Welsh, Irish and Scottish nationalism have points of difference but are alike in their anti-English orientation... One symptom of it is the delusion that Eire, Scotland or even Wales could preserve its independence unaided and owes nothing to British protection.... No modern Irish writer, even of the stature of Yeats or Joyce, is completely free from traces of nationalism.

True enough, on the last point, but this would rightly have included the editors and polemicists in the still UK unionist *Irish Times*. SNP took note of lessons from Ireland, as it did from Norway, Denmark and the Netherlands but rejected the cult of violence revered by the 20th century Irish nationalism victorious in the 1918 election that obliterated the non-violent Irish Home Rule constitutionalists. The Irish victors thereafter demanded the six Unionist-controlled Ulster counties for most of the rest of the century, while knowing and caring less and less about them. SNP nationalism makes their fulfilment of Orwell's nationalism impossible, since they have no desire to possess themselves of territory beyond the limits of Scotland as they were before James VI of Scotland became James I of England. Hugh MacDiarmid declared the permanent limits of Scottish nationalism:

> The rose of all the world is not for me.
> I want for my part
> Only the little white rose of Scotland
> That smells sharp and sweet – and breaks the heart.

James VI, Bonnie Prince Charlie, and Prime Ministers the Earl of Aberdeen, the Earl of Rosebery, the Earl of Balfour, Sir Henry Camp-bell-Bannerman, James Ramsay MacDonald, the Earl of Home, and Gordon Brown were all nationalists from Scotland yearning to rule England (Tony Blair is irrelevant having been 'from' Scotland in a purely geographical sense of the term). Theirs was not a 'narrow' nationalism. Neo-Toryism, Celtic Nationalism, Communism, Political Catholicism, Zionism, Colour Feeling, Class Feeling, Pacifism, Anglophobia, Antisemitism, Trotskyism were all singled out in Orwell's essay as examples of nationalism. Presumably he and his readers in 1945 would have taken it for granted that Nazism and Fascism were automatically included. On the other hand, it seems well on the road to my conclusion that nationalism is a universal human trait. As Bernard (the junior Secretary in the BBC political Soap-opera 'Yes, Minister') might put it:

> I am a patriot
> You are a nationalist
> He is a chauvinist.

The unspeakable Scot

You may find the foregoing discussion of Gordon Brown at odds with what the media told about him. He was, from the beginning, black-guarded by London political media, and it would seem principally because he was Scottish, not simply because he was born in Scotland. London media in general resent being forced to think beyond their all-embracing metropolis – apart from exotic postings 'abroad'. SNP annoy them by making Scotland more than merely a location of midwinter news reports about expensive idiots climbing largely inaccessible mountains. Whatever the benefits of Oxbridge housetraining and London rule, in their prime they called their United Kingdom of Great Britain and Ireland 'England' and discouraged any serious study of its history outwith the *real* England. Nationalism may often wish to distort history in the interest of its present propaganda. Nevertheless, Scotland's professional historical writing was transformed by the impact of SNP, and the consequent epic historical debates between the country's great historians made a former desert bloom with fascinating results.

Sir Tony Blair was Edinburgh-born, but thanks to Scotland's most English public school (Fettes) and Oxford he easily self-Anglicised. Gordon Brown attended Kirkcaldy High School and Edinburgh University. This was probably crucial (though naturally not admitted) when on the death of Labour Party leader John Smith, Blair and his ally Peter Mandelson bluffed Brown into permitting the much less well-qualified Blair go for the Labour leadership instead of himself. Being a good historian Gordon was genuinely modest. He believed the Blair–Mandelson 'confidence-man' trick that the Labour Party would vote for an English voice, rather than a Scottish voice. In other words, Blair and Mandelson convinced him that, despite *The Red Paper on Scotland,* UK Labour was but English nationalism writ large, though gallantly and selflessly he has remained devoted to it. In fact, they made him believe he was a predestined victim of English Scotophobia although in loyalty to the party he must never admit it. The Labour Party had accepted a Welsh leader in Neil Kinnock and then a Scotsman in John Smith. Kinnock had been somewhat undermined by anti-Welsh sentiment coyly popularised by Thatcher and her nursery, and Smith, a finer debater than any of his contemporaries, bubbled over with laughter in the faces of Scotophobes in and out of parliament. Gordon Brown was too innocent to see through creatures so inferior to him in intellect. He was being outflanked by snobbery on all sides, which he couldn't measure. Gordon really enjoyed the fun of being an intellectual and never spoke of himself as such, except in self-mockery.

London media, accustomed to defer to loud-mouthed graduates of Eton and Oxbridge, gave themselves the luxury of despising the unreconstructed Scot. (A Scotland complicating binary politics with a party only operating electorally in Scotland made it much more difficult for the media to pontificate, and it wasn't helped by having to outsmart much too canny Scots.) As President 'Dubya' Bush made clear when entertaining Prime Minister Gordon Brown, a Scot is expected to be dour. First-class intellect is not appreciated by banal commentators. In fact, Brown's puritan demeanour, often quite involuntary, probably made the media feel they had been discovered smoking behind the bike-sheds. I was once being interviewed for some television programme about Gordon Brown, and stopped the interviewer and told the producer that that question had been designed so that no answer could be given to it which would not be hostile to Gordon. Unless at least lip-service was given to fairness the interview was over and the use of what had been filmed would be prohibited. My terms were accepted, we continued more objectively. The interviewer afterwards remarked apologetically that he had behaved as he had because Gordon had once refused him an interview. London was not prepared to allow Scots to get above themselves without punishment.

Antiquity of London Scotophobia

Long before the Union of 1707 – and even more after the '45 – English popular culture ridiculed Scots as barbarians and increased its own nationalism in doing so whether in border forays or national conflicts, especially after Scottish nationalism had been kindled by Edward I from sparks to forest fire. The English resented the Union of Crowns brought by James's succession to Elizabeth in 1603, and prevented it for a century from becoming a Union of Kingdoms. Thomas Babington Macaulay in his second essay on 'William Pitt, Earl of Chatham' (in *Edinburgh Review* 1844) found London informants to tell him what London had said when George III appointed a Scot (Bute) as Prime Minister in 1762, with bitter memories of Scottish Jacobite insurrections:

> The events of 1715 and 1745 had left painful and enduring traces. The tradesmen of Cornhill had been in dread of seeing their tills and warehouses plundered by bare-legged mountaineers from the Grampians. They still recollected that Black Friday, when the news came that the rebels were at Derby, when all the shops in the city were closed, and when the Bank of England began

to pay in sixpences. ... The favourite did not suffer the English to forget from what part of the island he came. The cry of all the south was that the public offices, the army, the navy, were filled with high-cheeked Drummonds and Erskines, Macdonalds and Macgillivrays, who could not talk a Christian tongue, and some of whom had but lately began to wear Christian breeches. All the old jokes on hills without trees, girls without stockings, men eating the food of horses, pails emptied from the fourteenth story, were pointed against these lucky adventurers. To the honour of the Scots it must be said, that their prudence and their pride restrained them from retaliation. Like the princess in the Arabian tale, they stopped their ears tight, and, unmoved by the shrillest notes of abuse, walked on, without once looking round, straight towards the Golden Fountain.

English colonies devoured Scotophobia with all the zest with which they devoured other English fashions. One of the causes of the American Revolution was resentment against the Scots who held improvident Virginians and Carolinians to their legal contracts. The Scottish Enlightenment intended to make its mark in profitable missionaries amongst English readers who devoured such education but resented the authors' awareness of how deeply the southerners needed it. 19th century humour in *Punch* and such popular prints perpetually depicted Scots as drunken misers (and, like its successor *Private Eye*, it honoured its jokes by their endless repetition). TWH Crosland's *The Unspeakable Scot* began the 20th century with bitter resentment of Scots in English communications media advancing one another's fortunes at English expense.

Gordon Brown at Edinburgh University could have heard Scotophobia freely ornamenting lectures from English dons resenting their own failure to gain Oxbridge posts, or laments from English undergraduates rejected from Oxbridge places. Sir Tony Blair, by contrast, hardly troubled the inferiority complexes of the media. Dr Brown was left to work his way into the service of UK nationalism while silently resenting Blair's attempt to Anglicise himself: an obvious requirement for English success. The resultant mutual hostility was ascribed by the voracious media to childish rivalry, biased in favour of Blair's assiduous conformity to its model of the modern Prime Minister. Blair's repackaging of the Labour Party amid his chatter of 'New Labour' was construed as statesmanship with appropriate eyes on the potential conversion of Surrey stockbrokers. Dr Brown undertook his own quest, for Britishness. His Edinburgh history studies must have given him excellent groundwork for he was trained by the late Paul Addison, author of the leading histories of UK politics in the 1940s. Intellectually, Addison may have been the Englishman Gordon knew best, and he could not have found a finer representative, courteous, industrious, brilliant, modest and truly kind. It meant that the Britain on which Gordon had received the finest teaching was the Britain where British nationalism visibly and audibly existed in what its national hero Winston Churchill singled out unforgettably as its finest hour. Gordon himself became a major historian of Labour in Scotland between the World Wars. Ironically, it reflected his Scotland and his Britain moving out of synchronisation. Scottish nationalism seemed to create a different time-zone appearing more progressive yet more devoted to hard-won social values. Politically speaking Gordon remained the symbol of Labour in Scotland in all three Westminster elections during the Blair government. In many Labour candidates' election literature in Scotland Blair was not even mentioned, but he and his entourage were happy to take the credit for the victory Brown and his followers achieved. On the other hand, Blair was entitled to credit for Labour's Scottish losses. The Britain Gordon Brown sought to discover – and was forced to invent – had become a different country. Its glories of World War II were now shovelled out in vile semi-racist Europhobe attacks by the popular press on the whims of its plutocrat proprietors paying few UK taxes, if any. The freedom of the press had become the tyranny of its capitalists, before whom today's politicians were required to grovel, in which proceeding Sir Tony outstripped all of his contemporaries. The very fact that Gordon had been trained as a historian in perpetual pursuit of truth made him the better statesman but the worse politician.

Coronavirus revolutionises

Professor JH Elliott in his fascinating *Scots and Catalans : Union and Disunion* remarks judicially:

> As the Anglo-Irish Treaty of 1921 made all too clear, nationalism and separation were two sides of the coin.

Cliché is the death of intellect, but the late Reverend Dr Ian Paisley and the happily living Dr Gordon Brown are unmistakeable nationalists, the UK being their imaginary community, and neither of them countenancing separation. This reduction of nationalism to a formula in chemistry packaged by the pharmacist will not serve. Benedict Anderson was right that any attempt to think, talk, and write in favour of nationalism inevitably works the imagination hard, since we cannot hope to know ourselves, let alone the people we see enlisted in our nationalism. The more interesting prophets of unionism are in precisely the same situation. Dr Brown (whether he knows it or not) tried to invent British nationalism as fast as he could. He should have been inventing UK nationalism, Northern Ireland requiring honest attempts to assert its inclusion. In the end, Scottish independence will probably be caused by Whitehall and Westminster continuing to set Scottish nationalism on fire, just as Irish independence was made possible in Easter Week 1916 by the Irish capital, Dublin, being demolished by UK bombardment. The country's future was handed over to an incompetent general who promptly imagined martial law was real law. Not that Scottish independence will be won by violence from its proponents: if it does not remain non-violent, it will not be worth having. Unfortunately, UK nationalism prides itself on its violent record and did what it could to absorb the nationalisms of its component parts by rejoicing in such slaughter in UK service as was required of them. So deeply-rooted is the cult of slaughter in the shop window of UK nationalism that the Rt Hon Philip Hammond speaking as Secretary for Defence during the Independence Referendum in 2014 declared that even if Scotland became independent it would have to retain TRIDENT and its like in Scottish waterways. By the principles of Scottish nationalism, it may not. Nevertheless, Mr Hammond has his uses. Commentators are apt to classify brexiteers as UK nationalists and exempt the rest of the Tory Party. But all the Tory Party or parties are UK nationalists or, as they would prefer to put it, unionists.

Encircled by the world-wide plague known as Covid-19 (or Coronavirus), Dr Brown addressed the UK on 19 March 2020. The house style of the current government obliged him to explain:

> [T]his is a global problem... it's not just a national problem, it needs global action and not simply national action. We've had too much of America First, China first, India first.

This address was both true enough and urgent enough, with that self-styled nationalist President Donald Trump using the plague to pump up a self-destruct American chauvinism to offset his own initial ridicule for the reports of its imminence. Dr Brown also sought to improve the shining hour by stating we had had too much of this 'populist nationalism' and that we should believe in our UK administrators. We must certainly labour to have confidence in today's con men, and grant that at least some of them may rise to the occasion. Yet, we must fight the plague together, working with our fellow-Scots, fellow-English, fellow-Welsh, and fellow-Irish on both sides of the Irish border. We must maintain SNP internationalism, and bring UK nationalism up to SNP levels. We must all be internationalists, rather than leave it to the diplomats. We must all keep thinking and working for our fellow-humans across the world. Populism was most obviously defined by the American Populist party in the early 1890s whose legislative programmes, like those of their predecessors the UK Chartists, advocated reforms almost all of which are standard law today. They preached real politics of human improvement while the major parties simply competed to get jobs for the boys and protection for capitalists.

As for nationalism, whether in Scotland, the UK, throughout Europe, or across the globe, Coronavirus insists on all of us being nationalists. Virtually every government under the sun is decreeing nationalism to its people, both in declamations and in decrees. Nationalism's most eloquent enemies such as France's Emmanuel Macron today lead the enactment of nationalism. As so often with

nationalism's critics, the criticism in itself often becomes nationalism, as in President Macron's charismatic Armistice Day address
whose celebration of patriotism as the antithesis of nationalism
struck nationalism's chords via the nationalist cults of Charles Peguy,
Charles de Gaulle, Joan of Arc, and others. Few of today's rulers
could hope for much more tolerance for themselves by their dis-
illusioned electorates, and hence in one form or another they seal
the borders of their countries in so many respects, and justify it by
appeals to idealism. The unit of overall national government – or
that of devolved national government – is the simplest method of
organising society to meet the threat of the Coronavirus pandemic.
We have to be good nationalists working for the survival and welfare of all of our people, here and throughout the planet. It is the
people alone who can ensure that the necessary decrees by its rulers
(where wise) are accepted, enforced, and carried through. Coronavirus is making socialists of the Tories, and may yet make Dr Gordon
Brown recognise his own status as hero and martyr of nationalism.
His heroism and his martyrdom are both ancient and familiar, ideal-
istic but idiosyncratic, moody yet marvellous, exploited by popular
frauds and trivialised by weasel-wordsmiths, old as near-universally
forgotten magic, modern as the rhapsodic revival of reading among
children. He is today's Harry Potter, a well-taught wizard, conscientious, courageous, bewildered by the difficulty of discovering who
he is, mocked by snobs, exploited by frauds, endangered by crooked
media, suspicious of apparent enemies who may ultimately prove
real friends, and perpetually innocent.

CHAPTER THREE

Is God a nationalist?

God heard the embattled nations sing and shout
   '*Gott Strafe England!*' and 'God save the King!'
God this, God that, and God the other thing –
   'Good God!' said God, 'I've got my work cut out!'

JC Squire, 'The Dilemma', *The Survival of the Fittest, and other poems* (1916)

'Ye see the distress that we are in, how Jerusalem lieth waste, and the gates thereof are burned with fire: come, and let us build up the wall of Jerusalem, that we be no more a reproach.'

Nehemiah 2:17, *Holy Bible,* quoted on National Party of Scotland General Election Campaign Leaflet May 1929 for John MacCormick

---

St John, Gospel 11.47–52 in King James Version, *Holy Bible*

Then gathered the chief priests and the Pharisees a council, and said, What do we? For this man doeth many miracles.

If we let him thus alone, all men will believe on him: and the Romans shall come and take away both our place and nation.

And one of them, named Caiaphas, being the high priest that same year, said unto them, Ye know nothing at all,

Nor consider that it is expedient for us, that one man should die for the people, and that the whole nation perish not.

And this spake he not of himself: but being high priest that year, he prophesied that Jesus should die for that nation:

And not for that nation only, but that but that also he should gather together in one the children of David that were scattered abroad.

ST JOHN MADE it clear that he was witness to what he described in his Gospel, or else witness to witnesses who saw what he did not. He was probably very young and may have been a boy: a mascot among the disciples of whom Jesus was particularly fond, an honorary son or brother whom He would bestow on His mother from the Cross. He grew up in an oral culture, knowing prayers and Jewish records by heart, and able to repeat what others told him. Pharisee Nicodemus was his source for what the High Priest Caiaphas told the Sanhedrin. John may also have had an account from the former High Priest Annas, at whose house he was welcome. Annas as the father of several boys could naturally converse with him and evidently enjoyed their acquaintance enough to offer an open door at any time. John as a Galilean, not being a permanent resident in Jerusalem and hence a Jew but not a Judaean, was likely to feel a little like a young Scot visiting London, repelled by the sophistication of the metropolis however spiritually attached to it.

When speaking, Caiaphas certainly referred to the Jews, at home and around the world. From the beginning of his Gospel, John was creating work so far into the sublime as to be unique. The ultimate meaning of what Caiaphas claimed John declared included salvation for the 'nation' – the Jews. Caiaphas certainly did not mean all 'the children of God that were scattered abroad', converts to Jesus in the future, however remote. John's nationalism was built from the 'nation' as spoken by Caiaphas. Caiaphas had a very different and much more earthly nationalism making the most of a colonial status where Jews worshipped by Roman permission under his stewardship appointed by Pontius Pilate's predecessor, the Roman governor Valerius Gatus who had dismissed his father-in-law Annas. Yet the Zealots offered another kind of nationalism: to rebel against Rome by force of arms. Pilate's condemnation of Jesus would free the Zealot Barabbas to walk free despite his patriotic murders; and the nation that was Rome subjected most of the known world to its nationalism orchestrated in Roman propaganda from the greatest known poets, historians, philosophers in the world.

At the heart of the prophecy of Caiaphas lay the ugly principle of the scapegoat: 'expedient that one man should die for the people'. Nationalism would follow Christendom in enrichment by the blood of its martyrs, Joan of Arc for the French, William Wallace for the Scots, the Easter insurgent leaders for the Irish, King Charles I for the English; and beyond them the thousands to die for the nations in endless wars. Caiaphas prophesied something else, the eradication of the entire Jewish nation if Jesus did not die, the awareness that sooner or later a holocaust awaited them had Jesus never appeared, however successful Caiaphas himself might be in keeping some peace. The endless centuries to unfold horrific Christian persecution of the Jews might attempt impossible justification by blaming Caiaphas. In reality, the Saviour whom they claimed to vindicate had uttered what may have been His utmost condemnation on hypocrites. Caiaphas may have been primarily dominated by anxiety to keep his job, which meant keeping in with Pilate better than his father-in-law Annas had managed with Pilate's predecessor who had fired him. Caiaphas's demand for Jesus's death was consistent with his own Jewish nationalism: to save the nation from Roman destruction while retaining as much Jewish dignity and self-respect as he could, and conveniently eliminating what he saw as a dangerous competitor. Caiaphas's prophetic fears for the Jews would have been conscious and genuine, while remaining unaware of its Christian implications. He was clearly a devious diplomat, playing Roman politics as cleverly as Pilate, as well as keeping his own flock in order. As Jesus said from the Cross, His killers did not know what they were doing, which obviously includes the one who began the killing process, Caiaphas. That divine plea for forgiveness destroys the whole basis of Christian anti-Semitism, which unlike Caiaphas did not kill in a cause of defensive nationalism.

Nationalism from the beginning

Nationalism may seem hostile to God by obviously being His competitor, as well as by the crimes committed in its name. The Bible quickly declares nationalism's origin – in competition.

Genesis 11:1–8, King James Version, *Holy Bible*:

And the whole earth was of one language, and of one speech.

And it came to pass, as they journeyed from the east, that they found a plain in the land of Shimar: and they dwelt there.

And they said one to another, Go to, let us make brick, and burn them thoroughly. And they had brick for stone, and slime had they for mortar.

And they said, Go to, let us build us a city and a tower, whose top may reach unto heaven: and let us make us a name, lest we be scattered abroad upon the face of the whole earth.

And the LORD came down to see the city and the tower, which the children of men builded.

And the LORD said, Behold the people is one, and they have all one language; and this they begin to do: and now nothing will be restrained from them, which they have imagined to do.

Go to, let us go down, and there confound their language, that they may not understand one another's speech.

So the LORD scattered them abroad from thence upon the face of all the earth: and they left off to build the city.

Nationalism is therefore God's creation, invented to counter human pride and greed. It begins as a weapon in humanity's seemingly endless attempts to compete with God, which damns competition in itself, important for us to remember in our present climate where governments slaver in deification of competition. Daniel O'Connell could tell William Joseph O'Neill Daunt in 1833 that:

> [A] diversity of tongues is of no benefit; it was first
> imposed on mankind as a curse, at the building of Babel.
> It would be of vast advantage to mankind if all the inhab-
> itants of the earth spoke exactly the same language.

Since O'Connell had already moved the Irish Catholic lower classes from Jacobite fantasy to pressure a hostile UK government to yield Catholic emancipation in 1829, why did he reject one of the major nationalist impulses? O'Connell was not one but several nationalists. He had rejected nationalism as defined by the French Revolution from which, as a schoolboy, he had been a fugitive. He shared some of the condemnations against it from his greatest – and most profound – precursor as apostle of Catholic emancipation, Edmund Burke. Burke naturally opposed Revolutionary French attempts to abolish history from the cathedral and the calendar, and denounced its official violence at home and abroad. Their childhoods in rural Kerry and Cork empathised with local nationalism, engendering zeal to eradicate the British-Irish Government's exclusion of Roman Catholics from citizenship. O'Connell won Catholic emancipation for Britain as well as Ireland, and thence demanded a liberal nationalism for both. He sought to repeal the Union enacted in 1800 if possible but, in any case, demanded emancipation for the Jews and an end to racial enslavement in UK and USA.

Nationalism created to bring down Babel by babble is neither good nor bad, but O'Connell's idea of unilingual unity shared atmosphere with apocalyptic redemption. Emancipating his Catholic followers from the opium of Catholic Stuart restoration, O'Connell's nationalism shared some of their dream cloud-edges fashionable amidst the European romanticism of the 1820s. It coincided with an exceptionally high tide of secret society agrarian violence, which O'Connell abominated but the roots of whose anger he understood. His mass meetings for Repeal in the 1840s were simultaneously inventions of democracy and promises of miraculous bloodless victory which UK rulers answered with false justice, and debilitating imprisonment. He was an Irish nationalist and simultaneously a UK nationalist, keeping reform governments in power in Westminster, showing by his masterly deployment of Irish Catholics using common ground with Protestants where possible to show how Britain must also adapt itself to politics 'out-of-doors'. He drew in financial support for his political machine from the poorest, forcing his foremost opponents Sir Robert Peel (future repealer of the inhuman Corn Laws) and Lord Stanley (father of the 1867 Reform Act) to liberalise their own programmes in trying to prevent his. The three of them were the greatest Commons orators of the 1830s, which in O'Connell's case testifies to the strength of Gaelic inspiring the grand mastery of English. One of the most rewarding popular roads from Gaelic to English was made by Robert Burns. Scots as a language shared common ancestry with English, much more so than with Gaelic, but Burns's music and songs became vernaculars for countless Gaelic speakers to find space as their minds grappled with alien new worlds. Twentieth century Irish story-tellers and scholars recognised Burns as an Irish favourite: from Protestant Antrim to Catholic Cork. It brings home another lesson to us. Nationalism may take its most active form in enabling migrants to move from one culture and environment to another, just as religion – especially the Irish Catholic religion – was the firmest form of psychological stability as the Mass remained unchanged in its ritual and its Latin language.

Carlton JH Hayes, 'What Nationalism is', *Nationalism: A Religion* (1960):

… a nationality receives its impress, its character, its individuality, not, unless very incidentally, from physical geography or biological race, but rather from cultural, and historical forces. First and foremost among these I would put *language*.

Language is peculiarly human, and at least ever since the legendary Tower of Babel there has been a wide, fluid, and baffling variety of languages. Anthropologists have shown that primitive tribes are marked off from one another by differences of speech. And alike to scholars and laymen it should be obvious that language is the surest badge of nationality.

Language begins nationalism

Carlton Hayes – Professor of History in New York's Columbia University, President of the American Historical Association, and convert to Roman Catholicism – was writing his last book after 40 years' pioneer work in the history of nationalism. If we bring his view to bear on our archipelago: Latin was our common language from Julius Caesar to various forms of learning in recent times, Welsh is our strongest living link with the remotest past, English our common destination, Ireland enlivened by two conflicting languages down the centuries, Scotland four – Gaelic, Scots and English and forms of Scandinavian. Many more recent arrivals to our archipelago retain their original nationalism by speaking or revering the languages of their origins. The saying 'there ain't no Black in the Union Jack' grimly reminds us of the failure of historical nationalist icons to represent the modern nations to which they refer.

The flags of our archipelago are more monitors of individual nationalisms than they used to be. The Union Jack carries the cross of St Patrick despite his greater identification with Protestant and Catholic imaginations in the Republic to which it does not apply. The green, white and orange flag of the Republic was flown during the Easter rebellion of 1916 honouring, and perhaps even annexing, the colour of extreme Protestant politics here united in a tradition of violent republicanism by the white symbol of peace. The green derives from the old green flag which was an 18th century idealisation of unity for Ireland, being taken to mingle orange (for William III) and blue (for St Patrick whose flag, before inclusion in the Union Jack, was blue). The symbol of a golden harp on a blue background also existed as a flag of Ireland. Ignorant 20th century reproductions of the Irish tricolour showed green, white and yellow, which Orangemen declared to be a mingling of the green flag with the Papal colours of white and yellow, which some Catholics were pleased to believe. The conflict in interpretation symbolised Irish Catholic nationalism's dilemma as to whether its loyalties were primarily Catholic or Irish. Flags were trophies to rally followers in battle and humiliate the enemy when captured, as Roman standards had been, and as above all the Ark of the Covenant, bearing the ten commandments on the stone of their adoption, was carried into battle by the ancient kings of Israel. The problem nicely illustrates the variety of uses of nationalism whether to proclaim peace or defy opponents.

In 20th century Scotland the Union Jack was flown without much question, although it was agreed that the Royal Flag of Scotland (the Lion rampant) and the Saltire (the St Andrew's Cross) were appropriate flags for certain occasions. The term 'saltire' presumably became common in the late 16th century to remove Roman Catholic associations. This was not necessarily elbow-jerk anti-Catholicism. Protestantism protested against what it saw as pagan and superstitious as well as corrupt clerical rackets, and cults of the saints which were felt by many – Catholics as well as Protestants – to displace devotion to God, and to imitate the many gods of the Roman Pantheon. St Andrew, first known disciple to be called by Jesus Christ and brother of St Peter, became identified with Scotland in the 8th century initially being honoured by the Christianised Picts and then taken up by the Irish-Scots. Pilgrimages to the shrine housing supposed relics of his body at what became St Andrews in Fife were active in the 10th century, greatly facilitated by transport improvements ordained by St Margaret at North and South Queensferry over the Forth in the late 11th century. The saltire became accepted as the Scottish flag with warriors told to wear the St Andrew's Cross when fighting against Richard II of England in the late 14th century. St Andrew had received exceptional honour even for a medieval national saint, what with a university founded in his honour, town, and a cathedral. He was also a very shrewd choice for a people who would become fixed on a Christianity based on Scripture. Unlike most medieval saints St Andrew has very firm presence in the four gospels, Jesus's first disciple having been directed to Him by St John the Baptist. Ironically the most visible expression of his cult with least Scriptural foundation is the supposition that he was martyred on a cross with his limbs forced into an X-shape, whence the flag. Bearing in mind how ruthless the proscription of Catholic worship was in Scotland, St Andrew seems directly responsible for some phenomena of Scottish Catholicism lasting down the Protestant centuries. In medieval times, like many other saints he was a special figure to be invoked in time of war, utilised by Walter Scott in *The Talisman* and made a clear card of Scottish identity in its movie version *King Richard and the Crusaders*.

The Union Jack itself began as Scottish comprising of the St Andrew's Cross with its blue ground on which the red upright St George's Cross was imposed. James ('Jacques') VI of Scotland inherited England in 1603 and went on to prescribe the Union Jack, with the Saltire providing the blue background and white diagonal on which St George's Cross was allowed its place. If James proved unable to unite the island's parliaments, he succeeded in uniting its name as Great Britain in 1604, its Bible to his authorised version in 1611, and its flag bearing his name in 1606 – without future generations remembering who was the Jack of the Union Jacques. St Patrick's Cross, the diagonal red cross, was included after the Parliamentary Union of Great Britain and Ireland from 1801 but referring only to Northern Ireland after 1922, although Northern Ireland Presbyterians mostly thought of St Patrick as an Irish Catholic icon.

St Patrick, as a national saint, had the advantage of being based on very real personal documents. His autobiographical *Confessio* and *Letter to Coroticus*, and his testament as a kidnapped and runaway slave should have received far more use by historians of slavery than it has. St George was an importation from the crusades, winning significance as an order of chivalry vulgarised as the Garter. St Patrick was almost certainly British (and whatever he was he wasn't Irish), being from a romanised people making Latin his native language in which he wrote. He must have also conversed in old Irish after the Irish kidnapped him and he later returned as a missionary. St David the only native patron saint of the four must have functioned in Latin and old Welsh. St Andrew spoke in Aramaic, Hebrew for worship, and Greek. St George if he was indeed a soldier martyred under the Emperor Diocletian may have had Greek as his native language but must have also spoken Latin. St Andrew was a significant force in uniting Scotland by the disparity of his cult across the several nations. St David certainly united south Wales, with 60 churches in his name from Pembroke to Hereford by 1200. Before the Reformation all western Christians would worship in Latin, in which intellectuals would dispute and delight. The proclamation of Scotland's nationalism, the Declaration of Arbroath in 1320, won its converts when translated into English but was formally born in Latin, being a Roman Catholic document addressed to the Pope: a foretaste of the internationalism of much of Scottish nationalism which would be reasserted in linguistic terms in the 1920s by Hugh MacDiarmid notably in his *A Drunk Man Looks at the Thistle*. The Tory MP and master story-teller John Buchan saluted MacDiarmid's first book.

God enters from the Left

John Buchan, 'Preface' to Hugh MacDiarmid, *Sangschaw* (1925):

Once upon a time the Scots vernacular was a national speech, and men like Henryson and Dunbar used it for the highest matters of poetry. But at the Reformation it was rusticated from court and college, and by the eighteenth [*recte* nineteenth] century it had become a tongue only for familiar conversation, and in literature it was confined strictly to the homelier humours and affections. It was still capable, as Burns showed, of heights and profundities, but its lateral range was narrow. As a consequence vernacular literature suffered from the fault of provincialism, a contentment too often with the second-rate in thought and style. In our own day we have seen the speech in its idiomatic form slowly dropping out of use, and Scots poetry becoming more and more of an antiquarian exercise. The inspiration may be from the heart, but the words are an effort of memory and scholarship.

My friend, the author of this book, has set himself a task which is at once reactionary and revolutionary. A preface is not the place for criticism, but I may be allowed to emphasise the boldness of his purpose. He would treat Scots as a living language and apply it to matters which have been foreign to it since the sixteenth century. Since there is no canon of the vernacular, he makes his own, as Burns did, and borrows words and idioms from the old masters. He confines himself to no one dialect, but selects where he pleases between Aberdeen and the Cheviots. This audacity may make some of the pieces difficult for the reader, and it may be that he does not always succeed, for a man with a new weapon rarely hits the mark at the first shot. But I welcome the honest hope and faith which inspire the experiment. It is a proof that a new spirit is to-day abroad in the North, which, as I have said, is both conservative and radical – a determination to keep Scotland in the main march of the world's interests, and at the same time to forgo no part of her ancient heritage.

John Buchan hit the mark in seeing MacDiarmid in the vanguard of a revolt against provincialism. Above all, his nationalism vituperated against the provincialism eclipsing the world by obsession with England. MacDiarmid was officially an atheist, but God was essential to the making of his poetry. Buchan saw the necessity that MacDiarmid be at once reactionary and revolutionary: as a poet remaking the Scots language his nationalism had to be micro and macro, from the smallest Scottish flower to the cosmos.

Hugh MacDiarmid, 'The Innumerable Christ' in *Sangshaw*:

> Wha kens on whatna Bethlehems
> Earth twinkles like a star the nicht,
> An' whatna shepherds lift their heids
>   In its unearthly licht?
>
> 'Yont a' the stars our een can see
> An' farther than their lichts can fly,
> I' mony an unco warl' the nicht
>   The fatefu' bairnies cry.

> I' mony an unco' warl' the nicht
> The lift gaes black as pitch at noon,
> An' sideways on their chests the heids
>   O' endless Christs roll doon.
>
> An' when the earth's as cauld's the mune
> An' a' its folk are lang syne deid,
> In countless stars the Babe maun cry
> And the Crucified maun bleed.

Jesus Christ: where extremes meet

Scottish nationalism means an atheist Christianising the universe. This was one of Hugh MacDiarmid's earliest poems, but – under his own name – Christopher Murray Grieve had written several precursors stemming directly from his experience and perceptions during and immediately after service in the Great War. We should seek him first among the Jewish Isaac Rosenbergs and Siegfried Sassoons, the English Wilfred Owens, the Welsh David Joneses, and may find deeper affinities still with Patrick MacGill, the Irish navvy, whose earliest poems and autobiographical *Children of the Dead End* recreated life among Scotland's construction workers and tramping artisans, followed by verses written among his fellow-soldiers on the European battlefront. MacGill saw suffering Christs within his immediate wartorn 'red horizon'. MacDiarmid found them potentially omnipresent throughout the universe. So he wrote in his epic psycho-analysis of Scotland *A Drunk Man Looks at the Thistle*:

> I'll ha'e nae hauf-way hoose, but aye be whaur
> Extremes meet – it's the only way I ken
> To dodge the curst conceit o' bein' richt
> That damns the vast majority o' men.

To be an atheist and to create the largest poetic vision of Christ of which humanity is capable, anticipated that declaration perfectly.

MacDiarmid did it in what Buchan rightly diagnosed as a revolutionary act: declaring Scottish independence of the hitherto all-conquering English language. For all of his careerist Toryism and UK nationalism Buchan might take refuge in Scots verse, or send his Richard Hannay in *The Thirty-Nine Steps* fleeing from police and German spies back to the Scotland he had left as a six-year-old. The Scots language in capable hands towered in the beauty of simplicity. When on Earth, Jesus Christ spoke with a divine clarity and charity amidst clerics' self-glorifying pomposities, and in contrast even simple devotional terms such as 'the Holy Innocents' might distance the reader or worshipper from the reality of the infants massacred by Herod, but 'the fatefu' bairnies' conquers heart before head. The simplicity of Scots unveils with maximum economy the inverse to St Luke's Gospel narrative (with its shepherds about to receive word of Jesus's nativity), integrated with St Matthew's star (which the three wise men followed), but making Earth become the star bringing pilgrims to the newly-born Jesus. MacDiarmid recognised the crucifixion as the counterpart: Jesus's life began with a star lighting the way to his birthplace, and the lights of all the stars including Earth's were extinguished at His death. MacDiarmid's capture of millennia across the universe, by use of a Scots vocabulary recruited across the centuries, was suddenly hurled into his audience's faces in its most famous form, Burns's 'Auld Lang Syne', but here directing a chilling confrontation facing his audience's expectations of reunion with the certainty of their oblivion. His high mockery inverted another reassuring familiarity, Jane Taylor's century-old nursery rhyme 'Twinkle, twinkle, little star' plundered with a probable schoolboy grin: it was Jane Taylor and her sister Ann whose *Hymns for Infant Minds* had saddled 19th century schoolchildren of Scotland, Ireland, and Wales with the duty of learning by heart

> I thank the goodness and the grace
> Which on my birth have smiled,
> And made me, in these Christian days,
> A happy English child.

The Taylors' God was firmly an English nationalist.

God multiplied by enlightenment's children

Science was supposedly undermining, discrediting, and demolishing Christianity: MacDiarmid, the atheist poet, asserted that science might fulfil it. He had given the poem the epigraph 'Other stars may have their Bethlehem, and their Calvary too' adapted from *Man and the Attainment of Immortality* by James Young Simpson, professor in Natural Science, New College, Edinburgh. Simpson asserted the mutual support of science and religion. With nationalism of a more obvious kind, MacDiarmid deliberately saluted a descendant of the Scottish Enlightenment who in person and professorship united religion and science under Scottish Presbyterian auspices. Whether atheist or not, Scottish nationalism at this time derived some of its creative impulse from intellectuals in revolt against the Church of Scotland sometimes deepening the rebellion by attraction to Roman Catholicism, the journalist Moray McLaren (author of Penguin's mass-circulation *The Scots*), the novelists Fionn MacColla, Compton Mackenzie, George Scott-Moncreiff among them, reacting against English inter-war cultural isolationism. The roots of SNP hostility to Brexit are visible there. MacDiarmid in *Sangschaw* had common ground with them. The poem is also intensely evangelical in its implications: as a nationalist MacDiarmid would always evangelise, but 'The Innumerable Christ' also gives Christian evangelism a universal implication far beyond the range of any other pastor. Not only did Jesus Christ die to save humankind from the punishment we deserve, have deserved, and will deserve, to the end of Earthly time, but the same divine atonement for sins like ours may be necessitated throughout the universe. The poem is a parable telling us that however much it thinks it is perfecting itself, human nature on this or any other planet will continue in its sins and need the death of Jesus Christ to save it.

CS Lewis tried using science fiction for a nationalist message, to cleanse the UK of its fanatical zeal to subjugate other peoples, however scientific its self-justification. Like Swift putting Gulliver in Brobdingnag or among the Houyhnhnms, he was creating greater and more exemplary peoples in Christian parable. Lewis's anti-imperialist UK nationalism would be brought alongside his youthful Belfast Protestant Unionist nationalism in *The Last Battle* where his imaginary Narnia is invaded by a hostile neighbouring people pretending friendship egged on by an ancient ape evidently inspired by the nonagenarian Pope (sometimes Ulster-pronounced 'Pape') Leo XIII: a demon pseudo-Christian figure whom Protestant infants believed master-minded attempting to break-up the UK by Irish Home Rule. When Lewis was writing the book, IRA raids on Northern Ireland were starting up again while cold war continued between its six counties and the 26 in the Republic. By contrast, MacDiarmid's indictment of our perpetual crucifixion of Christ was more courageous. It preaches the need for a redemptive nationalism as well as the linguistic nationalism clothing it. Is the agent of those soul-destroying sins the potential or actual speaker of Scots? Or is it all of humanity especially when the poet's language is Scots and his subject universal? Or is there any difference between Scotland and humanity? What it doesn't have is a partial redemption limited to predestined favourites. Atheist as he liked to call himself, MacDiarmid was catholic and, in that sense, also Catholic. In his later years he declared that in the impossible event of him embracing Christianity, it would be the Roman Catholic variety. English Catholic nationalism also inspired his Scottish nationalism, such as GK Chesterton's 'The Rolling English Road' in *The Flying Inn* telling of the rolling English drunkard:

> His sins they were forgiven him; or why do flowers run
> Behind him; and the hedges all strengthening in the sun?
> The wild thing went from left to right and knew not
> which was which,
> But the wild rose was above him when they found him in
> the ditch.
> God pardon us, nor harden us; we did not see so clear
> The night we went to Bannockburn by way of Brighton Pier.

This last line constituted a challenge from an Englishman who had made a Scotsman's challenge to a duel the basis of his novel *The Ball and the Cross*, and it was logically answered by the title declaring that in Scotland *A Drunk Man Looks at the Thistle* thus launching MacDiarmid's epic. If that is a clear succession of one nationalism inspiring another, Chesterton forgot a third nationalism – the Welsh. His song began:

> Before the Roman came to Rye or out to Severn strode,
> The rolling English drunkard made the rolling English road.

A spendidly paradoxical, anti-bourgeois proclamation, save that the rolling English drunkard never saw a rolling 'English' road until half a millennium had passed after the first Roman landing. The ancient Briton made what roads existed before the Romans. Welsh nationalism may shelter in pride behind the great curtain of the Welsh language, but another variety of nationalism with which it shares some common ground is the knowledge that this isle was its, or at least a southern portion of it stretching up to Strathclyde, and that Welsh nationalism could best realise itself by reconquering its old Caer Lydd renamed Londinium by the Romans. Chesterton may have deliberately forgotten that the rolling English drunkard actually made his own roads amidst his genocide of the ancient Britons.

The innumerable Christ's innumerable fellow-Jews

In the 1990s the University of Edinburgh students' History Society hosted a lecture by David Levi. For nearly half a century, the Glaswegian served his city's synagogues after having survived the Nazi concentration camps of Auschwitz, Dachau, and Belsen. He described the systematic murder of his fellow-Jews in tones of sorrow rather than anger, and his very economy strengthened his lament for the murdered millions. He himself was so wasted by starvation that when the Americans arrived in Belsen he was no longer able to stand up. When the student Chair, Mohammed Hameed, sought questions for the speaker, an innocent girl from the home counties asked 'But where was God while all this was happening to you?' 'God?' said Mr Levi. 'God was lying on the ground beside me in Belsen.'

The 20th century produced innumerable Christs in the shape of His murdered fellow-Jews, victims of Christians or former-Christians. For two millennia Christians first quarrelled with their doctrinal cousins, then persecuted them to countless deaths. For each Jew killed, Christ suffered and died again, and His self-styled followers tortured, lynched and burned Him while insisting in their proclamations and prayers that they were torturing, lynching and burning in His name. Jesus died as so many of his fellow-Jews had died in the most squalid and painful of deaths the imperial Romans could devise for the inconveniently monotheistic Jews, who refused the compromise of trading their God for a pantheon where He could be included as a new administrative concession supported by business consultants. The murdered and martyred Jews died for being Jews, honouring their own religious and ethnic identity in one form or another. They gave excellent examples to their persecutors, showing how defenders of a religion or a nationalism must die without betraying their faith, whatever form it might take. Their Christian persecutors were inflamed even more if the Jews they were injuring pointed out the Jewish identity of their enemies' Christ, as the Citizen in Joyce's *Ulysses* goes berserk when Leopold Bloom declares it so. The logic – insofar as so subhuman a thing as anti-Semitism can – is that Jews who did not accept Jesus as God, and Barabbas's followers who called for Pilate to crucify Him, had His blood on themselves and on their children. Hence Jews were accursed and appropriate objects of Christian persecution for all time, they were Christ-killers.

To all Christian anti-Semites Jesus has spoken the words He spoke to Saul (later St Paul): 'Saul, Saul, why persecutest thou Me?' The prayers of the Good Friday Mass before the advent of Pope St John XXIII in 1958 included pleas for God's mercy on all humanity listed in various categories, but the prayer for the Jews alone virtually reproved God for being ready to forgive the people in question: 'O God who dost not refuse Thy mercy even to the perfidious Jews ...'. The prayer was normally uttered in Latin amidst the other Latin prayers, but its translation confronted Good Friday worshippers in their Missals alongside the Latin in modern times, and seems to have won little anger until John XXIII began its sanitation by demanding the removal of the word 'perfidious' at once, and when the priest celebrating Good Friday in front of him retained it, stopped the Mass and ordered that the prayer be said without that supreme foulness. Latin was a second language to all Roman priests before the Second Vatican Council which John XXIII would convene, and some pogroms had started with clerical inflammation from sermons preached during Mass (as in Limerick in 1907). Sometimes the movers and shapers of nationalism made anti-Semitism a prominent part of their agenda, as though a doctor might include leprosy amongst his habitual cures.

King Fernando of Aragon and Queen Isabella of Castile united Spain by their marriage in 1469, established the heresy-hunting inquisition in their dominions, expelled Jews (other than Jewish converts to Christianity) from 1492, and expelled Muslims from 1496. Isabella added most of America to her dominions, the whole constituting nationalism's largest acquisition. Edward I of England, whose nationalism bloodily forced the Welsh and (until his death in 1307) the Scots under English rule, expelled the Jews in 1290. Previously the Jews had been exploited and persecuted notably in the massacre of Jews in York in 1190; its human implications were grimly depicted by Scotland's leading literary romantic nationalist Sir Walter Scott in his *Ivanhoe* whose wise and brave hero, Rebecca, is Jewish. The English nationalist historian Thomas Babington Macaulay and the Irish Catholic nationalist Daniel O'Connell spoke passionately in the House of Commons for repeal of restrictions injuring the Jews, after both had campaigned for similar emancipation of the Roman Catholics; but Parliament did not unfetter the Jews until 1858. Macaulay rightly declared that true Christianity lay in defending the Jews.

Thomas Babington Macaulay, 'Civil Disabilities of the Jews', (*Edinburgh Review*, January 1831):

> We have... learned the doctrines of Him who com-
> manded us to love our neighbour as ourselves, and
> who, when He was called upon to explain what
> He meant by a neighbour, selected as an example
> a heretic and an alien. Last year, we remember, it
> was represented by a pious writer in the *John Bull*
> newspaper and by some other equally fervid Chris-
> tians, as a monstrous indecency, that the measure for
> the relief of the Jews should be brought forward in
> Passion Week. One of these humourists ironically
> recommended that it should be read a second time
> on Good Friday. We should have had no objection;
> nor do we believe that the day could be commemo-
> rated in a more worthy manner. We know of no day
> fitter for terminating long hostilities, and repairing
> cruel wrongs, than the day on which the religion of
> mercy was founded. We know of no day fitter for
> blotting out from the statute-book the last traces of
> intolerance than the day on which the spirit of intol-
> erance produced the foulest of all judicial murders;
> the day on which the list of the victims of intoler-
> ance, that noble list in which Socrates and More
> are enrolled, was glorified by a yet more awful and
> sacred name.

The prince of darkness is a gentleman (Shakespeare, King Lear*)*

Some anti-Semites cited the New Testament as justification: there can in reality be no justification for anti-Semitism. Biblical verses tripping off the bigot's tongue may have very different implications. Luke 13:30 has been interpreted as meaning that Jews, long the chosen people, would be repudiated by God for not publicly acknowledging Christ as Messiah or at least as a true prophet:

> And, behold, there are last which shall be first, and there
> are first which shall be last.

This conclusion may mean that Jews who kept their faith, however interpreted, against endless persecution might be preferred for entrance into Heaven to their Christian persecutors. That passage opens with Jesus saying in reply to an enquiry as to whether few would be saved:

> Strive to enter in at the strait gate: for many, I say unto
> you, will seek to enter in, and shall not be able.

The strait gate, or the hard road, was taken by many Jews in fidelity to their religious or social identities. Jesus's prophecy that 'the master of the house' might say tell aspirants that he knows them not, despite their claim of having eaten and drunk in his presence, could apply all too well to Christians trading on previous but infertile acquaintance with Him. Matthew 21:28–32 recorded Jesus's parable of a man's request to his two sons to work in his vineyard, the first refusing but then working, the second accepting but not working: He applied this to harlots and publicans who believed John the Baptist while nominally virtuous persons did not. This parable would also apply to Jews rejecting Jesus who then died for being Jews, while complacent Christians showed no such fidelity in practice or serious resistance to the anti-Semitism of Hitler.

The New Testament was translated into Scots by William Laughton Lorimer, completed after his death by his son Robin Lorimer. Its Gospel of St Luke was recited in public performance during the Edinburgh Festival by the actor-director Sandy Neilson, with the simplicity of a Scots-speaking Christ taking on a new dimension. It made good the strange absence of a Bible in the Lowland and urban Scots people's language up to that time, although Scots-Gaelic translation had been available since the late 18th century, preceded in Irish-Gaelic and Manx from the 17th, and Welsh from the 16th. Non-Gaelic Scottish Presbyterianism was thus tied to the somewhat alien English language for its Biblical groundwork, and the archipelago in general received the beautiful prose of the King James Bible, an expression of British nationalism imposed although thankfully adopted. This placed even greater emphases on the sermons and *ex tempore* prayers of the

Presbyterian clergy, strengthening stress on Scots personal relations to God, and church superiority to the state, all the more because of Presbyterian hostility to ritual and hierarchy.

The Lorimer Bible was triumphantly nationalist in language of the Scots people, not that of the UK rulers. Lorimer Senior had left a draft translation of the temptation of Jesus in the wilderness by Satan, in which the Devil's was the only voice speaking in English. This was a neat nationalist joke and highly appropriate, since English had always known itself to be more sophisticated than Scots, and cities supply paramount nests for Satan throughout the Bible: the dialogue became honest peasant against the urban conman. The Anglophone Devil was later discarded, presumably in a spirit of Christian clemency. The English-born dramatist Bill Dunlop produced an astonishing translation of Aeschylus's *Oresteia* into Scots *Klytemnestra's Bairns* its first play *Agamemnon* staged in Riddle's Court in and then the entirety on Calton Hill the following year, both in the Edinburgh Festival Fringe. The effect was to make Agamemnon, his family, court and locals seem like primitive Scots whose king has just destroyed a remote Anglophone city Troy, bringing a captive Princess Cassandra as bed-companion on his return; her impeccable English makes the Scoto-Greeks think of her as mad, but the theatre audience would find her accent one of an upper-class English lady bewildered by her surroundings and shrewd in their assessment but relatively sane. The Lorimer Bible and the Scots *Oresteia* show the transformative effects of linguistic nationalism operating among international bi-millenarian classics.

Religion, nationalism and its linguistic determination

In Welsh nationalism, Saunders Lewis, President of Plaid Cymru 1926–39, was a convert to Roman Catholicism in 1932. In the newly-established Irish Free State and its successors Eire and the Republic of Ireland, all party leaders made their Roman Catholic devotion almost painfully and permanently visible. In Northern Ireland, nationalism of Catholics was wholly identified with similar devotion, all the more powerful because adherence to the faith kept its practitioners second-class citizens, frequently boycotting the Unionist government and legislature in the manner of the Papacy boycotting the government of the united Italy which had seized the Papal states in 1860 and Rome in 1870. Unlike the Pope from 1929, Northern Irish Catholic bishops, clergy, and laity kept up their anger, increasing the sharpness of their Protestant oppressors frequently enlivened by reverend demagogues. Contrary to what both parties imagined, the Bible was much used by both Catholics and Protestants, and it may have transmitted a sense of its users acquiring a special form of self-approved salvation even when atheist. Certainly MacDiarmid was but one of many supposedly atheist Scots to have become culturally as well as spiritually enriched by study of the Bible. In the USA too the atheist HL Mencken revered its prose though not that of its modern translators or commentators. He once described as one of his happiest memories the night he spent marooned in a Buffalo hotel alone with a Bible. His nationalism resembled MacDiarmid's in its anger against the dishonesty and cowardice of his fellow-countrymen with force kindled by reading Old Testament prophets, particularly Jeremiah. Mencken was also a literary nationalist, defining a separate American language in several editions and volumes of *The American Language* from 1919, an ominous date officially ending a war in which Mencken had seen bland Anglo-American propaganda habitually strangling truth while the USA's moral judgment was taken prisoner by its increasing ignorance in an increasingly alien English language. Mencken's fellow-American, Ernest Hemingway, remembered in *A Farewell to Arms* the war's devaluation of language:

> There were many words that you could not stand to hear and finally only the names of places had dignity. ... Abstract words such as glory, honour, courage, or hallow were obscene beside the concrete names of villages, the numbers of roads, the names of rivers, the numbers of regiments and the dates.

It is a divine heart-cry on the use of language to evade God and thus do Satan's work.

It complemented MacDiarmid's post-war search for a linguistic nationalism to liberate his country.

Hugh MacDiarmid, 'Talking with Five Thousand People in Edinburgh' (*Poetry No. 2* (1945)) :

> All who should help to open the way to true expression
> – The teachers, the ministers, the writers – are living like maggots
> On dead words in an advanced state of decomposition.
>   Big words that died over twenty years ago
> – For most of the important words were killed in the First World War –
> And Edinburgh has not given birth to any new words yet
> In which it can say anything worth saying, make anything but animal noises.

A religious inheritance

MacDiarmid, simply by being himself, led other Scots to build themselves in Scots poetry and drama like Sydney Goodsir Smith, or in a newly-reborn Gaelic whose landscape Sorley MacLean recreated in his language, or in the laughing magisterial ironies of Norman MacCaig, or in the Catholic spirit of George Mackay Brown reawakening Viking Orkney. Not all of them voted SNP: MacLean maintained his fidelity to Labour, and MacDiarmid sometimes voted for Labour's Judith Hart wickedly justifying it on the ground of her pulchritude. Flyting, a centuries-old form of Scottish poetic expression sparked fires as poets and scholars reacted against one another's work and play. Intense nationalist expression emerged from infuriated anti-nationalists in pubs, lecture-rooms, and confluences of both. The anti-nationalists may not have been converted by nationalists: most of them seem to have converted themselves. In different forms of folklore research and expression scholars, whether ex-Communists such as Norman Buchan and Hamish Henderson or academics in pursuit of wisdom for its own sake such as Alan Bruford, brought voices of the Scottish people asserting their own forms of identity: nationalist perhaps but often unclassifiable, ancient sometimes proving very modern. As for God, He was most evident when least visible, but His place in Scottish eloquence underlay so much artistic and political creativity.

The delivery of a long sermon requires a range of forensic and dramatic qualities to hold the audience, who may discuss it with the preacher afterwards. As Pope St John Paul II affirmed on his visit to Scotland, Scottish Protestantism deserved exceptional honour for its devotion to the Bible down the centuries. God therefore remained front and centre stage in Scottish identity back to St Columba's 6th century foundation of the Iona community, King Macbeth's 11th century voyage to Italy to honour Pope St Leo IX in 1050, and Hungarian-born English Queen of Scotland St Margaret's Christian leadership that stabilised the dynasty re-established by her husband Malcolm III from whom all subsequent Scottish monarchs (including all English after 1603) descended. John Knox became popularly synonymous with Scottish religion and nationalism against the French-educated Mary Queen of Scots. Knox's preaching dominated its popular reputation for many centuries, so much so that when the Maly Theatre of Leningrad brought over its opera on Mary Queen of Scots for the quatercentenary of her execution, its conscientious facsimile of the Canongate enabled staging an Aria from Knox singing on his balcony to symbolise his pivotal role in Mary's doom. After which, the assembled supposedly Protestant chorus crossed themselves Russian Orthodox fashion, Lenin or no Lenin.

The Bible remained the basis of Scottish religion. Once the Reformation gave it wider circulation it was pressed into the service of Scotland's new nationalism, whether Knox's, James VI's or those of other interested parties, pushing Scotland in different directions. Knox and his fellow-Protestants preached a nationalism liberating

Scotland from France driven by religion. When the Stuart kings inherited England, new forms of Protestant nationalism developed in rebellion against Stuart Episcopalianism which in James's elder two grandsons Charles II and James VII/II became Roman Catholicism and once more French-dependent. After the ousting of James VII/II in 1688–89, Jacobite nationalism developed in Scotland and Ireland in its turn, almost entirely Catholic in Ireland, much more mixed in Scotland between Roman Catholics, Protestant Episcopalians and some dissident Presbyterians.

Post-Mosaic nationalism

Nationalism in the New Testament is important but various. Roman nationalism itself took the life of Jesus when Jesus's enemies black-mailed Pontius Pilate by saying that Jesus's supposed claim to be King of the Jews defied the Emperor Tiberius Caesar:

> If thou let this man go, thou art not Caesar's friend: who-
> soever maketh himself a king speaketh against Caesar.

Pilate's action in having Jesus's Cross sport the legend 'Jesus of Nazareth King of the Jews' in Latin, Greek, and Hebrew acknowledged his own agreement with the charge of high treason, while enabling him to retain his dignity by resisting objections to the wording. This represents a template compromise in confrontations of warring nationalisms whereby one nationalism pretends to be a more virtuous form of its rival, however alien. St Paul used what scope Athenian polytheist nationalism allowed, by nestling Christianity within the cult of the unknown god. This might seem shallow compared to the nationalism of the Old Testament which courageously, if not always consistently, sustained the identity of the Jews through the centuries and proved a paradigm to the Christians. Originally this must have been oral testimony taught and learned down the generations, much of it in song institutionalised and celebrated with dancing. The song created by Moses and the great Jewish migration from Egypt – in Exodus 15:1–19 – rejoicing in the drowning of their pursuers in the Red Sea has been claimed as the oldest part of the

Bible. That nationalism is not simply a matter of Jews falling short of due fidelity to God and their own traditions of worship, diet, and conduct. It involves a protagonist trying to rally the Israelites, sometimes showing himself unworthy of God, sometimes answerable by ourselves, his audience, when he seeks to conceal his self-gratifying crimes. In their different ways David in his Psalms – 'O God, thou knowest my foolishness: and my sins are not hid from thee' – and Jeremiah in his lamentations – 'I am become vile' – have such epiphanies that give us ammunition for reply. This humanity is a great relief to a nationalist readership, and makes for more objective history (even if over-zealous preachers seek to explain away the honesty of the hero).

Robin Hood, perhaps the most obvious folk-hero, had the excellent habit of recruiting anyone who outdid him in combat, such as Little John or Friar Tuck. The medieval and early modern tradition of a great minister, often a cleric such as Richelieu, guiding and controlling heads of state did not require elaborate linkage with Old Testament prophets whose stories spoke for themselves in peoples' minds, Isaiah wise but friendly towards well-meaning kings and Elijah much more hostile to rulers hence sometimes endangered yet recognised as unwanted but unavoidable. The Old Testament as guardian of religious orthodoxy and social identity is one of the greatest weapons of nationalism history knows, and the tradition that it was begun by captives – specifically by their leader and emancipator Moses – gave it logical strength when its narratives, recited publicly or secretly, told captive or exiled Jews who they were and how they must continue to revere their identity and worship its deity, writing down the sacred narratives recited down the generations.

Biblical nationalism in practice

What kind of nationalism does the Bible portray or teach us? However authentic the Biblical texts, their original authors built their narratives for their own purposes. As an Israeli taxi-driver once remarked to me, we only hear the story of David from David's point of view and never hear it from Saul's. His Psalms show us his histories in composition, justify and indict him, and show his own readiness for all of his extraordinary success to complain of the supposed hostility of God. Scholars should treat the Bible as possibly authentic since its influence throughout history has affected people who believed in that authenticity. That differs from taking the text as statement of fact.

As with any other historical document we have to take what is being said as the statement of the author(s), not necessarily as the statement of God. The Gospel and First Epistle of St John, given the mutual love of himself and Jesus, may be the nearest we get to narratives from God. The book of Joshua ascribes genocidal commands to God when what we are reading are Joshua's commentaries on the war he led, as complacent, vigorous and horrendous as Julius Caesar's description of his conquest of Gaul. Joshua would have been as anxious to prove his actions by God's demands as Caesar would have been to prove himself the ideal Roman commander, and the Book of Joshua as we have it assumes that its events happened in the lifetime of its first hearers. The Gospels might seem in a similar category, since they record the doings of Jesus Christ who was and is God. Where He is directly quoted we must assume what is written is by His will, particularly in John's reports of his lengthy statements; but these quotations from Jesus are those from a God on earth whom many initial readers or hearers of the Gospels might have seen and heard, while God quoted in or by Joshua rests on Joshua's word, and military memoirs make the most of exalted patrons, whether to claim praise or to shift blame. Joshua's late master Moses had delivered and repeated his most important order from God – the Ten Commandments – on stone tablets, but Joshua at his last public appearance:

> took a great stone, and set it up there under an oak, that was by the sanctuary of the LORD. And Joshua said unto all the people. Behold, this stone shall be a witness unto us; for it hath heard all the words of the LORD which he spake unto us: it shall be therefore a witness unto you, lest

ye deny your God. So Joshua let the people depart, every
man unto his inheritance.

Joshua, 24:26–28.

The remaining five verses of the book cover Joshua's death, a kind
of sign-off convention acknowledging a posthumous editor just as
John's Gospel ends by saying in anonymous editorial verses 'we
know that his testimony is true', perhaps meaning that John was
dead or had disappeared when the final words were written.

The Book of Joshua was described to me by Rabbi David Rosen
(former Chief Rabbi of Ireland) as 'the most disturbing book in the
Old Testament'. To understand nationalism, it is essential to master the Bible whence so much inspirational nationalism has been
made: much of it good, much of it bad. The Reformation's reproach
against medieval clerics that they had kept the Bible from the people
had some truth – those with a little learning are anxious to declare
their monopoly – but the Bible, when let loose among the people of
England, was taken to justify the judicial murder of Charles I, the
Cromwellian massacres of Irish Catholics both lay and clerical, and
the confiscation of their lands leading Long Parliament profiteers and
gallant Cromwellian veterans unto their inheritance. Joshua, leading
a migrant nation felt their lack of stability, whatever their strength.
Richmal Crompton, the 20th century's foremost satirical English
writer of short stories for children told in 'Three Cheers for Sweetikins' of a corpulent Pom – Sweetikins – entrusted by his corpulent
owner to her nephew Ginger to take on a walk. Since the Pom won't
walk, Ginger and his friends William, Henry and Douglas leave it at
the bottom of a quarry until their games are over:

> Douglas felt some qualms of conscience, but he soon
> quieted them.
> 'After all', he said. 'it's what Joseph's brethren did to him,
> an' a thing can't be wrong if it's in the Bible.'

Joshua's nationalism emerged in victories over other nations and
his book seems to have been popular with 20th century Northern Ireland Protestant Sunday schools. Its enthusiasm for the

demolition of natives of the Promised Land would have married well with the history of Ulster Protestant plantations filled by hard-line Scots and frontier Calvinists starting in 1607. Nobody in the Old Testament talked of Home Rule for Canaanites or Philistines. James VI/I promised Ulster land to Protestant settlers since his double kingship eliminated the desirability of a deep thrawn border between England and Scotland. After Joshua some of the natives surviving his conquests rebelled with resultant slaughter. The Ulster Plantation suffered the equivalent in 1641 when Catholics driven from their former lands revolted, and Cromwellian reprisals appeared to have been inspired by Joshua's methods applied subsequently by Deborah, Gideon, Samson, King Saul and King David. 20th century Sunday schools bred boys who would join Northern Ireland's official paramilitaries, notably the 'B-Specials' recruited (sometimes by Protestant pastors) in support of the Royal Ulster Constabulary from the 1920s. Unlike the RUC, the B-Specials and their equivalents did not recruit Roman Catholics, although the RUC seldom promoted them.

Esther leaping the centuries

The nature of Judaic nationalism on Old Testament evidence turns drastically on its relationship to God, its relationship with monarchism, its reformation in exile complicated by its successes in the conquering state. The Book of Esther recorded Jewish history in Babylonian and Persian captivity whose message sustained Jews over the next millennia and profoundly stirred African Americans who within the1950s and 1960s would put *Esther* to first-class use as a manual of instruction for the civil rights struggle lying ahead. Aaron Henry, head of the Mississippi branch of the National Association for the Advancement of Colored Peoples (NAACP), lived in endless mortal danger in the state of Mississippi where he traded as a pharmacist in Clarksdale in the 1960s. His branch secretary Medgar Evers was killed on 12 June 1963, after which Henry campaigned for civil rights across the USA, and organised the 1964 Freedom Summer in Mississippi: a landmark in the civil rights struggle. Unlike his ideological leader Martin Luther King Jr and many of the African American civil rights leaders in the segregated South, Henry was not a clergyman, but his oratorical use of the Bible was comparably forceful.

He would speak about the Book of Esther for an hour, showing that it turned on a Jewish woman in personal good fortune as a Queen of Ahasuerus the Great King of Persia, and Persian Queenship was no sinecure. She was suddenly faced with the need to imperil her life to save her fellow-Jews threatened with annihilation. Henry would show with minute skill in dissecting the scriptural nuances that well-to-do African Americans were in Esther's situation, and that the future of their people depended on identifying with their poorer brothers and sisters trapped in the racist South. His cool, clear speeches were a perfect demonstration of Biblical mobilisation on civil rights, showing how the example of the ancient Jews and their conviction of God's will that they should be preserved was the moral armour which might shield them from their violent enemies, as it had sustained the African Americans seeking liberation from slavery a century earlier. Freedom Summer in Mississippi in 1964 included the murders of three civil rights activists, two New York Jews and one Mississippi African American. Jews were the most frequent whites to participate in the struggle for African American civil rights, all the stronger because of the fate of their cousins in Nazi Europe and their own determination to eradicate racism from the USA. The direction of the movement was always in African American hands: apart from anything else, they knew what segregation really meant, as a possible matter of life and death, and they knew far more about non-violence than we whites did.

King's mass movement was the great heart and soul of the whole struggle. African American figures who dissented from Martin Luther King and preached violence naturally won media attention. Violence sells newspapers and ups television-watching statistics, and white Americans were uneasy about non-violent proofs of African American moral superiority, so the media always make the most of any violence. Claims by various figures from Elijah Mohammed to Malcolm X that they were leading a black nation distracted from the reality. Of course there was an African American nation, however reluctant some of its more prosperous citizens were to acknowledge it. It was King and non-violence who proved its existence, orchestrated its common spirit, and won it power. His followers' reliance on the Bible was a perfect illustration of the way in which concepts of nationalism in various forms travelled through history. The civil rights movement kept before its eyes the fates of the Jews as a subject people whether in Egypt until liberated by Moses, in Babylon defending their religious identity, or in Persia gaining royal favour and the hope of return to the Promised Land. Throughout African American captivity and subjugation in the USA, that knowledge of the Bible travelled orally among the oppressed, in sermons, in conversation, and in teaching. Southern slaveholders had sought to use the Bible to assert divine justification of slavery, but their apparently docile slaves made it the instrument of their mental and, occasional, physical liberation.

The limits of Jonah's bravery

Inevitably, some humans misread the Bible or mistook its oral transmission, though African Americans had wiser perspective, being less impeded by wealth. The Book of Jonah is a good example. Supposedly set in about 800BCE, the story became sensational by the episode of Jonah being swallowed by a big fish (popularly rendered a whale). The story has often been retold as the tale of a coward fearful of following God's demand that he preach to the people of Nineveh, the Assyrian capital, famous for the brutality of its armies. Orson Welles's triumphant achievement as the preacher Father Mapple gave that version immortality in John Huston's movie *Moby Dick* so that the myth of the coward seems more real than the reality. We may also remember the striding ranks of fundamentalist Southern ladies in *Inherit the Wind* singing 'Give me that old time religion' usually including 'It was good enough for Jonah! It was good enough for Jonah! It was good enough for Jonah! And it's good enough for me!'. The Book of Jonah actually tells us Jonah decided the old time religion was *not* good enough for him. He was a brave man. He told the crew of the ship to throw him overboard because he was the cause of the storm about to wreck them. It took his own consumption by the great fish to make him return to God, since he evidently wasn't going to be given his own death as a means of proving his point. The central point was that if he prophesied death to the people of Nineveh and they repented, God would let them off and destroy Jonah's reputation as a prophet preaching truth. But Nineveh as Assyria's citadel was synonymous with evil empire whose inhabitants had oppressed, raided and otherwise persecuted Israel and Judah. Readers and listeners were to understand that Jonah would be delighted to avenge the wrongs of the Holy Land on Nineveh.

Jonah's nationalism does not speak of possible reward if he had prophesied its doom to Nineveh, and had survived – he was fully prepared to be killed for his unwelcome prophecy. He would thus have been the classic case of a nationalist hero sacrificing his life in the cause of his country and his God, but he retained the fear that God would deny him both Nineveh's destruction and his own martyrdom (or triumphant return home). His fear indeed proved well-justified, the Book of Jonah concluding with Jonah's renewed anger and God gaining the last verse with a direct appeal to Jonah to save himself by a sense of humour:

> And should not I spare Nineveh, that great city, wherein
> are more than sixscore thousand persons that cannot dis-
> cern between their right hand and their left hand; and
> also much cattle?

It was exactly what Jonah had feared, and it firmly declared God in favour of compassion in divine and human relations, and demanding the same of His missionaries. The moral is that your nationalism, if worthwhile, could mean your self-sacrifice in status for the betterment of other nations as well as for your own, including potential enemies; your nationalism should bring life, not death. Martin Luther King exemplified this when, with despite all the white support so painfully garnered over the previous ten years he denounced the war in Vietnam, although it was now being waged by Lyndon Johnson, the President who had done more to integrate Americans across colour lines than any of his predecessors.

Were you there when they crucified my Lord?

Religion has animated huge populations: sometimes from conviction, sometimes from social pressure, sometimes from state ukase, sometimes from sheer greed. Apart from religious observance firmly setting the mind of the worshipper spinning back through centuries and millennia, the thinkers, preachers, martyrs of its history, the sacred documents and holy books draw minds more firmly, reverently, and imaginatively into the past with far more concentration than an ordinary study of history. Forms of worship intensify the process. The Catholic Mass, whether celebrated according to the Roman, Eastern Orthodox or High Anglican forms, keeps the mind directly on Jesus Christ's crucifixion. Its worshippers believe that the bread and wine consecrated, elevated and consumed is Christ himself infinitely reproduced across space and time, so that believers are spiritually present at the Last Supper when Jesus blessed bread and wine and identified Himself with them, and the Crucifixion when he offered Himself as sacrifice and died, as well as worshipping in their own time. Here the past is not only invoked with piety, but Jesus's acts and words are intended to dominate the mind and soul of the participant.

If nationalism becomes identified with Catholicism, its impact can be tremendous. Its time situated it amongst other nationalisms – Imperial Rome, Herodian Jerusalem, Barabbas and his friends – with the complex variations from the differing rulers enjoying those leaderships. The time-wrinkling is of outstanding importance. Whether in the sacrifice of the Mass itself and in any other form of Christian worship, or in the clarity and vigour of Jesus in speech or action, the worshipper leaps the millennia, and these far-off events become of more importance than anything else. This gives us a clue to how nationalism, both religious and secular, can conquer intervening aeons as the Gaelic hero Cuchulain reached different kinds of immediacy on the nationalism of Yeats and of Pearse.

Suffering may conquer time, as the suffering of Jesus reached Oscar Wilde at the edge of self-destruction in jail, and won his self-identification as expressed in his *De Profundis* letter written in jail and in the

Ballad of Reading Gaol written after release in 1897. As the child of scholarly and poetic witnesses of the Irish Great Famine the dialogue of Death and Avarice in his 'The Young King' (*A House of Pomegranates*) had already indicted religion pampering itself from the profits of starvation labour. Nationalism finds its own wings when its parent nation loses one-third of its people in a single decade.

Whose nationalism owned the Pope?

Nationalism provided justification for much monarchical self-interest but endangered the security of the state and the integrity of the ruler who concluded what Louis XIV of France is alleged to have defined in 1655 as *'L'etat, c'est moi!'* In such circumstances God was likely to be conscripted as the invisible partner. It tempted kings to fasten their hold on their subjects by portraying themselves, and their regimes, as divinely supported or protected. It was a dangerous game to play.

Louis XIV took his identification with his territorial possessions so ruthlessly that he sought control of appointments of ecclesiastical as well as secular magnates. Hence Popes Innocent XI and Alexander VIII allied with Louis's most dangerous opponent, his (Protestant) cousin William of Orange Stadtholder of the Netherlands and ultimately King of England, Ireland and Scotland: the Pope was thus on William's side in the Battle of the Boyne in 1690 to the mortification of educated Orangemen for the next three centuries. It was a classic case of nationalisms in conflict, Louis's yearning to possess his northern neighbours the Netherlands, William's determination that he never would, Innocent's refusal to allow any nationalism make the Pope its stooge. He was upholding the traditions of Innocent III (who desperately needed the support of France in his struggles against England's King John and his cousin the Holy Roman Emperor Otto IV but refused to allow France's King Philip Augustus set aside his wife and enthrone his mistress), and of St Pius V (who needed the full support of Europe's foremost monarch of his time Philip II of Spain but nevertheless over-rode Philip's protests and wishes in condemning Spain's beloved bull-fighting). Other popes made miserable capitulations to the nationalism of Catholic powers such as France,

Spain and Portugal who had all suppressed the Jesuits in their dominions and bullied the wretched Pope Clement XIV into abolition of the order in 1773. It was later restored in 1814 by Pope Pius VII who had shown his independence in distancing the Papacy from the stifling imperial – and nationalist – embraces from Napoleon and from his father-in-law Franz I of Austria.

God doesn't want to save the king

This perpetually repeated pattern of the hero-king anxious to hold his subjects' allegiance by winning – and if he could, controlling – clerical sponsorship for his variety of nationalism is very old. It actually begins Homer's *Iliad* with Agamemnon's continuing rape of Chriseis, for which the god Apollo massacres the Greeks in considerable number. The Bible goes to the heart of royal relationship to God by God's contemptuous proto-Marxian exposition of the worthlessness of kings, and the artificial classes of toadies and profiteers they create. God asserts nationalism should retain its own integrity, and pictures the Israelites declining into an adulterated nationalism betraying itself by subjection to fashion rather than to God.

Future human history would show many comparable cases. The friendship between the high priest Samuel and God is among the most beautiful in sacred literature. At first, Samuel has so much difficulty realising it is God's voice that he is hearing. In Samuel's old age the clamour for a king makes him feel that he has failed, but God tells him his people have not rejected him, but have rejected God, and hurtful to God as that is, His first action is to comfort Samuel and in fine Jewish tradition to say that no blame attaches to him. God with possible elaborations from Samuel is thus the first known preacher of republican nationalism. This was recognised by Thomas Paine in his *Common Sense* when preaching the same doctrine for the British colonists in North America. It's interesting to reflect that the two other great sources of European culture, Athens and Rome, made the abolition of their kingships the bases of their identity: symbolically speaking, they followed God on the question where His chosen people the Israelites did not.

Holy Bible: 1 Samuel 8:1–22.

And it came to pass, when Samuel was old, that he made his
   sons judges over Israel.

Now the name of his firstborn was Joel and the name of his
   second, Abiah: they were judges in Beer-sheba.

And his sons walked not in his ways, but turned aside after
   lucre, and took bribes, and perverted judgment.

Then all the elders of Israel gathered themselves together, and
   came to Samuel unto Ramah.

And said unto him, Behold, thou art old, and thy sons walk
   not in thy ways: now make us a king to judge us like all
   the nations.

But the thing displeased Samuel, when they said, Give us a
   king to judge us. And Samuel prayed unto the LORD.

And the LORD said unto Samuel, Hearken unto the voice
   of the people in all that they say unto thee: for they have
   not rejected thee, but they have rejected me, that I should
   not reign over them.

According to all the works which they have done since the
   day that I brought them up out of Egypt even unto this
   day, wherewith they have forsaken me, and served other
   gods, so do they also unto thee.

Now therefore hearken unto their voice: howbeit yet protest
   solemnly unto them, and shew them the manner of the
   king that shall reign over them.

And Samuel told all the words of the LORD unto the people
   that asked of him a king.

And he said, This will be the manner of the king that shall
   reign over you: He will take your sons, and appoint them
   for himself, for his chariots, and to be his horsemen: and
   some shall run before his chariots.

And he will appoint him captains over thousands, and captains over fifties; and will set them to ear his ground, and

to reap his harvest, and to make his instruments of war, and instruments of his chariots.

And he will take your daughters to be confectionaries, and to be cooks, and to be bakers.

And he will take your fields, and your vineyards, and your oliveyards, even the best of them, and give them to his servants.

And he will take the tenth of your seed, and of your vineyards, and give to his officers, and to his servants.

And he will take your menservants, and your maidservants, and your goodliest young men, and your asses, and put them to his work.

He will take the tenth of your sheep: and ye shall be his servants.

And ye shall cry out in that day because of your king which ye shall have chosen you; and the LORD will not hear you in that day.

Nevertheless the people refused to obey the voice of Samuel: and they said, Nay: but we will have a king over us.

That we also may be like all the nations: and that our king may judge us, and go out before us, and fight our battles.

And Samuel heard all the words of the people, and he rehearsed then in the ears of the LORD.

And the LORD said to Samuel, Hearken unto their voice, and make them a king. And Samuel said unto the men of Israel, Go ye every man unto his city.

Good king Herod?

God and Samuel argued that monarchy makes a new class for its entourage, unproductive, artificial, and unnecessary. In so doing they wanted a nationalism which gave few openings to parasites. Granted that corruption existed and contributed to any demand for a king; granted, also, that it festered even among the children of saints. The demand for kings, because everyone else had one, is ironically akin to children demanding certain toys at Christmas because other children have them. The text itself constituted a camouflaged trap. The reader (especially if a king himself) might simply understand it as a stage to an inevitable monarchy. However, closer reading might suggest that God's critique of kingship was as valid for later times as it had been when He enunciated it. God was also warning us about artificial nationalism, something imposed rather than evolved, liable to corruption in trying to make up the resultant deficiencies. It is liable to borrow what it takes to be useful bits, some from its predecessor superseded by revolution, some from display in other regimes. It may work out, but nationalism ought to surge from the soul however wise to study its precursors and neighbours.

A future nationalism responsive to God must have doubts about kings, and just before the life of Christ the obvious king was the effective but questionable Herod the Great. Yet the king whether David, Herod or James VI/I will want to be accepted as the prime channel to and from God. If modern chronology is correct in dating Herod's death to before Jesus's birth, he doesn't qualify for his most enduring infamy, the 'fateful bairnies', and scholars who dismiss their massacre for want of documentation ignore Herod Archelaus's 3,000 victims, easily including 2,000 children. The second chapter of St Matthew's Gospel notes Archelaus as the reason why Joseph, Mary and Jesus could not return to Bethlehem and went directly from their refuge Egypt to Nazareth. The return of Jesus's family from Egypt followed the demotion of Archelaus, but not by his, or his father's, death. Matthew's sources may have included Mary herself, or else the apostle and future evangelist John with whom she resided after the crucifixion.

Thanks be to Mary, for we know the details of Jesus's birth lit up for us across two millennia, but having lived through several dangerous Herods she was probably less concerned with the genealogical details of which Herod wanted to murder her Son, and which actually murdered her cousin John the Baptist. Herod the Great had created the visible and invisible political foundations for the dynasty. He restored the Temple from near-destruction under several alien empires and survived in limited power under several rival Romans – Gnaeus Pompeius

Magnus, Julius Caesar's officials, Caesar's murderer, Caesar's avenger Marcus Antonius and his ally Cleopatra, then the victorious Caesar Augustus. When preaching, Reverend Alex J MacDonald – former Moderator of the Free Church of Scotland – sometimes takes on a character of some witness of Jesus's life, thus firmly establishing the proximity of Scottish Presbyterian sermons to theatre arts. His *Tell Me the Story: The Carpenter* carries a dozen alleged autobiographical recollections from Jesus's mother Mary to Marcellus, the Roman Governor replacing Pontius Pilate. They are all luminous, eloquent studies in miniature stressing the simple humanity in MacDonald's voice. His unpublished performance as Herod the Great firmly put conventions on the defensive, since he declared Herod a nationalist and, while giving politics little room in his homilies, he is an affectionate believer in independence for Scotland.

Herod faced dangerous competition from nationalisms clerical and lay: the Temple priests condemned him privately for too many concessions to the Romans at the cost of the true Jewish religion, and Zealots condemned him publicly for butchering their faith to make a Roman holiday. His own nationalism led him to bring as much peace as possible to the land he loved, as much devotion to the Temple he had rebuilt, and as much independence within the Roman Empire whose control he exploited. Alex MacDonald in his sermon showing Herod a persuasive advocate in his own defence prayed for our deliverance from an ultimately murderous pride in our own success, however humanly beneficial it might be. As Conor Cruise O'Brien argued in his solo play *King Herod Explains*, while Herod might have been innocently dead by the time the 'fateful bairnies' were killed, his reputation as child-murderer was nonetheless true. He was above all a mortal danger to children in his own family. To preserve his noble achievements several had to die as potential security risks or as bribes to slake the lusts of necessary allies. It might be wise to consolidate power by gaining what clerical support might be possible but a seemingly successful secularised spirituality could produce the most dangerous adversary. Martyrs will not be puppets, and nationalism in the king's name faces the ultimate adversary in a nationalism for God.

The Church of Scotland as mother of her country

Priests, rabbis, imams and ministers may recover their country's nationalism and revive their people when suddenly finding themselves conscripted by an alien usurper. Recent Scottish history supplies a fascinating example of this. Margaret Thatcher was an English nationalist whose rule over Wales, Scotland and Northern Ireland must always subordinate them to English interests. She did, however, note the reduction of her Tory MPs in Scotland from 21 to ten in the general election of 1987. Her view of other countries in or out of the UK was largely schooled by images on comic postcards: Scots to her were primarily producers and consumers of whisky, but she retained enough imperial spirit to cultivate relevant witch-doctors. The monarch is an ordinary member of the Church of Scotland, not its head (as opposed to her headship of the Church of England). She nonetheless has the right to address the annual meeting of its General Assembly in what is actually a fringe event, but never so described. If the Queen does not personally fulfil this role she may appoint one of her children or grandchildren to represent her, but otherwise the prime minister nominates a Lord High Commissioner.

For the first General Assembly after the 1987 general election Thatcher had her chosen commissioner invite her to address it on 21 May 1988 which thereafter she and her entourage would term an invitation by the General Assembly itself. The speech touched fairly traditional stops, ticking the boxes, so that the right thing would seem to have been said and the wrong thing rejected. She is said to have written almost all of it herself, and it reads like it. At an early point she quoted without attribution 'Christianity is about spiritual redemption, not about social reform'. Whilst she did not directly endorse it, she left it within contagion distance of her approval, and being widely credited with its endorsement. The distinction is in fact ridiculous: spiritual redemption is impossible without social reform, and the converse is also true. She sharpened her implied separation of spiritual redemption from social reform with '"If a man will not work he shall not eat" wrote St Paul to the Thessalonians'. St Paul is a fairly dangerous man with whom to play selective truncation of quotation, the passage actually being (2 Thessalonians 3:8–11):

> Neither did we eat any man's bread for nought: but wrought with labour and travail night and day, that we might not be chargeable to any of you: Not because we have not power, but to make ourselves an ensample unto you to follow us.
>
> For even when we were with you, this we commanded you, that if any would not work, neither should he eat.
>
> For we hear that there are some which walk among you disorderly, working not at all, but are busybodies.

The last line certainly described Thatcher in Scotland. The 'sermon' was delivered with the prime minister's best condescension, the great lady graciously quizzing the village idiot. It greatly enraged the patronised clergy, and left them worried that their congregations would fear complicity with her turning the Church of Scotland into a fat-cat church. God is not mocked, neither are his more altruistic ministers. It was the Reverend Willie Storrar who found the answer. Almost a year later, the Church of Scotland opened her Assembly Hall to all political parties and churches to create a constitutional convention determining Scotland's future direction. The direct analogy, and antecedent, was the action of the retired General George Washington and a few friends meeting to talk about necessary changes for the USA's constitutional condition in 1785. The US feared the possibilities of a reinvigorated Great Britain winning a return match against a disintegrating USA, squabbling amongst its individual states and bereft of its former European allies. This almost invisible but morally unassailable pressure from Washington resulted in the Constitution of 1787.

The Church of Scotland was similarly an impeccable source of moral pressure. It was made all the stronger because, in the absence of a Scottish Parliament since 1707, the Annual Meeting of the General Assembly of the Church of Scotland was its nearest equivalent in popular image. The Church had become what it had so long claimed, but never with so much support and affection from so many people outside its doctrinal votaries. Contrary to her will, or knowledge, Thatcher had revived Scottish constitutional nationalism as a spiritual act instead of a mere parliamentary device. Under the Church's welcome the warring political parties and rival churches created the conditions making a far stronger Scottish Parliament than devolutionists had ever envisaged, and so it came into being in 1997–99, appropriately housed in the Assembly Hall until the new Parliament building was ready to receive it.

The Church of Scotland had rediscovered its own nationalism to lead its people into a moral regeneration in place of a Thatcherite frontier kitsch-market Vanity Fair. The convention under the Church of Scotland roof was initially chaired by Reverend Kenyon Wright, a Methodist Canon, who on 30 March 1989 produced its great rallying-cry:

> What happens when that other voice we know so well says 'We say No, and we are the State'? Well, We say Yes and We are the People.

It was a heartwarming distinction, and it spoke for the 58 of Scotland's 72 MPs, and as Neal Ascherson recorded in his *Stone Voices* it also spoke for the:

> Trade Unions, the churches, the Gaelic lobby, army of single-issue leagues for the reform of this or that, the ethnic minorities, the educators, the planners.

In fact, what became known as the Scottish anti-establishment establishment. It was the Church of Scotland existing to be an audience for Thatcher, becoming the Church of Scotland calling the people together, one might say a pillar of cloud transfigured into a pillar of fire. Thirty years later, the Scottish Parliament has evolved and the SNP has ruled it for over 14 years, the repentant prodigal son enjoying the fatted calf. Tory Prime Minister of the UK, Mr Boris Johnson, has trained his kindergarten-style Cabinet to answer unwanted questions by saying 'the people' are not interested in whatever may be the thorny thistle presented by press persons for comment, what the people want is to be told whatever is convenient for Mr Johnson to tell them. In cold UK law, the devolution settlement after the 1997 general election and referendum was enacted as a decision of the House of Commons which has the right to withdraw what it has conceded, and with his present 73-strong majority Mr Johnson may one day decide that 'the people' want the suppression of the Scottish Parliament. His insistence that he knows what the Scottish people want is not so much Louis XIV as Queen Victoria, when Gladstone told her in 1885 that if Ireland sent 80 or 90 MPs to Westminster pledged to Home Rule it might be very difficult to resist such a demand, and she told him that these people would only be low, disreputable persons elected by order of Parnell and not representative of the true feeling of the country. God save the Scottish Parliament!

During the 1964 Republican convention in San Francisco, a satirical performance by 'The Establishment' cabaret declared that if the candidate Barry Goldwater became President and accidentally pressed the nuclear button he would send a prompt message to Moscow regretting the mistake but adding 'It's all right. God is on our side.' As a parable it captures the essence of nationalism's relationship to God down the centuries: ostentatious reverence perpetually manipulating. Even when God is not directly invoked, supposedly secular states use obvious authoritarian substitutes. Atheism and agnosticism make gods of themselves.

CHAPTER FOUR

Nationalism from Homer's workshop

To one only among the countless millions of human beings has it been given to draw characters, by the strength of his own individual hand, in lines of such force and vigour, that they have become from his day to ours the common inheritance of civilised man. That one is Homer.... Like the sun, which furnishes with its light the courts and alleys of London, while himself unseen by their inhabitants, he has applied with the illumination of his ideas millions of minds never brought into direct contact with his works, and even millions totally unaware of his existence.

William Ewart Gladstone, 'Homeric Characters in and out of Homer', *Quarterly Review* CII (July 1857)

The subject of our narrative was born upon the 15th day of August 1769 at his father's house in Ajaccio. We read with interest that his mother's good constitution and bold character of mind induced her to attend mass on the day of his birth, it being the Festival of the Assumption, obliging her to return home immediately, and, as there was no time to prepare a bed or bedroom, she was delivered of the future victor upon a temporary couch prepared for her accommodation and covered with an ancient piece of tapestry, representing the heroes of the *Iliad*. The infant was christened by the name of Napoleon, an obscure saint...

Walter Scott, *The Life of Napoleon Buonaparte* (1827)

What was Homer?

DOWN THE CENTURIES the Bible, the Quran and other sacred writings millennia old, have profoundly influenced their auditors, readers, and prayer-makers – and even their more sceptical students – in their political, social and erotic opinions. Can we encounter the Book of Joshua without seeing its nationalism? Can we hear or read the Psalms without recognising their place in shaping nationalism as the thought and ambition of future kings. The Psalms created their own nationalism by identifying their state with their nation and their nation with themselves. Can we ignore their self-justification, their attempts to manipulate God, their readiness to hint that the fault might be God's, their hints that God should produce a little more clarity, their cunning as to whether David is their author, their bullying, whining, avoidance of blame at others' expense, and their greatness of heart, mind and soul? Can we study the Gospels without seeing the insistence of Jesus on purifying nationalism, respecting the nobility of aliens, building a people by loving all humans as much as ourselves, being ready if necessary to die – but never to kill – for our nation which is all humankind? Conor Cruise O'Brien's *God Land* showed the Latin word *patria* – fatherland – initially used in Christendom to mean 'Heaven' as our hoped-for destination, gradually became identified with the territorial aspirations of its users. St Thomas Aquinas's Hymn to the consecrated Host, commonly sung to begin Benediction of the Blessed Sacrament which Catholics believe to be Jesus, crowns its text with *patria* as the ultimate destination for which we yearn: this is eternal nationalism.

ST THOMAS AQUINAS 'O *Salutaris Hostia*' (mid-13th century).

O Salutaris Hostia	O saving Host who opens wide
Quae coeli pandis ostium:	The gates of Heaven to men below:
Bella premunt hostilia,	Wars press on us from every side,
Da robur, fer auxilium!	Give strength to us, and aid bestow!

Uni trinoque Domino	To Thy great name be endless praise,
Sit sempiterna Gloria!	Immortal Godhead, One in Three,
Qui vitam sine termino	Oh, grant us endless length of days
Nobis donet in patria.	In our true native land with thee!

Homer's epics may or may not have constituted a part of religious belief, but the *Iliad* and the *Odyssey* explore divinity whether in the ultimate Fates, in their inferiors the great Olympian gods, and in the divine ancestry of a few mortal heroes, and assume that superior gods may be manoeuvred by the considerable diplomatic powers of goddesses. Neither Zeus, nor Priam, nor Agamemnon dare declare themselves – like Louis XIV or Friedrich the Great – to be the state, to proclaim a nationalism coterminous with their identity. Louis and Friedrich would have done their successors a service to remember the limitations on Homeric monarchy long before Louis. For almost 3,000 years Homer's epics were transmitted orally and then in writing, often simplified, permeating Greek, Latin, Christian and post-Christian cultures, accurately or erroneously, elaborately or childishly. Inevitably nationalism, often dramatic in its expression of faith, took form partly because it proved to be a child and a parasite of religion.

We may say that nationalism was anti-religious, or non-religious, but that is because we are afraid to look at religion in case it might bite us. Giuseppe Mazzini insisted nationalism must be non-religious, but a close scrutiny of his own nationalist theory shows its clear evolution from Roman Catholicism in ritual perhaps even more than in politics. Homer lay at the heart of so much European education such as Greek tragedy and Roman poetry, and naturally nationalism reflected its epiphanies in his epics – the nationalism of a city under siege, the nationalism of a loosely confederated army besieging it, the nationalism of a fugitive king hungering to return to his home and re-establish himself despite usurpers. On *Newsnight* Tom Holland suggested that the classical education of the UK governing classes led to heroic self-identification, austere aloofness from the masses, and celebration of defeat by falling on one's sword: and in certain cases it certainly might. But we must remember that Homer is where all classical ladders start. The great tragedies of Greek and Roman drama are spin-offs, mutations, kith and kin to *Iliad* and *Odyssey*, and resemble heroic tales told in far-off places across the globe where their origins are unknown. Tutors in nationalism to train future governing classes could use the last books of *Iliad* and *Odyssey* to show the value and beauty of reconciliation, magnificent empathy between Priam and Achilles in the *Iliad*, and pragmatic acceptance of arbitration between king and dead suitors' relatives in the *Odyssey*. The Olympian deities (for once benign) command those processes, which Christian clerics a millennium after Homer could find useful in illustrating the wishes of God for peace. Byron, frivolously translating Horace, announced in *Don Juan* Canto 1 (1819):

> Brave men were living before Agamemnon
> And since, exceeding valorous and sage,
> A good deal like him too, though quite the same none;
> But then they shone not on the poet's page,
> And so have been forgotten...

Disraeli's father clinched the case for unknown precursors arguing:

> Undoubtedly there were good poets before Homer; how absurd to conceive that a finished and elaborate poem could be the first!

Modern politicians seldom fall on their own swords: nationalist leaders who do, in the sense of contriving their own destruction to achieve their ambition or to entomb their failure, are more spiritual figures akin to Patrick Pearse of Easter 1916 in Dublin. The two most important Etonian movers and shakers of the UK towards democracy: Edward George Geoffrey Stanley, afterwards 14th Earl of Derby who led the enactment of the Reform Bill of 1867, and William Ewart Gladstone who led that of the Reform Bill of 1884, cherished Homer all of their lives resulting in Derby's dozen years translating the *Iliad* into blank verse and Gladstone writing studies of Homer for half a century. They learned what democratic nationalism might be from

Daniel O'Connell as Odysseus in Homeric combat against a Hector, or an Achilles, as old Nestor in occasional affectionate tutorials to his nominal Tory enemy Gladstone, recorded in Gladstone's beautiful memoir 'Daniel O'Connell'.

O'Connell's achievement in 1829 placed him personally in the Westminster Parliament visibly arising from his previous mobilisation of thousands of Irish Catholics to vote for Protestants pledged to support Catholic emancipation. If not voters, then financial contributors to O'Connell's machine, or crowds at his meetings, or mutual psychological support, egged on by some (though not all) priests, and finally rallying behind the forbidden Catholic candidacy of O'Connell himself in Clare. O'Connell's crusade for emancipation had been constantly driven by hopes of influential and perhaps irresistible Protestant support in Britain and Ireland. This came notably from the Scottish Presbyterian leader Thomas Chalmers whose evangelical yearnings for intensifying personal religious devotion amongst his fellow-Scots publicly entailed supporting, contributing to, and learning from O'Connell's movement. Chalmers reflected Scottish readiness to learn from the Irish Catholics, his Presbyterianism and their Catholicism deriving from popular belief rather than from power bestowed by princes: and both were believers in Christian non-violence. For a time, O'Connell, however much nationalism's Irish tribune, dreamed of support from the Regent later George IV for Catholic emancipation, hoping for its realisation from George IV's state visit to Ireland in 1821 (the first made by any of its kings since James VII/II and William II/III). Byron's 'The Irish Avatar' angrily pointed out that making the Catholic Earl of Fingall a Knight of St Patrick and treating O'Connell as a bosom friend meant nothing, George was merely playing Shakespeare's scapegrace Prince Hal with inevitable treachery towards his Falstaff:

> Wear, Fingall, thy trappings – O'Connell proclaim
> His accomplishments! *His!!!* And thy country convince
> Half an age's contempt was an error of fame,
> And Hal's the rascaliest, sweetest *young* Prince!

O'Connell subsequent relied, above all, on his popular following in Ireland, and took pride in his enemies' sneer that he was 'King of the Beggars'. He campaigned in Ireland thereafter under banners quoting from Byron's *Childe Harold's Pilgrimage* Canto II:

> Hereditary bondsmen! Know ye not,
> Who would be free themselves must strike the blow?

The effectiveness of this, originally directed to the Greeks still under Turkish rule, grew powerfully from 1824 when Byron died enlisted for Greek liberation. There was irony as well as identity in that: Byron, like O'Connell, hated war, yet himself ended in arms. O'Connell, perpetual opponent of violent nationalism found his reliance on belligerent Irish mythology had armed the intellectuals publishing historiographical war-cries whether in their best-selling weekly *Nation* from 1842, supporting his campaign for Repeal of the Union but ultimately rejecting him in favour of physical force. Byron and O'Connell were simply preaching self-reliance as a prerequisite for worthwhile nationalism, but 'striking the blow' unwisely surrendered to military metaphor. In the 1830s O'Connell advanced politics in the direction of democracy partly through alliance with aristocratic Whigs and Irish mass support to extract needed reforms from the ruling classes. It would follow that however attractive Repeal might seem as an underlying unifying faith in O'Connell's politics after emancipation, Irish peasants could perfectly understand that day-to-day concessions had to be won by bargaining.

The Irish Catholic underclasses had survived the hopelessness of their 18th century powerlessness amid Jacobite dreams. Yet, the dreams gave them some sort of political sense on whose perceptions O'Connell could build. He could become Homeric as well as practical in parliament, creating rivalry as well as anger in Peel and Stanley, both of whom were driven to justify their Homeric leadership by what benefits for the Irish masses they could produce amid warfare against O'Connell. Stanley as Chief Secretary for Ireland in 1830–33 was usually at vituperative loggerheads with O'Connell and resented O'Connell's skill in making friends with Stanley's Whig cabinet colleagues ultimately driving him back to the Tories. Achilles also became so angered with his fellow-Achaians that he found him-self wanting the enemy to win, at least for a time. He also protested against the corruption in army administration by Agamemnon, and Stanley in Dublin Castle discovered that the preceding century's anti-Catholic oligarchic rule had meant endless corruption in apparent longevity, which Achilles-like he opposed in winged words and actions. O'Connell showed his Odysseus-like genius in turning the Irish Catholic popular memory of the normally anti-Catholic 18th century Irish Parliament into a dream of lost glories to be redeemed on its return. Achilles when not in angry abdication earned his heroic stature, and Stanley battled incessantly and triumphantly to give the Irish Catholics a system of education denied to them for the preceding century. As Whig Secretary of State for the Colonies in 1833 Stanley abolished slavery within the British Empire. As Derby he gave the UK a Reform Act in 1867 which would prove its first real legal step towards democracy. Gladstone gradually became the supreme standard-bearer of Irish constitutional nationalism in his last years carrying the Second Irish Home Rule Bill to victory in the Commons in 1893, and exposing its contemptuous dismissal by the Lords as naked self-interest leaving their veto an obvious target in future democratic advances. By then Gladstone himself had passed from party manoeuvre and diplomatic alliances to absolute belief in the necessity of Home Rule for Ireland, perhaps to be followed by Home Rule for the Scotland whence his parents came, and the Wales in which he lived. He now believed that English nationalism in its own interest had to relinquish authority derived by dishonour: Helen, abducted in violation of hospitality, ought to be returned to the Achaians, as Troy's greatest hero, Hector, believed.

JL Hammond, *Gladstone and the Irish Nation* (1938):

> Gladstone the great Englishman sleeps with the great English dead beneath the solemn beauty of the Christian dream that gave his strength its patent power. That Gladstone was the loyal Minister

of the Queen, the faithful servant of the nation, the glory of its Parliament. But the other Gladstone belongs to a world older than the world of England's life: that Gladstone was the heir of Europe's centuries of hope and sorrow, her tempests in his blood, her ancient wisdom in his eagle eyes. His place is among the mighty shadows that people the distant memories of man; the memories of the twilight towers of Priam's Troy, once sad with Helen's gaze watching the battle; of the plain, once bright with swift chariots and the glancing beauty of the horses from Thessaly and Argos in the hollow ships; of Scamander, once a sea of surging wrath when the son of Peleus tempted the anger of a god, as he himself had tempted the anger of an empire.

Homer for the young

As to the more numerous students of Homer's greatest and most ungrateful disciple Virgil, Sir Robert Peel played the part of Aeneas's ultimately vanquished last rival Turnus in Harrow School's staging of the *Aeneid* in which his classmate Byron had a small part. The classics, in whatever form, played great parts in educations obtained far beyond the English public schools. Homeric Greek is less easy to master than Xenophon's *Anabasis* whether studied in Britain or Ireland or Europe. O'Connell was confronted as a schoolboy by magisterial demand for his skills in the original Greek of Homer as well as Xenophon when, aged 16 he had been smuggled to St Omer in north-eastern France for a Catholic education in 1791. Homer's pace is good, his formulaic adjectives reassuring, and content frequently absorbing. O'Connell would have encountered Homer initially in Kerry where his uncle Maurice, wealthy from smuggling, could lay his hand on a few books, and where Gaelic poets took liberties with Homeric analogies. Homer was the master story-teller whose art lies behind all teaching, and while we know nothing about him (or possibly her or them), he showed us himself at work. The *Odyssey* time and again brings us Odysseus (and occasional others) telling tales, frequently altered or invented for specific purposes: Odysseus may not have been in the least like Homer, but the art of storytelling in which he radiates his proficiency was his creator's profession. And Homer was clearly proud of his epics, pride sprinkled with captivating humour. In the *Odyssey's* last book the ghost of Agamemnon bitterly remembering his own murder by his own wife mockingly addresses the absent and still surviving killer of Penelope's unsuccessful suitors whose ghosts reveal their fate as translated by Emily Wilson (2018):

> Lucky you,
> Cunning Odysseus: you got yourself
> a wife of virtue – great Penelope.
> How principled she was, that she remembered
> her husband all those years! Her fame will live
> forever, and the deathless gods will make
> a poem to delight all those on earth
> about intelligent Penelope.

There is a grand impudence in this, since the preceding section of the *Odyssey* is Penelope's sublime identification of Odysseus, which Homer's audience had probably heard yesternight if not earlier tonight. Homer might be saying to us:

> You do not know who I am, but I have shown you what
> I am, and it may be that at least some things you learn or
> imbibe from my account of them in action – what you call
> 'nationalism', for instance – may still be told in one way
> or another to the last syllable of recorded time, as one of
> my successors may phrase it some day.

Shakespeare, the successor who so phrased it in *Macbeth* knew his Homer as *Troilus and Cressida* shows, and bound his audience closer in *Julius Caesar* when after murdering Caesar first Cassius and then Brutus prophesies the acting of that scene endless times for endless audiences across endless ages. Brutus at least kills Caesar for a nationalism insistent that for its own survival a nation must not have a king, the very point we saw God making to His friend the aged Samuel. God kills nobody to prove His point, saying kings are deplorable but apparently inevitable, while the play shows Brutus's regicidal actions resulting in the establishment of a super-king, a future emperor, Octavius, the young Augustus, who speaks the play's last line as is consistent with the form of nationalism his real-life original would have his poets preach. That passage in the *Odyssey*'s last book teaches another lesson in nationalism: the first place to establish your security is in your home. Professor Mary Beard ('Sappho Speaks', *Confronting the Classics*) sardonically points out how severely Telemachus reprimands his mother Penelope when she attempts to cut a bard short. As Professor Emily Wilson equally disdainfully translates Telemachus:

> Mother, no,
> you must not criticize the loyal bard
> for singing as it pleases him to sing.
> Poets are not to blame for how things are:
> Zeus is; he gives to each as is his will....

One might claim this as Homer's unscrupulous bardic propaganda, and no doubt it is, but the delicious humour implicit in the translation as well as in the comment invites us to suspect that Homer began the joke, which might make him, or her, the original progenitor of the old saw about teaching one's grandmother how to suck eggs. There is an assumption of bardic integrity which coheres with the singular objectivity of Homer's work. Nationalism has been widely accused of poisoning history with bias, and bards in the service of patrons (especially kings) have been commonly assumed to make truth the first casualty. Telemachus is rude and ridiculous; but his benevolent view of bards does not seem to be questioned, although his manners are, and the *Odyssey* in part concerns his coming of age, given the adolescence with which he ends his instructions to his mother:

> ... It is for men
> to talk, especially me. I am the master.

After which he talks to the abominable suitors with such folly that he sets them off in an attempt to kill him; and it takes gods from Olympus to extricate him successfully. Telemachus is a symbol of immaturity and its need for education, notably in Archbishop Francois Fenelon, *Les Aventures de Télémaque*, and in James Joyce's *Ulysses* where Stephen Dedalus is still a very young man requiring protection. Leopold Bloom is pseudo-deified by rescuing Stephen, the rescuer here more akin to Athena/Minerva in Homer and Fenelon than to Odysseus/Ulysses. Both *Télémaque* and Joyce's various portraits of the artist are studies in nationalism. *Télémaque* by exposure of the vices and blemishes disgracing Louis xiv's France, Joyce by exposure of the pettiness and betrayals damning his own Ireland. Joyce's magnificent biographer Richard Ellmann found in him a nationalism yearning for an Ireland reconciling Jew and Catholic regardless of their cultural disavowals. Nationalism knows itself above all in the creation of its own students, the younger the better.

Versions of Homer and Virgil circulated down the centuries in Gaelic Ireland and Scotland. The Gaelic Irish scholars, poets and story-tellers usually seem to have been pro-Greek claiming their bronze-age heroes and gods the *Tuatha de Danaan* to be Danaians. The British were more pro-Trojan (including claims of descent and nomenclature from a mythical Brutus great-grandson of Aeneas, much flourished by Edward I in his pursuit of bogus genealogy to justify his conquests). Bishop Gavin Douglas's early 16th century Scots was the oldest surviving English-related language into which the *Aeneid* was translated. Scotland had many a Hector and the faint snobbery of legal Anglicisation sometimes substituted Aeneas for Angus or Aonghas. (During the Burke and Hare trials William Burke's brother Con (Conchubhar in their native Gaelic) was rendered as 'Constantine' by the legal authorities who significantly saw nothing odd in primitive peasants' classicism.)

The great epics may certainly shape nationalism's leaders and prophets however unconsciously. Prime Minister Boris Johnson, an Oxford graduate in Classics, has resembled Agamemnon whilst imagining he is Achilles – a self-absorbed commander-in-chief preferring to think of himself as a wronged but invincible hero. He might have recognised himself more aptly as a cheap tourist-trap Odysseus, the trickster ready to sacrifice anything especially truth to his self-protective nationalism, occasionally plausible in his lies while incapable of detailed truth-telling, and sacrificing everyone in his unfailing instinct for his own survival. As Odysseus Prime Minister Johnson remains a hero modelled by cosmeticians such as Mr Dominic Cummings in modern equivalents of the goddess Athena's prettification services. To date, Odysseus remains the more convincing story-teller. Down the centuries self-styled heroes or victims of nationalism have seen Homeric heroes in their mirrors, and caricaturists have raided Homer to deride their doing it. Nationalism by its nature encourages its votaries to imagine their own potential heroism, which is far the richer when Homer fuels dreams of action. His epics have the advantage that none of the leading male characters are largely unblemished, other than Eumaeus the slave swineherd in the *Odyssey*, and perhaps Patroclus in the *Iliad*, necessary virtuous sidekicks for tarnished Homeric heroes, although changeable in modern identity as the hero may require. We are all children, and nationalism in many ways caters to our childishness.

Homer enslaved

Homer through his two epics or their spin-offs dominated Greek culture and, more indirectly, Latin. We cannot call him a nationalist either celebrating Greek victory or bewailing Trojan defeat. We cannot deduce his beliefs from his texts in most particulars, not knowing was he man or woman, islandman or landmass-dweller, intentional subverter of monarchy or its apologist, one poet for both epics or two. But we know what he meant by poetry and how he produced it in performance. *Odyssey* Books 8–12 show that, firstly in the court poet of Phaeacians Demodocus whose blindness may have induced the traditional belief that Homer himself was blind, secondly in Odysseus's four-book narrative of his adventures since the fall of Troy. It is not narcissism, but Homer wants to celebrate his own craft. It is not nationalistic in itself. Witness Odysseus unable to conceal his grief for brutalities led by himself while sacking Troy, on which Homer leaves us amid the possible ambiguities where Virgil's *Aeneid* perpetually damns the Greeks. Nationalism percolated from Homer over nearly three millennia, perpetually inspiring readers and hearers to take from the epics what interested them, leaving to them the work of deciding what lessons nationalism thought best learned from the texts or from memories of their recitation. The story-teller in the baronial hall or by the peasant fireside might be no Homer, but his art enlivened and inspired in keeping with the Homeric tradition.

Naturally nationalism was a welcome evangel enlivening the story and compelling its audience. Nationalism failed one Homeric test. Homer was quite phenomenally objective as between Achaians and Trojans: has any historian surpassed his objectivity? Gladstone thought Homer preferred the Trojans, but admired the Achaians more: there are several other opinions. But three centuries after Homer, Athenian nationalism if not objective saw that room must be made for self-criticism. Once the Greeks had established themselves as Greek, Homer was recreated in Greek tragic drama. Revulsion against the Peloponnesian war of the 5th century BCE and sheer artistic independence of mind led all three major Athenian tragedians Aeschylus, Sophocles and Euripides to continually see the sack of Troy through the eyes of defeated Trojans whose Greek despoilers meet harsh Nemesis, or showing Greek commanders at their most despicable. Their audiences were learning a nationalism purifying its people by readiness to see the anti-heroism of their heroes, Homer having shown their evil as well as their good, and pettiness no less than magnanimity.

Euripides is often singled out for his anti-heroes, but Sophocles could be as brutally iconoclastic, and Aeschylus's *Agamemnon* is even darker. He is murdered by his wife, true, but partly for having murdered their eldest daughter Iphigeneia as a war necessity, and for bringing home a captured princess and priestess Cassandra for regular rape virtually in his wife's presence. Nationalism in Virgil's *Aeneid* was there because Virgil and his master Caesar Augustus wanted it to be there, and took pains to make it unavoidable. Curiously, Irish Gaels unconquered by the Romans occasionally included

Augustus in litanies of classical and Gaelic heroes where the Romans had merely deified him.

Latin came with the authority and organisation of the Roman Empire and its medieval clerical heirs. Greek may have civilised Latin, but Latin determined the presentation of Greek for 1,800 years after Virgil. We have already seen a flicker of Roman ownership of Homer when Horace lays down the law about Agamemnon as lightened – or enlightened – by Byron. To the middle of the 19th century AD, Greek was kept in a Latin refrigerator, to be removed by its translators into various languages but returned after transplant surgery. When the planet Neptune was discovered in 1846 its English and French discoverers agreed that the formidable sea-god, implacable foe of Odysseus, seemed a good choice but in his Latin name rather than that used by Homer, Poseidon. The adoption of 'Odysseus' in place of the intrusive 'Ulysses' only became UK convention after Oxbridge professionalised Greek studies and even then it persisted into the early 20th century, James Joyce's *Ulysses* being the prime example. Nobody enjoyed his own obscurities more than Joyce but he had no intention of letting his readers miss the point of his masterpiece's origin. Latin weighed more heavily if the political orator wanted to be understood and was not merely showing off, for instance the original name of the planet Ares was forgotten after the Romans had declared it was now Mars. Republican Rome had adopted the gods of the conquered Greeks, with some changes of identity: significantly Mars was venerated by the military-minded Romans, credited with the paternity of their mythical local founder Romulus, second only to Jupiter in importance where Ares in Homeric and subsequent Greek mythology is a more contemptible figure.

It is an instructive test of nationalism to see what a culture retains and discards of its borrowing and thefts from another culture whose people it has conquered. Rome had conquered, where Greece had succumbed. Therefore great Mars, as open god of war, replaced mean Ares, its profiteer, just as a lion makes a more respectable predator than a jackal. Nationalism, as it derived from the Greeks, drew lessons hostile to its furtherance by violence. Nationalism in Roman hands celebrated its own triumphant growth as a warfare state. At the same time Roman nationalism told itself that Troy, alleged fatherland of Rome's alleged founder Aeneas, had been savagely sacked by Greeks from Greece, not what Homer called them, Achaians or Argives. Rome had defeated Greece as a totality in the 70 years before Virgil's birth in 70BCE. Therefore, Virgil's *Aeneid* is partly a justification of Rome's conquest of Greece as appropriate revenge for Greek cruelty to Rome's ancestor Troy over a thousand years earlier. The *Aeneid*'s pillage of Homeric myth and tradition symbolised Rome's actual loot and tyranny in Greece, as did the Latin language's subjection of the Greek and consumption of its words, names and terms. But there had to have been a Greece to establish Roman piety towards ravished Troy culminating in '*pius Aeneas*', and so the *Aeneid* as a poetic lesson in Roman nationalism was obliged to invent Greek nationalism, for an imaginary Greek nation.

Rome's voracity dominated the next millennium regardless of its political decline and fall. Medieval western Christendom preferred Latin, especially as its second millennium rapidly separated Greek and Eastern Orthodox Catholicism under the Emperors in Constantinople, from Roman Catholicism under the Popes. At the same time Christianity, by Jesus's doctrines, should have disdained vengeance which so actively sustained Roman nationalism, but vengeance was virtually practised as a medieval virtue, whether by governments in developing kingdoms or by nomadic warriors. Virgil's *Aeneid* finishes abruptly on an act of vengeance by Aeneas, Virgil's Dido curses her deserter Aeneas and thus is declared progenitor of a pattern of vengeance from Carthage against Rome only capable of conclusion by the destruction of Carthage and the defeat of Cleopatra.

Nationalism comfortably translated itself from fallen Rome to nascent Scotland, England, France, or Spain, as well as to resurgent Wales under Owain Glyn Dwr, and in individual Irish locations. Homer was Latinised to almost Roman military standards. English translators – from the Jacobean pioneer George Chapman to the Victorian statesman Derby – naturally prided themselves on bringing Homer to the people much as pioneer translators of the Bible from John Wycliffe to the divines directed by James VI/I had done. Virgil's texts probably reached our islands before Homer's, with Bishop Gavin Douglas's Scots-language *Aeneid,* of 1513, the first surviving translation in our archipelago. Shakespeare kept the Homer heroes Latinate in *Troilus and Cressida* in 1602, notably 'Ulysses' for 'Odysseus'. If, as his friend Ben Jonson declared, he knew little Latin and less Greek, he adjudged this to be the condition of his audience at all levels. 'Ulysses' also displaced 'Odysseus' in Thomas Hobbes's unintentionally hilarious translation of Homer's epics in 1673. For an author who took nationalism into its most spectacular and scholarly worship of totalitarianism in his *Leviathan*, Hobbes certainly provided readers of his Homer with comic relief, such as description of the ogre Polyphemus who devoured several of Odysseus's sailors in *Odyssey* Book IX:

> It was a huge and ugly Monster, and
> > Look'd not unlike a rocky Mountains head
> That does' mongst other hills asunder stand
> > With a great Periwig of Trees o'erspread.

Hobbes also domesticized the omen of the goose-devouring eagle seen by Odysseus's son Telemachus and the court of his host Menelaus in Book XV:

> As he said this, an Eagle dexter flew
> > And seiz'd a great white tame Goose grazing near.
> The standers-by shouted and cried, Shue, shue.

A team of scholars is currently at work on the detailed pursuit of Homeric origins in Hobbes. Their findings should deepen our awareness of Homer as wellspring of Hobbesian nationalism: an appropriate fate for the author of the judgment in *Leviathan* that 'The Papacy is but the ghost of the old Roman Empire sitting crowned on the grave thereof'.

The original Polyphemus episode became immortal partly because of humanity's need to cherish myths of weakness outwitting strength – and any nationalism is going to need rejuvenation with stories like that. Folk-legends are thronged with them, Tom Thumb, Jack the Giant-Killer, the Brave Little Taylor – and (as George Orwell noted) 20th century mass culture continued the tradition with Mickey Mouse, Charlie Chaplin, and Popeye the Sailor. Most of such victories are those of the trickster using language to make the gigantic bully trap himself. The cleverness of defeating the seemingly all-powerful Cyclops partly with word-play would fascinate philosophers in infancy or age. Odysseus delights Polyphemus with the sweetness of his wine for which, Polyphemus having demanded his name and being told it is 'Noman', promises that Noman will be the last of his captives to be devoured. This was appropriated by the rebel American Congress in 1775 in the American Revolution, writing to tell the Irish people that if they do not join the rebellion they will simply be the last to be devoured. They obviously assumed that Homer meant as much to the Irish parliamentarians as to the American Continental congressmen, and that the Irish would automatically understand the Americans as declaring the Westminster government to be a huge, homicidal, cannibalistic, greedy, stupid tyrant imprisoning and killing those it claimed as its lawful prey. They were inventing Irish nationalism in the process, since the Protestant Irish Parliament and the Catholic masses hardly thought of themselves as a totality. James Joyce's 'Cyclops' episode in *Ulysses* lacerated an Irish nationalism degenerating into racism as exemplified by Michael Cusack the great father of Gaelic athletic revival caricatured in *Ulysses* as 'the Citizen' whose homicidal anti-Semitism is magnificently frustrated by the triumphantly Jewish and Irish Leopold Bloom. Nationalism only deserves to survive culturally if it will find common humanity with other nationalisms. Homer also warned against the potential folly of nationalism which, at the moment of victory, sows the seeds of its own destruction. Odysseus, having blinded and eluded the Cyclops, shouts his own name in vaunting celebration which leaves himself and his crew open to incessant vengeance from Polyphemus's father the sea-god Poseidon. The episode itself warns against nationalism vindictively giving way to the pleasures of vengeance, as Joyce's countrymen were discovering in 1922, the year *Ulysses* was published, when their growing belief in military solutions tore them asunder in the Irish Civil War.

The size of Homer

Homer has captured his hearers and readers with varying intensity over the last 2,800 years and nationalism made his epics permanent building-blocks for their minds. John Keats proved the best mathematician to measure Homer's stature, once shown George Chapman's translation (1616), and promptly creating his sonnet 'On First Looking into Chapman's Homer':

> Much have I travell'd in the realms of gold,
> And many goodly states and kingdoms seen,
> Round many western islands have I been
> Which bards in fealty to Apollo hold.
> Oft of one wide expanse had I been told,
> Which deep brow'd Homer ruled as his demesne;
> Yet never did I breathe its pure serene
> Till I heard Chapman speak out loud and bold.
> Then felt I like some watcher of the skies
> When a new planet swims into his ken;
> Or like stout Cortez when with eagle eyes
> He stared at the Pacific – and all his men
> Looked at each other with a wild surmise –
> Silent, upon a peak in Darien.

It is terrific. It is a perfect meeting of poetic imaginations. The richness of its beauties may initially eclipse the subtlety of its ironies. By all means compliment the poets of our archipelago from Shakespeare and Milton down. The symbolism of gold lit up the natural association of ideas with the greed of the European conquerors of the Americas encircling the sonnet to culminate in Hernan Cortes and his Spanish troops in 1519 first catching sight of Tenochtitlan (whose Aztec ruins became the ground of the future Spaniards' Mexico City) imposed on Vasco Nunez de Balboa's 'discovery' of the Pacific Ocean. But this globalism itself is dwarfed by Keats's self-likening to the Hanoverian immigrant Friedrich Wilhelm Herschel at his telescope in 1781 descrying the first new planet beheld by humanity since prehistory when Saturn, Jupiter, Mars, Venus and Mercury were first beheld from Earth. Since Hanover's elector was Britain's King, Herschel might seem an immigrant of relatively acceptable origin, but from 1760 the king – now George III – had been English-born, speaking English as his first language, so Herschel felt the need to display his new-found English nationalism with all of an immigrant's defensiveness. After all, 'England' in 1781 was at war facing a Europe hostile or malevolently neutral, so he Christened the new planet '*Georgium Sidus*' [George's star] the name it retained in the UK until 1850 although from 1781 the rest of the world called it Uranus. As galactic nationalism, it is less foolish than President 'Dubya' Bush selling pieces of the moon or President Donald Trump proclaiming his intent of similar rapacity on Mars. Keats symbolised in himself the hordes of readers past present and future ignorant of Greek yet enchanting themselves by translations as faithful as Chapman's, or else (like Pope's) gaining in beauty what they lose in fidelity.

Pitt Conscripts Homer

Thomas Babington Macaulay's last completed work, his biography of William Pitt the Younger written in 1858 for the *Encyclopaedia Britannica,* described the 22-year-old Pitt elected MP in January 1781 faultlessly invoking Macaulay's beloved Homer with surgical precision in a debate in mid-December 1781:

> Pitt spoke in the committee of supply on the army estimates. Symptoms of dissension had begun to appear on the Treasury bench. Lord George Germaine, the Secretary of State who was especially charged with the direction of the war in America, had held language not easily to be reconciled with declarations made by the First Lord of the Treasury. Pitt noticed the discrepancy with much force and keenness. Lord George and Lord North began to whisper together; and Welbore Ellis, an ancient placeman who had been drawing salary almost every quarter since the days of Henry Pelham, bent down between them

to put in a word. Such interruptions sometimes discompose veteran speakers. Pitt stopped, and, looking at the group, said, with admirable readiness, 'I shall wait till Nestor has composed the dispute between Agamemnon and Achilles'.

The faithful Commons should have easily remembered the original episode from the first book of the *Iliad*. Macaulay ended Pitt's life on his despair at the news of Napoleon's victory at Ulm in 1805 offset four days later at the news of Nelson's victory at Trafalgar and, still Prime Minister, making his last public appearance at the Guildhall where he replied to the toast of his health:

> England has saved herself by her exertions, and will,
> I trust, save Europe by her example.

As Macaulay said, it was one of 'those stately sentences of which he had a boundless command'. It was, in itself, a perfect statement of English nationalism at its most truly altruistic and desperate. It probably sustained Churchill at the finest and darkest hour through the Battle of Britain and Blitz in 1940–41, and it is a tragedy of our time that its altruism has been so little honoured by the Tory Party founded by Pitt's 19-year premiership. Pitt's countrymen have too readily followed his titular indifference to the Union he made in 1800, 'England' meaning but dishonouring the 'one country' which the entire archipelago now was. He meant 'Britain', he surely also meant Ireland, but England was the heart of his meaning. Pitt expected Scots like his bosom friend Henry Dundas, and Irish Protestants like his promising junior minister Robert Stewart Viscount Castlereagh, to say 'England' as their country, regardless of their birthplaces. He had desperately tried to make it a much more real union by emancipating the Catholics, and had temporarily resigned when George III's veto created a new Irish and far more Catholic 19th century nationalism, animating millions under Daniel O'Connell in the teeth of Tory government hostility, to draw on traditions of secret agrarian activists, Jacobite smugglers and recruiters, eloquent Irish Protestant parliamentarians in opposition, and French revolutionary sympathisers.

Pitt by himself was English nationalism: a nationalism taking its being from his European sense strengthened in the 1790s by the Irish-British Edmund Burke, but partly shaped by Homer, as his conscription of the *Iliad*'s first book showed. For at the time in Pitt's parliamentary youth when he was speaking in December 1781, the last British army in the field against the Americans had surrendered under General Lord Cornwallis two months previously but the news had not yet reached Europe. Lord George Germaine fell from office two months after Pitt dubbed him Achilles, to be succeeded by Welbore Ellis, whose tenure lasted a further month and then ended as did his new office the Secretary of State for the American Colonies and the 12-year-old government of Lord North. Pitt had evidently foreseen that the rupture between North and Germaine would take more than Westminster mutterings to alleviate. Achilles's subsequent refusal to fight might also remind hearers of Germaine's disgrace 20 years previously when he had failed to support a British offensive at the Battle of Minden in 1759, a court-marshal in 1760 ruling that he was thereby 'unfit to serve His Majesty in any military capacity whatsoever'. Indeed, Pitt's own assurance in his deployment of Homer asserted a personal nationalism declaring that as son of the elder William Pitt, Britain's triumphant leader in 1759, he knew what leadership Britain required in 1781. As his eloquence and skill won him attention from the House of Commons he might have recalled Telemachus defying the present unworthy occupants of the house once commanded by his father Odysseus, but the relevance of Homer cut deeper.

The *Iliad* tells of two kinds of nationalism: that of a king like Priam of Troy trying to balance dignity with wisdom and summoning the general (but not universal) loyalty of its subjects due to a city attacked by an army of hostile invaders; and that of a variety of warlords uneasily allied in besieging Troy, several of whom defect from their self-centred commander-in-chief Agamemnon. These contrasting nationalisms were both fundamentally animated by spurious cults of honour, and both cults were present in the war of American independence, as many Americans would have recognised. The Americans were in their way as disparate as the Achaeans and as capable of letting selfishness override nationalism thus endangering their cause, and as aware as the Trojans that their nationalism might be on weaker grounds than they liked to tell themselves, but that honour dictated going to war and staying in the field. There was a further and more ominous descent from Homer, the fact that the future USA would continue divided into individual states with political leaders sometimes as hostile to central command as Achilles or Ajax could be, with some advocates of greater federal power being as capable but as unscrupulous as Odysseus (in this case prefiguring Alexander Hamilton). Nationalism made the USA and pulled it apart, depending on whether its citizens took their identity from their states or from their country, and (while federally linked by documents that became icons of nationalism, the Declaration of Independence and the Constitution) the United States of America never succeeded in giving itself more than a generic name. Although, New York, South Carolina, Ohio, Missouri, Washington, DC and the Pacific Northwest river attempted Columbus or Columbia as national names shown by usage for universities, state capitols, waterways, the district chosen to house the federal government centre, and the first spaceship to carry earthlings to walk on the moon.

2nd Lieutenant Alexander Douglas Gillespie *(Argyll and Sutherland Highlanders) – who would be killed at Loos on 25 September – extract from letter home 5 May 1915 republished in his* Letters from Flanders *(1916):*

> This day began for me about midnight, as I lay in my dug-out in the breastwork watching the Plough swing slowly round. I shall remember that night; there was a heavy thunder-shower in the evening, but when we marched down it cleared away for a warm still summer night; still, that is, except for the snipers' rifles, and the rattle of the machine-guns, and sometimes the boom of a big gun far away, coming so long after the flash that

you had almost forgotten to expect it. The breast-work which we held ran through an orchard and along some hedge-rows. There was a sweet smell of wet earth and wet grass after the rain, and since I could not sleep, I wandered about among the ghostly cherry trees all in white, and watched the star-shells rising and falling to north and south. Presently misty moon came up, and a nightingale began to sing. I have only heard him once before, in the daytime, near Farl[e]y Mount, at Winchester; but, of course, I knew him at once, and it was strange to stand there and listen, for the song seemed to come all the more sweetly and clearly in the quiet intervals between the bursts of firing. There was something infinitely sweet and sad about it, as if the countryside were singing gently to itself, in the midst of all our noise and confusion and muddy work; so that you felt the nightingale's song was the only real thing which would remain when all the rest was long past and forgotten. It is such an old song too, handed on from nightingale to nightingale through the summer nights of so many innumerable years. ... So I stood there, and thought of all the men and women who had listened to that song, just as for the first few weeks after Tom was killed I found myself thinking perpetually of all the men who had been killed in battle – Hector and Achilles and all the heroes of long ago, who were once so strong and active, and now are so quiet. Gradually the night wore on, until day began to break, and I could see clearly the daisies and buttercups in the long grass about my feet. Then I gathered my platoon together, and marched back past the silent farms to our billets.

Ceasefire

Gillespie was but one of hundreds, perhaps thousands, of the volunteer soldiers of 1914–15 who thought of Homer's heroes, images, and similitudes up the line to death, sometimes as battle-cry, sometimes as companion, sometimes as witness to the pity and futility of war, brilliantly critiqued in Paul Fussell's *The Great War and Modern Memory* and admirably surveyed in Elizabeth Vandiver's *Stand in the Trench, Achilles: Classical Receptions in British Poetry of the Great War*. Sometimes letters and poems from or about the war used Homer as code whence fellow-Homerists could read expressions of gay love. Gillespie commemorated his friend Isaac Baillie Balfour by three names from the *Iliad* – Hector (the *Iliad*'s supreme sacrifice of a hero), Patroclus (the beloved of Achilles for whose death he kills and dishonours Hector), Nireus (surpassed in beauty only by Achilles himself). The *Iliad* ends in compassion triumphing over hatred and vengeance for the killing of lovers and children when King Priam of Troy risks his own life and majesty to beg Hector's body of Achilles. Ireland's supreme classicist poet Michael Longley wrote 'Ceasefire' in 1995 when a cessation of IRA warfare seemed in sight. The supreme lesson nationalism learned from Homer is the recognition of common humanity beyond murderous frontiers:

I.

Put in mind of his own father and moved to tears
Achilles took him by the hand and pushed the old king
Gently away, but Priam curled up at his feet and
Wept with him until their sadness filled the building.

II.

Taking Hector's corpse into his own hands Achilles
Made sure it was washed and, for the old king's sake,
Laid out in uniform, ready for Priam to carry
Wrapped like a present home to Troy at daybreak.

III.

When they had eaten together, it pleased them both
To stare at each other's beauty as lovers might,
 Achilles built like a god, Priam good-looking still
And full of conversation, who earlier had sighed:

IV.

'I get down on my knees and do what must be done
And kiss Achilles' hand, the killer of my son.'

CHAPTER FIVE
Romanising Britain

I.

Roman Virgil, thou that singest
Ilion's lofty temples robed in fire,
Ilion falling, Rome arising,
wars, and filial faith, and Dido's pyre;

II.

Landscape-lover, lord of language
more than he that sang the 'Works and Days',
All the chosen coin of fancy
flashing out from many a golden phrase;

III.

Thou that singest wheat and woodland,
tilth and vineyard, hive and horse and herd,
All the charm of all the Muses
often flowering in a lonely word;

IV.

Poet of the happy Tityrus
piping underneath his beechen bowers;
Poet of the poet-satyr
whom the laughing shepherd bound with flowers;

V.

Chanter of the Pollio, glorying
in the blissful years again to be,
Summers of the snakeless meadow,
unlaborious earth and oarless sea;

VI.

Thou that seëst Universal
Nature moved by Universal Mind;
Thou majestic in thy sadness
at the doubtful doom of human kind;

VII.

Light among the vanish'd ages;
star that gildest yet this phantom shore;
Golden branch amid the shadows,
kings and realms that pass to rise no more;

VIII.

Now thy Forum roars no longer,
fallen every purple Caesar's dome –
Though thine ocean-roll of rhythm
sound for ever of Imperial Rome –

IX.

Now the Rome of slaves hath perish'd,
and the Rome of freemen holds her place,
I, from out the Northern Island
sunder'd once from all the human race,

X.

I salute thee, Montovano,
I that loved thee since my day began,
Wielder of the stateliest measure
ever moulded by the lips of man.

Alfred 1st Baron Tennyson, 'To Virgil', written at the Request of the
Mantuans for the 19th Centenary of Virgil's Death, *Nineteenth Century* (September 1882).

Tennyson as Virgil's Keats

'TO VIRGIL' IS SUBLIME, as worthy of author and subject as is Keats's 'Chapman's Homer'. John Mackinnon Robertson ended 'The Art of Tennyson' (*Essays Towards a Critical Method* (1889)) by saluting:

> the old-time Tennyson giving us his swan-song, a worthy one indeed, in the nobly beautiful lines 'To Virgil'... In some such temper, borrowing his own melodious acclaim let us to the last salute that singer of our youth who is the Virgil of our time.

Robertson, born on the Isle of Arran and raised in Stirling, wrote as 30-year-old deputy editor of the first atheist MP Charles Bradlaugh's *National Reformer* and declared that 'national animosity' ought not become a 'critical standard'. He deplored the aged Tennyson's rejection of Gladstonian liberalism (including Home Rule for Ireland) in his Victorian Jubilee poem 'Locksley Hall 60 Years After', but welcomed 'To Virgil' as enabling surviving votaries of the young Tennyson to rejoice in their poet-prophet of ancient times, his own and Virgil's. Virgil had preached his Augustan nationalism so shrewdly that subsequent generations could rejoice in his supposed proto-Christianity or in his possible religious freedom, depending on one's own personal preference. Tennyson sometimes seemed haunted poetically by doubt rather than dogma, and in 'To Virgil' credited such refreshing ambiguity to himself and to Virgil alike. Robertson saw the poem's rich, if rationed, identification of the British poet with the Italian, whence Tennyson had asseverated UK nationalism the true heir of 1,900-year-old Augustan nationalism.

'To Virgil' certainly was magnificently representative of Victorian culture, in its courage as in its capitalism. With a fine commercial eye, it crassly declared the superiority of Virgil and his pastoral poems over Hesiod and his *Works and Days*. Hesiod had been a pioneer vital for Virgil's pastoral, but to depend on pioneers and then proclaim one's superiority to them had been standard competitive practice long before Queen Victoria. Tennyson owed far too much to Homer for such ingratitude, playing with marginal Homeric themes. Tennyson had also translated four or five *Iliad* passages of 20 lines

or so in 1863–4. 'To Virgil' might conclude commercially competitive as to Virgil's supremacy beyond all humanity in the 'stateliest
measure': Homer tells his story with pace too great for his *dramatis
personae* to over-stress the stately, while Virgil's work as Augustan
propagandist demanded stateliness to set the tone for the pomp of
empire and emperor. The Victorians enjoyed pomp, nowhere better in verse than when wielded by Tennyson the Poet Laureate as
necessary, particularly for the enhancement of salesmanship, acquisition and investment given a virtuous clothing in nationalism. 'To
Virgil' opened in good shopkeeper style by itemising the product's
high points while losing none of their magic when calling the total.
That window display started with the first verse high-lighting the
best-known glimpses of the *Aeneid*: Hollywood trailers work on the
same principle. 'To Virgil' then had the nerve to enter Virgil's pastoral
kingdom, work as a critic and deliberately play a Virgilian note, glo-
riously, the nine-Muse collaboration in the lonely word, the word in
question being evidently 'lonely'. It then happily stood capitalism on
its head by dreaming the supposedly Christian prophecy in Virgil's
Eclogue ('Pollio') which Dryden rendered (IV. 28–29, 22–24, 45–48):

> The serpent's brood shall die; the sacred ground
> Shall weeds and poisonous plants refuse to bear;
> ...
> Unbidden earth shall wreathing ivy bring,
> And fragrant herbs (the promises of spring),
> As her first offerings to her infant king.
> ...
> But when to ripened manhood he shall grow
> The greedy sailor shall the seas forego:
> No keel shall cut the waves for foreign ware;
> For every soil shall every product bear.

One charm of the fourth Eclogue is that the Christian may happily discover proof upon proof that it prophesies the Virgin birth of Christ, and
the secularist may tell himself with equal confidence that it does not.
Tennyson has more in mind than ambiguous compromise, and knows
that Virgil may haunt his reader with apprehensions of the future not

found in Homer. Tennyson plays with Virgil's possible doctrines and actual images then salutes Virgil himself as the golden bough, passport to Hades for Aeneas which alone can take its bearer among the dead to discover the history of past and future, thus making Virgil both the poet of Augustan nationalism and its guarantor. It mocks the complacency of the 18th century Enlightenment by declaring Virgil its great and superior progenitor, Eclogue and Georgic having prepared the horticultural ground on which Voltaire ended *Candide*, and Thomas Jefferson preached the agrarian ideal; but 'To Virgil' also made rich harvest from the Enlightenment's younger-spirited rival, Romanticism. Tennyson was uneasy with the Celtic heritage whether among ancient British or modern Irish rebels, but accepted the Norman appropriation of Welsh legends of King Arthur, anglicising him comfortably though not absurdly. 'To Virgil' naturally expected its readers to know, or at least know of, Tennyson's *Idylls of the King* drawn on Welsh Arthurian legend retold across a millennium from the original versions of what Lady Charlotte Guest would edit, translate and popularise as the *Mabinogion* to the vast-ranging if exhilarating narrations *King Arthur and his Knights* for Victorian children by Sir James Knowles who as editor of the *Nineteenth Century*, published 'To Virgil' in September 1882. Professor WW Robson claimed that *In Memoriam* 'unites the romantic and the classical. A personal voice, while never ceasing to be a personal voice, becomes at the great moments of the poem the voice of all humanity.' But Robson in 'The Present Value of Tennyson' (*The Definition of Literature and Other Essays* (1982)) declared the *Idylls*:

> a remarkable document rather than a remarkable poem. As an epic it seems factitious. It should be said in Tennyson's defence that no English writing has succeeded in making a whole epic out of the Arthurian material.... The Arthurian material still awaits its Virgil. Tennyson came nearer to being that than any other writer. But for me the *Idylls* live only in episodes and fragments, though a few of them contain some of Tennyson's finest poetry. They are not convincing evidence of his architectonic powers.

So Tennyson's was an impressive attempt to build a national myth for UK nationalism. Thomas Carlyle wrote Ralph Waldo Emerson on 27 January 1867:

> We read, at first Tennyson's *Idylls* with profound recognit[io]n of the finely elaborated execut[io]n, and also of the inward perfect[io]n of *vacancy*, and, to say truth, with considerable impatience at being treated so very like infants, tho the lollypops were so superlative.

His scorn was shrewd, showing the *Idylls*'s natural appeal to less exalted minds thus developing their UK nationalism, among them Charles Dickens meeting the first four *Idylls* in 1858 while creating *A Tale of Two Cities,* new in both theme and style, climaxing on English nationalism's triumphs over newly nationalist revolutionary France by Sydney Carton's self-sacrifice at the guillotine to save Charles Darnay and Miss Pross's killing Madame Defarge to save Lucie Manette: inspired by Carlyle's *French Revolution* yet also influenced by the *Idylls* of which he wrote to Wilkie Collins on 16 August 1859:

> I have just been reading Tennyson's *Idylls of the King.* Most gallant and noble. I doubt if any thing were ever done finer than the last – Guinevere. But they are all wonderfully fine – chivalric, imaginative, passionate, admirable.

Men died in World War I buoyed up by Virgil (and still more by Homer) rather than by King Arthur or his knights. Yet Tennyson's art could also reach beyond Virgil whom he had honoured so perceptively. Robson makes a startling contrast between Tennyson's *Idylls* and his 'Specimen of a Translation of the *Iliad* [VIII.550–54] in Blank Verse' (*Cornhill,* December 1863):

> But sometimes, as in Tennyson's translation of a famous passage of Homer, this very largeness is what gives consolation and perspective.

> As when in heaven the stars about the moon
> Look beautiful, when all the winds are laid,

And every height comes out, and jutting peak
And valley, and the innumerable heavens
Break open to their highest...

It follows a speech by Hector to the assembly of all the Trojans, a classic exercise in the rhetoric of nationalism in its fullest sense, where every person of the nation in question is told they have a vital task: that of the women is to light fires to prevent an Achaian counter-attack in the darkness, the fires when lit being analogised as stars in Tennyson's translation, or in Derby's full-length version:

As when in Heav'n, around the glitt'ring moon
The stars shine bright amid the breathless air;
And ev'ry crag, and ev'ry jutting peak
Stands boldly forth, and ev'ry forest glade;
Ev'n to the gates of Heaven is open'd wide
The boundless sky...

Robson takes us back to Keats's astronomical and globalised measurement of Homer. Tennyson and Derby did their bests, but nationalism in defence reaches artistic heights perhaps denied to nationalism in aggression, for all that Homer was describing, Virgil instructing. What nationalism we get from Homer, we take; what nationalism we get from Virgil, he gives us. 'To Virgil' had to be sublime: it could not spell out Virgil's genius in harnessing underworld and afterlife to Roman politics by having Aeneas – the ancestor and by implication the prototype of Augustus – behold Augustus himself as humanity's reward for the travails of Aeneas and the Trojans and of all subsequent Roman history. Instead 'To Virgil' cleverly takes the journey where Virgil could not go, forward from Augustus to imply the *Aeneid*'s prophesies still enlightened Britain. Homer remained immune, for all of Virgil's lootings and lacerations. Gladstone ('Homer and his Successors in Epic Poetry', *Quarterly Review* ci (January 1857) p. 84) saw the contrast as what his juniors might call professional as against amateur:

The sustained stateliness of diction, metre and rhythm
in the *Aeneid* is a feat, and an astounding feat; but it is
more like the performance of a trained athlete, between

trick and strength, than the grandeur of free and simple Nature, as it is seen in the ancient warrior, in Diomed or Achilles; or in Homer, the ancient warrior's only bard.

The poet from the machine

Gladstone excited rude remarks on his Homeric studies both in his time and since: in fact, he has had to wait until our time to receive his due credit. Gladstone's Homeric essays are frequently a delight to read, and his theses however questionable are developed with a master orator's skill. He would admit no superior to Homer in the creation of human character, but made clear his admiration for Virgil's victims of Aeneas – Dido and Turnus – and as for the hero so vital for nationalist epic:

> Upon the whole we are thrown back on the supposition that this crying vice of the *Aeneid*, the feebleness and untruth of the character of Aeneas, was due to the false position of Virgil, who was obliged to discharge his functions as a poet subject to his higher obligations and liabilities as a courtly parasite of Augustus. As the entire poem, so the character of the hero, was, before all other things, an instrument for glorifying the Emperor of Rome. It at once followed that in no respect must that character be such as to suggest a comparison disadvantageous to the person whose dignity, for political ends, had already been elevated even into the unseen world; nay, whose forestalled divinity was to be kept in a relation of absolute and broad superiority to the image of his human ancestor. Aeneas [actually his son Ascanius] is himself addressed in the action of the *Aeneid* [by Apollo] as '*Dis genite, et geniture deos*' [*Aeneid*.IX.42: 'begotten by gods, and begetter of gods']. First, take the measure of the cold and unheroic character of Augustus; then estimate the degree of relative superiority, which it was essential to Virgil's position that he should preserve for him throughout; and thus we may

come to some practical conception of the straitness of the space within which Virgil had to develop his Aeneas, or, in other words, to run his match against Homer. All the faults, and all the faultiness, of his poem may be really owing, none can say in how great a degree, to this original falseness of position.

The date – 1857 – is important here. Gladstone would subsequently prove one of the great – if not always the most consistent – critics of empire, especially of Disraeli's empire, and certainly ended his public life in awe-inspiring denunciation of Tory attempts to rule Ireland with the comparable imperial authoritarianism and unscrupulousness to those denounced by Roman authors. Anthony Trollope might disagree with Gladstone on many things in different ways at different times, and in *Phineas Redux* proved the supreme caricaturist of Gladstone and Disraeli in parliamentary conflict, but when reviewing Charles Merivale's *History of the Romans Under the Empire* (volume 3) for the anti-Catholic *Dublin University Magazine* (June 1851) Trollope sought to speak for his England – perhaps for his UK – first quoting Merivale's defence of the young Octavius, not yet Augustus:

> 'And it is difficult', says Mr Merivale, 'to pronounce a harsh judgment on his ambition. The security that was promised to him he felt to be illusory. His lot was cast in an age of revolution, in which Caesar's nephew must be the mark for all the bolts of fortune. The fearful alternative was manifestly forced upon him; he must grasp Caesar's power to secure himself from Caesar's fate.'
>
> We will agree with our author that it is difficult to blame his ambition; we may, perhaps, also acknowledge that after having entered on his ambitious career, it became impossible for him to save his own head without taking those of thousands of his countrymen; we may even have to declare that Rome required a despotic ruler, and that there was no one then on the world's stage so fit to rule as the young Octavius; but arguments such as these will not

reconcile the English reader to the character of the man. We will leave it to casuists and divines to say whether or no Octavius was wrong, and if wrong, when first he commenced his fault; but we want no casuists or divines to tell us that his character was odious to humanity and unworthy of sympathy. But what Roman ever required the sympathy of any one?

Merivale was an attractive writer, whose differences with Gladstone on Augustus did not prevent the offer of Cambridge's Regius Professorship of Modern [*sic*] History in 1869 when Gladstone was Prime Minister; he refused it but accepted the Deanship of Ely. Augustus and therefore Augusta became popular names in aristocratic England after the Hanoverians imported German tastes. Their most formidable impact on UK nomenclature appears in Wilde's *The Importance of Being Earnest*: Aunt Augusta (otherwise Lady Bracknell) – and, of course, Ernest. The *Aeneid* was but a part, though probably the most immortal part, of reinventing Roman nationalism to establish Augustan tone which then outlived the Emperor, his reforms, his dynasty, his Empire, and his language. The *Aeneid*'s form of nationalism proved immensely durable, animating the Empires of Rome, Constantinople, the Papacy, Charlemagne, the Habsburgs, the Stuarts, the Bourbons, Napoleon and Victoria. Caesar of Caesar Augustus was transmitted in the various Kaisers of various German regimes, and the Czars of Russia.

From Aeneas onwards countless persons of consequence in the history of Rome (with such notable exceptions as Julius and Augustus Caesar) came from somewhere else, which helped make devotion to the metropolis a sacrifice into which one's birth, religion, language or other bases of original piety were dissolved. The metropolis at the heart of one's nationalism and its consequent impatience with the provincial cultures it outgrew, characterises the UK nationalism of today, especially when Oxford and Cambridge are included as outlying metropolitan posts. Dublin was notoriously the least Irish part of Ireland from its Norse foundation to its English administrators, but even as rural guerrilla forces made gains during the Anglo-Irish war of 1919–21 they sang 'We're off to Dublin in the green, in the green'. Judaeo-Christian scriptures carry perpetual denunciations of the cities as hearts of corruption from Sodom to Rome, but temples and bishoprics settled among them with majestic complacency. Monarchy under Augustus changed from identification with archaic tyranny or barbarian superstition, so that today the monarchical principle is taken to bestow excessive power on kings, sultans, dictators, party leaders, business tycoons, and university principals. Gladstone smouldered with anger in 1857 at the *Aeneid's* veneration of Augustus, which fuelled his own subsequent far-sighted view of the perils of politicised monarchy under Disraeli and its cultural evangelists such as his old friend Tennyson, but he might have been more appalled by a recent scholarly thesis that Virgil was not just flattering a patron but adoring a lover. Bard and chieftain had such relationships in Celtic civilisation, metaphorically or physically, and if true of the making of the *Aeneid* it gives Virgil a nobler motivation.

Pius Aeneas accurately designated Aeneas as having constantly exhibited his devotion to his household gods as well as to the Roman versions of the Olympian gods, notably his mother Venus. Schoolchild Anglophones would naturally render it 'pious Aeneas', thus feeding cults of Victorian imperial generals indistinguishable from Sunday-school models. The *Aeneid*, sweated in classrooms of all Christian denominations, warmed the juvenile imperial mind and conveyed the Heaven-sent superiority of the adult imperialists. Popular fiction for children followed its recipe: clear partisanship for the imperial heroes, and endless thrilling adventures, monsters galore, hairsbreadth escapes by which Virgil won the concealed admiration of his conscripted youthful scholars. Nationalism often progresses by identification with a woman, such as the eponymous *Cathleen Ni Houlihan* in Lady Gregory's and WB Yeats's play where Ireland as an old woman is rejuvenated by a bridegroom when he leaves his intended bride so that he can fight and presumably die supporting the invasion of Connacht by Revolutionary French soldiers in 1798. The play notoriously made young men feel they ought to go out and die for Ireland. The yearning for bloodshed was omnipresent throughout Europe in the early 20th century among nations at the zenith of their power or nations not yet states.

St Augustine Bishop of Hippo, from *CONFESSIONS* (397–400 AD), translated by Edward Bouverie Pusey (1874):

I was forced to learn about the wanderings of one Aeneas, forgetful of my own, and to weep for dead Dido, because she killed herself for love; the while, with dry eyes, I endured my miserable self dying among these things, far from You, O God my life.

What is more miserable than a miserable being who commiserates not himself; weeping the death of Dido for love to Aeneas, but weeping not his own death for want of love to You, O God? You light of my heart, You bread of my inmost soul, You whose power gave vigor to my mind, who quicken my thoughts. I loved You not. I committed fornication against You, [Psalm lxxii.27]; and all round me thus fornicating there echoed 'Well done! well done!' [Psalm xxxiv.21; Psalm xxxix.16] for the friendship of this world is fornication against You [James iv.4]; and 'Well done! well done!' echoes on till one is ashamed not to be thus a man. And for all this I wept not, I who wept for Dido slain, and 'seeking by the sword a stroke and wound extreme', myself seeking the while a worse extreme, the extremest and lowest of Your creatures, having forsaken You, earth passing into the earth. And if forbidden to read all this, I was grieved that I might not read what grieved me. Madness like this is thought a higher and a richer learning, than that by which I learned to read and write....

If, again, I should ask which might be forgotten with least detriment to the concerns of life, reading and writing or these poetic fictions, who does not foresee what all must answer who have not entirely forgotten themselves? I sinned, then, when as a boy I preferred those empty to those more profitable studies, or rather loved the one and hated the other. 'One and one, two'; 'two and two, four': this was to me a hateful singsong; 'the wooden horse lined with armed men', and 'the burning of Troy', and '[Aeneas's first wife] Creusa's shade and sad similitude' were the choice spectacle of my vanity.

We are St Augustine

Augustine's *Confessions* teach by Platonic dialogue, but where Plato has Socrates triumph over the other interlocutor, God is in dialogue with Augustine and by definition must triumph. There is of course a third party, the reader or hearer, of whom Plato or Augustine must be supremely – if silently – conscious. The relation of each one to the others will change as their identities change. We probably know far less about God than Augustine did, but some – no doubt very few – may know Him better. We are Augustine's schoolmates in preferring stories to grammar while believing we are wrong to do so. God – as Jesus Christ – taught by telling stories in which he warned against thinking the formalities of worship – its grammar – are superior to what a story tells. He also warned that we may not realise the true lesson that a story teaches. Augustine knows that God is truth and only truth can be heard from Him and only truth should be spoken to Him. The *Confessions* not only tell the truth, but they also give it away. They show that when remembering and abominating his youthful sins, something fairly harmless may remain still holding ghostly charm from original sin.

Dido still lives for Augustine not simply in Books I and IV of the *Aeneid*, the obvious clue being his continued necessity to express his contempt for Aeneas who betrayed her: he may no longer love her, but he can at least hate her greatest enemy, whom the young Augustine saw was less worthy of her than *he* would have been. Her place as Queen of Carthage gave her an ideal location on which local traditions looked back strengthening themselves into nationalism. Carthage was the great former great seaport 150 miles eastward of his own birthplace Thagaste and of his bishopric Hippo north of Thagaste on the Mediterranean coast. Thus to him in his boyhood Dido appealed as a martyr myth and a local landmark. Virgil held his readers of posterity, friends and enemies alike in thrall, to affirm however critically that the Augustan state defined political society. In 410AD Alaric the Goth sacked Rome. In 415, Augustine started on Book V of his monumental *The City of God* in which his ideal nationalism proclaimed the city of God in heaven (*patria*), but while on earth God would permit a nationalism to exist apparently as the best of inadequate choices. Here Augustine's wild schoolboy oats, harvested with the *Aeneid*, could testify to the world Augustus made and Virgil preached, now in 415 threatened by the Goths. The Second Book of the *Aeneid* naturally populated Augustine's imagination in facing up to the implications of the fall of Rome, and probably returned as he was dying during the Vandal siege of his own episcopal city, Hippo. *The City of God* (413–26AD) recorded Roman history as beginning with love of liberty becoming zest for domination, quoting Virgil first from *Aeneid* VIII.646–49 where Aeneas's shield prophesies Rome's thwarting the Etruscan king Lars Porsena's attempt to restore Rome's expelled royal family the Tarquins (Dryden version):

> There, Porsena to Rome, proud Tarquin brings;
> And would by force restore the banished kings:
> One tyrant for his fellow-tyrant fights:
> The Roman youth assert their native rights.

Turning back to *Aeneid* 1.279–85 Augustine found a good example of liberty turning to tyranny in Jupiter's promise to Venus that all would go well with her son Aeneas the Trojan refugee and his Roman descendants:

> E'en haughty Juno, who, with endless broils,
> Earth, seas, and heaven, and Jove himself, turmoils,
> At length atoned, her friendly power shall join,
> To cherish and advance the Trojan line.
> The subject world shall Rome's dominion own,
> And, prostrate, shall adore the nation of the gown.
> An age is ripening in revolving fate,
> When Troy shall overturn the Grecian state,
> And sweet revenge her conquering sons shall call,
> To crush the people that conspired her fall.

Roman nationalism invited sympathy when struggling for liberty but in itself found dominion so attractive as to be counted amongst its greatest glories. Augustine noted that Virgil's method represented Jupiter prophesying the future while the poet himself recalled the past (mythological, historical and theological inextricably inter-mingled) in the light of the present which he sought to control. He asserted Rome's superiority to other nations in the priority it placed on rule, command, conquest, subjection, for which above all Augustine returned to Aeneas's reception of prophesies from his dead father (*Aeneid* VI. 847–53, Dryden version):

> Let others better mould the running mass
> Of metals, and inform the breathing brass,
> And soften into flesh a marble face;
> Plead better at the bar; describe the skies;
> And when the stars descend, and when they rise.
> But Rome! 'tis thine alone, with awful sway,
> To rule mankind, and make the world obey:
> Disposing peace and war thy own majestic way.
> To tame the proud, the fettered slave to free,
> These are imperial arts, and worthy thee.

St Augustine then pointed out that Romans maintained skill in command better when they were less self-indulgent in greed, in swindling, and in buying responsive stage-actors. These lines from the *Aeneid* attracted many future readers, notably builders of UK nationalism beginning with its father, James VI/I, who concluded his *Basilikon Doron* ['the kingly gift' in Greek] with a quotation of the passage in its original Latin: a virtual proclamation that he saw his own kingship as the descendant of Augustus's empire according to Virgil. The prolific English thriller-writer Edgar Wallace began his *Room 13* on a satirical note with prisoners parading from their daily labour under the archway bearing the words '*parcere subjectis* [to spare the vanquished]', which Wallace pointed out was meaningless pretension however self-gratifying to the UK authorities building it to house convicts who would neither be vanquished nor spared. Professor Richard Jenkyns's magisterial *Virgil's Experience: Nature and History; Times, Names, Places* accords with Wallace's irony, pointing out that Virgil knew all too well how little the Romans spared the vanquished. If the thesis of Virgil's love for Augustus is correct, the words are a pitiful prayer rather than a prophecy.

And a little child shall lead them

Macaulay was prompted by the same passage in the last of his four *Lays of Ancient Rome* 'The Prophecy of Capys' supposedly sung by the victorious Romans when they had at last defeated King Pyrrhus of Epirus and his south Italian ally Tarentum (275BCE). Their celebration imagines a prophecy supposedly made to Romulus future founder of Rome about his militaristic posterity whose preference for war partly derived from Romulus's having been fathered by Mars and wet-nursed by a wolf:

> '... And such as is the War-god,
>   The author of thy line,
> And such as she who suckled thee,
>   Even such be thou and thine.
> Leave to the soft Campanian
>   His baths and his perfumes;
> Leave to the sordid race of Tyre
>   Their dying-vats and looms:
> Leave to the sons of Carthage
>   The rudder and the oar:
> Leave to the Greek his marble Nymphs
>   And scrolls of wordy lore.
>
> 'Thine, Roman, is the pilum:
>   Roman, the sword is thine,
> The even trench, the bristling mound,
>   The legion's ordered line;
> And thine the wheels of triumph,
>   Which with their laurelled train
> Move slowly up the shouting streets
>   To Jove's eternal fane. ... '

Macaulay wrote his *Lays* as an experiment, to imagine what songs the Romans of the early Republic might have made up about their own history, but the book rapidly became a UK best-seller. *Lays* was recited by teachers and schoolchildren across the British Empire, and almost invisibly identified with UK nationalism and each of its component parents. But in popularity, in recital, and when performed in children's games, the first lay, 'Horatius', was the favourite, and then 'The Battle of Lake Regillus', successive episodes in the fabled defence of Rome against return of the Tarquins' tyranny. Those lays were songs of liberty, as was the class conflict when the plebeians revolted against patrician lust and law, 'Virginia'. The cult of liberty was necessary to enhance the cult of domination, insular and imperial. Macaulay's great-grand-nephew Theodore Macaulay Trevelyan who died aged five in 1911 had organised endless games enacting while reciting 'Horatius' and later 'Lake Regillus', the supreme line being Horatius's own declaration before leading two others to defend the bridge to Rome until behind them the consul and citizens had torn it down so that Rome would be secure behind the river Tiber:

> Then out spake brave Horatius
> The Captain of the gate.
> 'To every man upon this earth
> Death cometh soon or late.
> And how can man die better
> Than facing fearful odds,
> For the ashes of his fathers,
> And the temples of his gods,
>
> 'And for the tender mother
> Who dandled him to rest,
> And for the wife who nurses
> His baby at her breast,
> And for the holy maidens
> Who feed the eternal flame
> To save them from false Sextus
> That wrought the deed of shame?...'

The story of Horatius came from the history of Rome by Titus Livius, *Ab Urbe Condita* II.10, probably written in 30BCE or shortly thereafter.

Horatius's war-cry may have been originated by Macaulay, English but reflecting his Scottish Highland ancestry. It partly evolved from the personalisation of nationalism with Ireland, England, Scotland, Britain, each treated as a resolute but vulnerable virtuous woman or else a bardic seer. It was deeply personal to Macaulay himself, his sisters living and dead and his infant niece being those persons he loved most in all the world. It was nationalism defending liberty minimalised within every grasp, preserving sibling or offspring, confronting the enemy as a physical personal enemy. In perhaps the most ceremonial literary occasion recording the zenith of UK criticism on UK nationalism's self-described leadership, *The Times Literary Supplement* on 30 April 1954 captioned its massive front-page review of the sixth and last volume of Winston Churchill's *The Second World War*: 'AND HOW CAN MAN DIE BETTER?' Churchill, a devoted reader of Macaulay, had named the Battle of Britain in contemporary broadcast and the Blitz in memorial retrospect as the finest hour of UK history, and Horatius in mid-19th century English verse commemorating glorious Roman mythology was exactly the requisite expression of nationalism. There was a reciprocal element. In Theo's lifetime his father George Macaulay Trevelyan, popular prolific Whig historian, produced three action-packed volumes on Giuseppe Garibaldi, best-selling narratives of Italian nationalism appropriately followed by *Scenes from Italy's War* created after his service as ambulance-driver where the Italians fought in World War I.

Nationalism likes untarnished heroes written up by reasonably sophisticated historians celebrating relatively simple men, inspired by the dangerous superstition that a soldier is in some way more virtuous than men without military service. Garibaldi's honest paganism and innocence of intrigue contrasted with both the ideologue veteran Giuseppe Mazzini, leader of the republicans ruling Rome after Pope Pius IX's flight to Gaeta in 1848–49, and the diplomatic genius Count Camillo Cavour who turned Garibaldi's conquest of Sicily and southern Italy in 1860 into unification of the entire peninsula under his master King Victor Emmanuel. The Garibaldi trilogy happily rounded off boyhood dreams of Roman heroes headed by Horatius, commemorated in his wife

Janet Penrose Trevelyan's dedication of her *A Short History of the Italian People* to the memory of their Theo and his love of the Roman heroes. Rome was thus the ancestor and the protégé of UK nationalism.

The Garibaldi cult comfortably included the destruction of Papal secular power in Rome and nationalisation of the extensive mid-Italian Papal states. Garibaldi in history remained more agreeable to the atheist Trevelyans than the devious anticlerical but personally Catholic Cavour. Yet George Trevelyan took pains to show the heroism of the pathetic Irish brigade fighting for the Pope against the Italian nationalists in 1860 when 'the identification between [Irish] nationalism and Catholicism was securing new allies' (R Dudley Edwards, *Ireland and the Italian Risorgimento* (1960: p.40)), and although Protestant Britain had added a dimension to its nationalism by vociferous journalistic testimony for the Risorgimento GM Trevelyan was nevertheless a lifelong advocate of Irish Home Rule. The Whigs had ended Catholic rule in our archipelago in 1688 but they had championed Catholic Emancipation won in 1829 by Daniel O'Connell, as duly recorded with enthusiasm by Trevelyan in *British History in the Nineteenth Century* thus proving himself a UK nationalist, not merely English or British.

Scottish nationalism before Scotland

A delicate balance was required for UK nationalism, or its component parts, when looking at the beginning of the nation or nations' stories of Roman conquest. English nationalism glosses over the historical irrelevance of the Roman Empire to the English despite their zealous attempts to claim the inheritance. Our ancestors in this archipelago were either subjects, slaves, victims, docile creatures, servile in hopes of profit, and unsettled by urbanisation replacing their rural freedom – or else uncouth enemy raiders, thieves, pirates, smugglers, natives disappointing future seekers for snobbish ancestry, or ultimate butchers of the Romanised. Did many survive Roman conquest long enough to become anyone's ancestors? The English invaders were usually a subsequent post-Roman historical stage. The Welsh recalled that they had produced a number of Roman emperors themselves, the Irish that the Romans never reached Ireland (except when Romans or Romanized natives such as St Patrick were kidnapped to be enslaved by the Irish). The Scottish writer Naomi Michison showed that our real affinities with Roman times are probably with losers in *The Conquered*. Vercingetorix and the Gauls defeated by Caesar show what nationalism might have existed two millennia before us.

Peoples in what many centuries later became Scotland sustained an appalling defeat in 83AD, supposedly prefaced by an immortal speech from a Pictish commander, Calgacus. Its Latin translation appears in Publius Cornelius Tacitus's first work, *Agricola*: the life of the commander in that battle, Gnaeus Julius Agricola. Almost all classicists believe that Tacitus invented the text. It contains some phrases paralleled in major Latin writers. Historians from Herodotus and Thucydides onward invented what they thought appropriate when including a major speech, and in later writings so did Tacitus. *Agricola* was his first work, probably more personal than anything else he wrote, being the husband of Agricola's daughter. He seems to have liked his father-in-law, and used immediate personal sources in Agricola's wife and daughter. Professor Anthony Birley, translator and interpreter of *Agricola*, thought it likely that Tacitus had served in Britain under Agricola: hence he may even have heard Agricola's speech and been present when Agricola received an account of Calgacus's speech. Professor JB Rives (revising notes for the Penguin *Agricola*) credits Tacitus with also having forged Agricola's speech before the Battle of Mons Graupius: even if Tacitus had not heard that, his mother-in-law should have, or would have known its content, as might Tacitus's wife. Would they have allowed son-in-law or husband pass off his own work in place of their dead hero's last battle speech?

Agricola was born in 40AD and married Domitia Decidiana 21 years later, their first son born in dying in infancy the following year. Their daughter was born in 63AD and married the young Tacitus in 76–7AD. Agricola was Governor of Britain from 77 and the Battle of Mons Graupius was fought in Autumn 83, Agricola was recalled by the Emperor Domitian in 84, and died in 93. Tacitus mentions conversations with Agricola including reminiscences shared with the family, and whether or not he took notes he may have outlined a memoir long before Agricola's death. *Agricola* remembers Agricola's Governorship of Britain, his second son's death seen in recollection, indicating Domitia Decidiana accompanied her husband. Tacitus says his father-in-law showed nothing like normal male artificial 'stiff upper lip' or female open grief, which probably meant visible contrast between Agricola and his wife. Did Tacitus himself fight at Mons Graupius or receive accounts of it from his mother-in-law, in either case overhearing or being told reports from spies, interpreters, traitors, captives?

Calgacus may have addressed his troops in Pictish, old Irish, or old Welsh. The great Celtic scholar Kenneth Jackson found his name derived from Gaelic 'colgach' meaning 'swordsman': Celtic myths glorify chieftainly swordsmanship. Calgacus's speech has touches of possible authenticity in its mistakes. Why should a bogus Calgacus include things Tacitus knew were false, such as a rising from the Brigantes in north Britain, or saying the Romans had no wives with them? The entire speech is probably inauthentic. Agricola, Domitia Decidiana, their daughter, or Tacitus himself might easily remember certain phrases reported to the Romans in translation. The prime candidate is of course '*solitudinem faciunt, pacem appellant*', immortalising Calgacus's name far beyond Latinate circles. It was in active use as Scottish nationalism grew during the Thatcher era, when one Scottish aqueduct was ornamented at great danger to the lives and limbs of the perpetrators, with mighty lettering below the uppermost rim 'SCOTLAND FREE OR A DESERT'. The original read 'to rob, butcher, rape, the liars call empire, and where they make a desert call it peace'. If Calgacus's entire speech was an invention, the young Tacitus had a very well-informed imagination. Calgacus's last words were 'Into battle, thinking of your ancestors and descendants!'; the Easter Week Rising was justified as 'for generations dead and generations yet unborn!'. As for those natives self-conforming to Roman style, Mary Beard's *SPQR* ((2016) p. 495) conscripts *Agricola* 'They called it, in their ignorance, "civilisation", but it was really part of their enslavement'

From Conor Cruise O'Brien, *God Land: Reflections on Religion and Nationalism* (1988):

The decisive event in the territorialisation, and ultimately the nationalization, of Christianity was the reception, beginning with Constantine and codified by Theodosius, of Nicene Christianity as the official cult of the Roman Empire. Christ has said that His kingdom was not of this world, but the cult of Christ now becomes that of a worldly empire and is about to become the cult of many kings and princes. And official Christianity has to adapt itself to the heritage of classical antiquity. Between the Christian and his God there is now inserted a political layer, first in the form of the Imperial Court. Eusebius of Caesarea wrote: 'Invested as he is with a semblance [*mimesis*] of heavenly sovereignty, [the Emperor] directs his gaze above, and frames his earthly government according to the patterns of that divine original, feeling strength in conformity to the monarchy of God.'

The new intermediate political layer between Earth and Heaven is continuous with the old pre-Christian Roman Empire, which, in its most admired aspects, becomes partly Christianized in retrospect. Addressing an ecclesiastical assembly, according to Eusebius, Constantine developed an exegesis of Virgil's Fourth Eclogue (line 5): *Magnus ab Integro saeclorum nascitur ordo.* ['The last great age, foretold by sacred rhymes, Renews the finished course' – Dryden trans.] The newborn 'order of the ages' prophesied in the Fourth Eclogue is now identified with Christianity. This provided Christianity with classical legitimation, and made the Christian Emperor the fulfilment of the classical past, rather than a deviation from it. At the same time Christianity itself became contaminated – as some earlier Christians might have seen the nature of the change – by the classical and pagan heritage. And that heritage included the deliberately exalted Roman nationalism of the Age of Augustus.

The acceptance of Virgil as a central figure in the culture of medieval Christianity is of critical importance. In medieval iconography Virgil figures as a prophet, side by side with David and Isaiah. Not only the Fourth Eclogue but the *Aeneid* acquires quasi-Scriptural status. And the *Aeneid* is a school of Roman patriotism.

Virgil's special status long outlasted the Empire of Constantine and his successors; it even outlasted the Middle Ages. Italians like Dante were especially susceptible to nationalism in its Virgilian form. But other nations, too, could come to see themselves as the true heirs of the Empire, the new Romans. Medieval Germans saw themselves in that light, so did the French of the Revolutionary period, so did the Victorian English. And the American Founding Fathers ... could think of America as being the true Chosen People, the new Israel, and also as transfigured Romans, the true objects of the sibylline prophecy of the fourth Eclogue.

Nothing in the classical heritage was equivalent to the Old Testament concept of the Covenant. Yet classical antiquity had its own way of linking the idea of a given land to the idea of the divine. This was the cult of heroes who had died for the *polis*, the *respublica*, or the *patria*. Pericles placed the first victims of the Peloponnesian War among the immortals. And Virgil's Aeneas saw on the Elysian Plains the spirits of those who had suffered for the fatherland, 'their brows bound with snowy fillets', equivalents of martyrs' crowns. (The *Aeneid* had its own version of a Promised Land: Italy, as promised to the Trojans by the Cumaean sibyl.)

The classical cult of the *patria* and its martyrs was about to become part of the heritage of medieval Christianity, further despiritualizing it, localizing it, and binding it to the earth.

Initially, Christian thinkers had tried to cope with the cult of the *patria* by using the exact same strategy on what we may call the classical front as they had used on the Old Testament front. They had rejected the cult of the *patria* in its literal and earthbound sense, while adopting it in a new spiritual sense. Saint

Augustine is explicit both about the rejection and about the adoption. 'Why should that man be praised?' he asks. 'Because he was a lover of his city? That he could be carnally ... But he was not a lover of the city above.' In Book v of *The City of God* Augustine cites the great deeds of individual Romans for their purely terrestrial *patria* in order to encourage Christians to even more heroic deeds for their *patria aeterna*.

So the Roman *Patria* joins the Jewish Promised Land, and fuses with it in the Sky. Intellectually, and as an aspect of Christianity, the Augustinian celestial synthesis proved remarkably durable. Nearly a thousand years later Peter Abelard, in one verse of his great hymn *Sabbato ad Vesperas*, exhorts his hearers to lift up their minds to their *patria* in heaven and to return to the heavenly Jerusalem out of Babylonian exile.

> *Nostrum est interim mentem erigere*
> *Et totis patriam votis appetere*
> *Et ad Jerusalem a Babylonia*
> *Post longa regredi tandem exsilia.*

> We must lift up our mind
> And seek the *patria* with all our vows
> And return after long exile
> Out of Babylon to Jerusalem.

The hymn is set to the beat of the march of those same legions who had destroyed the earthly Jerusalem more than a thousand years before.

CHAPTER SIX

King James, Shakespeare and the Great British Play

'...You know my methods in such cases, Watson: I put
myself in the man's place, and having first gauged his intelligence, I try to imagine how I should myself have proceeded
under the same circumstances. In this case the matter was
simplified by Brunton's intelligence being quite first rate, so
that it was unnecessary to make any allowance for the personal equation, as the astronomers have dubbed it. ...'

Arthur Conan Doyle, 'The Musgrave Ritual' *Strand* v (May 1893)

A play for a Scottish king

CONAN DOYLE'S SHERLOCK HOLMES stories are exceptionally useful
to the working historian. For their teaching hints for research and
observation largely derived from the author's training in Medicine at
the University of Edinburgh: medical and historical diagnoses often
present similar and sometimes identical problems. 'The Musgrave
Ritual' partly turns on the intellectual contrast between employer
and servant:

'You will excuse me, Musgrave, if I say that your butler
appears to me to have been a very clever man, and to have
had a clearer insight than ten generations of his masters.'
'I hardly follow you', said Musgrave...

Conan Doyle's disciple, PG Wodehouse, was to make this the basis
of his Jeeves-Wooster stories. The historian should allow for differences in intellect between themselves and whoever they may

write about. Most of us are inferior in intellect to Holmes and Jeeves, and to the men who made them. William Shakespeare and King James VI and I, the most intellectual King to have ruled Scotland and England, are minds so much greater than mine, and probably than yours, that we are out of our depth and had better remember it. King James was absurdly undervalued by historians until recently. Like many other wise persons, he would make silly jokes and appear absurd to soothe or to exploit the stupidity of persons presented to him: Abraham Lincoln played this very same game. Having been King of Scotland for 35 years, James came peacefully to the English throne better trained for kingship than other kings ancient and modern. He succeeded Elizabeth I on 24 March 1603, set off for London on 4 April, reached it by 3 May, and on 19 May ordained that the Lord Chamberlain's [theatre] Company was now to be known as the King's Company. He was thus the patron of its playwright, William Shakespeare. His language could be decidedly theatrical, and he thought of kingship in stage terms, beginning the preface for new readers to the English edition of his *Basilikon Doron*:

> For Kings being publike persons, by reason of their office,
> and authoritie, are as it were set (as it was saide of olde)
> upon a publicke stage, in the sight of all the people; where
> all the beholders eyes are attentiuelie bent, to look and
> pry in the least circumstance of their secretest driftes.

This London edition was available to Shakespeare, almost inviting him to try his hand at staging kingship in performance by an intellectual king, or an intellectual Duke. *Measure for Measure* – first performed in 1604 – did not caricature James, but it was careful to bring to humiliating contrition any who tried to mock the Duke. The play's Duke of Vienna certainly revealed a dignified cunning in court intrigue, and it ruthlessly exposed his deputy – the puritan Angelo – as a hypocrite, a lecher, and a fortune-hunter. In fact, the play is a strong lesson on puritans' injustice when given authority. This detestation of puritans opened up common ground between king and playwright: James hated puritan rule over his boyhood, and puritan reprimand in his manhood, while Shakespeare stood in constant danger of puritans closing his playhouse down.

Shakespeare and Scotland (2004, edited by Willy Maley and Andrew Murphy) noted that James's first speech to the English Parliament in 1604 clearly showed study of John of Gaunt's dying speeches in *Richard II*, Shakespeare's most famous English nationalist oration. Where Shakespeare in 1595 had made Gaunt praise England while speaking of it as though England were an island, James used such rhetoric to make the island and its unification a God-given gift and demand. Moreover, he told Parliament that just as his great-grandfather Henry VII had united the feuding houses of Lancaster and York, so James would unite England and Scotland. Much the most attractive means available for James to study the Wars of the Roses would have been through the printed texts of Shakespeare's three *Henry VI* plays and *Richard III* (all printed between 1594 and 1597) as well as the other tetralogy, *Richard II*, the two *Henry IV* plays and *Henry V* (printed between 1597 and 1600). These plays seem the most likely explanation of his rapid adoption of Shakespeare's company, possibly on a tip-off by his London agents. They were, so to speak, beautiful and useful. In Scotland he had hosted poets and other artists in performance, and clearly looked forward to a London culture more favourable to theatre than Calvinist Scotland was. James, being a student of many written texts, should have been interested in the company playwright from the outset.

Had he seen or heard report of a first performance of *Hamlet* in 1601 including what from his vantage-point was a happy ending: namely Fortinbras, the prince of a neighbouring and frequently hostile country, being suddenly declared the new king, which James obviously hoped would happen when Queen Elizabeth Tudor died? He had to anticipate any number of political revolutions, intrigues and attempted regicides, had survived plenty in his time, and knew that plays by an intelligent observer of England might tell him a great deal. And why did this *Hamlet* end on Fortinbras Rex? Was its playwright making a propaganda point favouring a Scottish king for England? In any event, James became king but plague closed the theatres until 1604, and when reassembled his company determined to rise to the occasion with a Scottish play. King James had had prayers said throughout the Church of Scotland giving thanks to

God on every 5th of August for his own deliverance from the Gowrie conspiracy on that day in 1600, and gave similar instructions on becoming Supreme Head of the Church of England. So in December 1604 the King's Men staged *The Tragedie of Gowrie* whose author we do not know but may guess. It ran with great success for two nights, attracting 'exceeding concourse of all sorts of people' (wrote John Chamberlain in a private letter) and then was disappeared:

> Whether the matter or manner be not well handled, or
> that it be thought that princes should be put on the stage
> in their life time, I hear that some great councillors are
> much displeased with it.

This seems to have been all that Chamberlain heard. Other productions falling foul of the authorities were answered by censorship, imprisonment, or both. King James had commissioned prayers – not plays – to commemorate Gowrie, but he also wanted his King's Men to be his allies, not his enemies. He sought to unify the country partly by making its king an icon winning national reverence, and knew that Scots were staged to appear inferior of the English. He was too shrewd to ignore the potential value of theatre in his support, and initially turned to where theatre chiefly flourished in Scotland: the pulpit.

He demanded a sermon from every Scottish minister thanking God for his deliverance on every 5th of August. It was understood that congregations did not need to be told details of the Gowrie affair, not to be called a 'tragedy' since only the Earl of Gowrie and his brother had been killed. The delicate situation was that on 5 August 1600 James had allegedly been entrapped in Gowrie House, Perth, by James Ruthven 3rd Earl of Gowrie and his brother Alexander the Master of Ruthven with intent to murder him. The Ruthvens were tough nuts, certainly. Patrick 3rd Lord Ruthven had risen from his deathbed on 9 March 1566 to join in the murder of David Riccio, Secretary of Mary Queen of Scots killed in her presence whilst pregnant with the future King James VI, after which the repulsive Ruthven fled to England and died there. His son, William 1st Earl of Gowrie, kidnapped the teenage king in 1582 and held him for a year – he was later beheaded for it in 1584. *His* sons were the alleged miscreants killed during James's visit to Gowrie House on 5 August 1600. There were alternative hypotheses, such as James perhaps making a pass at the master, Alexander, a handsome 19-year-old, who might have rejected it with violence. As English king in London in 1603, James wanted English prayers for his deliverance at Gowrie without any English questions. James and his minions could be rough enough when taking a play in dislike: Shakespeare's friend and fellow-playwright Ben Jonson was imprisoned between August and November 1605 for *Eastward Ho!,* a play deploying anti-Scottish satire. No punishment fell on the King's Men for the *Tragedie of Gowrie* whatever its contents, save its disappearance. The King's Men performed *Othello* at Whitehall and *The Merry Wives of Windsor* at Court in November 1604, and *Measure for Measure* on 26 December 1604, a comforting signal that the King's Men were in the clear. James could hardly have met Shakespeare before the *Gowrie* production, but now was the time.

A British King for a play

What were the King's Men to do now? *Measure for Measure*'s premiere on the morrow of Christmas 1604 should have held James in some degree of appreciative benevolence, recognising himself – or rather his *Basilikon Doron* – as a major source. Having been caught wrong in a Scottish play, they needed to do something Scottish before somebody else cashed in on the idea and won higher favour in court. The obvious decision was to call on the King, quickly deplore their former ill-chosen subject, express their anxiety to honour him with a Scottish play, and enquire his Majesty's pleasure. A performance of *Measure for Measure* in front of the king might enable such a meeting. James might well have been pleased by the finale when Duke, almost universally merciful, orders Lucio to marry a whore for 'Slandering a Prince' which might neatly ask pardon for *Gowrie*. It's most likely that the king told the king's Company that if they wanted to stage a Scottish play, choose a subject 500 years earlier, such as the reign of Macbeth (more accurately Mac Bethad) 1040–57, of which

Raphael Holinshed's *Chronicles* presented a convenient account. The inevitable scholarly conversation with James would have established Shakespeare's frequent use of Holinshed. Macbeth would have been no casual choice for James, and after the *Gowrie* disaster Shakespeare knew James's choice must be honoured. The play would have a conclusion of political symbolism: England would save Scotland, the final symbol in this play. 'England' overthrowing Mac Bethad had actually been an invasion in 1054 by Earl Siward of Northumbria (more Viking than English), and Mac Bethad had been defeated rather than ousted, to be killed in 1057 by Malcolm III.

In 1604, James had a clear agenda: the invention of the nation of Great Britain, not simply a seat on two thrones, three if you included Ireland. To bring Great Britain to birth meant that its king must create a new nationalism to sway the English and Scottish Parliaments in favour of their union. The invention of a nationalism might seem involuntary: it naturally fell into place with James's Hampton Court Conference of January 1604 which initiated the authorised translation of the Bible by 50 scholars and aides (with some supervision from James himself) finishing their work by 1611 bringing Biblical data under royal licence into ready use throughout 'Great Britain'. British nationalism naturally justified itself by James's Bible, transcending normal political limits. John Milton, born in 1608 but no admirer of James, would be but one of many scholarly theologians to appropriate the place of chosen people for himself and his countrymen, quoting how God:

> [H]ath not dealt so with any nation, and as for his judgments they have not known them.

Alas, he and many thousands of others probably meant the English, not the British. All over Britain men and women brooded on God's promise of land to Abraham and his posterity. After the descendants of Abraham's grandson Jacob had suffered exile, degradation, enslavement and long march, they took possession of their Promised Land building their nationalism under Joshua's leadership, followed by judge-rule leading the future western world through the Old Testament in the principle of law first laid down in the Ten

Commandments. The decision to be ruled by kings (deplored by God to Samuel but twisted by James into advice from God) brought with it the inevitable human corruption of divine law in the royal interest, as later diagnosed by St Augustine evolving into the City of Man and the City of God. King David – for all of his sometimes ruthless self-interest – made his own nationalism in the Psalms with one eye on God and the other on Man. He was a useful precedent for James, more so than Solomon to whom royal propagandists compared James with his acquiescence when alive, but whose heterosexual polygamy James surely found distasteful. Homer let nationalisms take what they could find, and Virgil made a poetic system of such takings, but Augustus (whatever his limits) had been too intelligent to set out his nationalism. James needed his own Virgil, to teach lessons to national audiences from the past, with but a few genteel allusions to the present and future of the new nation. James had, of course, read Virgil in Latin in his earliest youth writhing under the discipline of his brilliant and sadistic tutor George Buchanan, and more happily in the Scots in which Bishop Gavin Douglas had rendered it 90 years before James accepted England, Wales, and Ireland.

Shakespeare had shown his proficiency in staging English nationalism while Elizabeth equated it with herself, proving herself the finest Tudor propagandist. Any actor or playwright might admire her last address to Parliament:

> You have had, and may have many Princes more mighty
> and more wise than I, sitting in this Seat, yet you never
> have had, nor shall you have, any that will love you better.

That height James could not reach, nor could he ever approach Elizabeth's popularity, deserved or not. Shakespeare's most famous uses of English nationalism were given to Philip Falconbridge bastard son of the dead Richard I to finish *King John*, and to the dying John of Gaunt in *Richard II*, neither speech having historical warrant. Richard I's only known bastard was called Philip but his career seems to have been entirely French, and John of Gaunt was born in Ghent with virtually no English ancestors apart from male kings, was detested in England, and his chief but frustrated ambition was to become King of Castile. Shakespeare had involuntarily produced a memorable – if derogatory – portrait of a French nationalist in *Henry VI Part One*, his first major character: Joan la Pucelle, otherwise Joan of Arc. In *Henry VI Part Three* he created the supreme tragic nationalist, the king himself, horrified at having been the cause of his beloved England tearing itself apart. *Macbeth* contains one Scottish nationalist, Macduff, whose speeches show a love and concern for Scotland itself deeper than anything from other major characters. Macduff's infant son is the bravest person in the play, trying to save his mother as he is killed, after trying to defend his father from her complaints about his absence in London: it may be a tragic memory of Shakespeare's own son Hamnet who died in August 1596. Lady Macduff is right in calling her husband a traitor: he has betrayed her and their children by leaving them in danger from a Macbeth who has killed their king and his own comrade-in-arms Banquo. This desertion may well result in Macduff's sacrifice of his wife, son, and all other offspring for his country, however involuntarily. This stage Scottish nationalism, however lethal to the families of its votaries, plays its part in the making of UK nationalism: these nationalisms ought no longer to be enemies, and must learn to work together.

Macbeth is not vociferated by stage Scots: James was too much of a figure of fun in the malicious eyes and ears of English courtiers to permit ridiculous Scots on stage. The whole play must be in English, if the English were to be converted to union. James sought to dispose of English and Scottish nationalism by his coup on 20 October 1604 when, regardless of parliaments, he had himself formally and legally proclaimed to be King of Great Britain, France, and Ireland, Defender of the Faith, etc. By 1605, Shakespeare was ready enough to think, speak and write British nationalism. Previously he had been ready enough for a little English nationalism to please instincts of audience and court sometimes nastier than the heroics of Falconbridge and Gaunt. The contemptible master-villain in *Much Ado About Nothing* – the bastard Don John – was obviously named to dishonour the great Spanish (bastard) hero Don John of Austria, who saved Europe from the Turks at Lepanto in 1571, and dying in 1578 as Spanish Governor-General of the Netherlands where he had defeated the rebel Protestants, thus becoming the soldier England had most reason to fear. Bernard Shaw (in the *Saturday Review* for 12 March 1898) wrote that Shakespeare

> with all his superficiality... knew that villainy is something simpler and deeper than a mere means to an end. Don John is a true natural villain: that is to say, a malevolent person. Only, he is Un-English, because he is quite conscious of his villainy, and disguises it neither from himself nor his accomplices.

Macbeth, we may thus conclude, is also Un-English, and is meant to be. Shakespeare amused himself and his audiences by a sequence in *Henry V* giving cameo visions of representative recruits from Henry's realms of Wales, England and Ireland and the unusually friendly Scot Captain Jamie. King James was all set to create UK union of Parliaments, and Shakespeare was ready to meet him. His first British play, *King Lear* (1605–6) is testimony against a broken Britain, Lear dividing his kingdom among his daughters with tragic consequences including invasion, civil war, mutilation, and attempted regicide. Audiences might not respond to the play with new zeal to unite the island of Britain as their foremost thought, but it was a useful contribution to unionist propaganda. The choice of realms for Lear's sons-in-law raised a curious question: in 1600 James declared his newly-born son Charles Duke of Albany, and on becoming King of England in 1603 he declared his eldest child Henry Duke of Cornwall. Use of the names in *Lear* forcefully symbolised a Britain broken up if parliaments were not united under James (as indeed they were not, to his great regret). Already the English Parliament was proving nasty about it: James had taken the English crown with high legality but if anything it exacerbated existing feelings amongst Scotophobes, one parliamentarian complaining that the Scots were a bad people with whom to unite, because they were always killing their kings. His Scottish history was wretched, as English Scotophobe history usually is, but it endured. When 19-year-old Queen Victoria asked Prime Minister Viscount Melbourne about her Scottish ancestors she was told:

I have found a book. It is all very sad, Ma'am, and very confusing. They were all called James, and they were all murdered.

Scotland's Duncan I and Macbeth were killed in civil war, Malcolm III was killed in battle against England as was James IV, James II was accidentally killed by an exploding gun, Mary Queen of Scots was killed by the English (as her grandson Charles I would be), only James I and James III were murdered by their fellow-Scots. As against this, the English had murdered their own Edward II, Richard II, Henry VI, and Edward V, Richard III was killed in civil war, and England unlike Scotland had been conquered (successively by Danes, Normans, and Angevins). English nationalism didn't like to talk of England's subjection, unlike Irish nationalism which fattened itself on memories of oppression by foreign invaders. James had not conquered England, but the omnipresence of Scottish profiteers from his accession to the English throne might make it seem that he had. The English Parliament might fear union with the Scottish Parliament as implying Scottish victory and hence many English parliamentarians sought to obstruct and prevent its union with the Scottish Parliament. It was always possible that the Scots might someday choose one son of James and the English another. *King Lear*'s first line (spoken by his most faithful vassal the Earl of Kent) pushed the names of Albany and Cornwall into the audience's faces:

> I thought the king had more affected the Duke of Albany
> than Cornwall.

These respectively were the official designations of James's sons Charles and Henry in 1604. In the play Albany, Goneril's husband, is rather a weak and impressionable man who only achieves stature by learning that his wife is an adulterer who means to murder him, while Cornwall is as horrible a sadist as his own wife Regan. Preceding versions by the 12th century Geoffrey of Monmouth and the Elizabethan Raphael Holinshed had used those ducal titles but in James's reign Shakespeare could not have done so without calling the new Princes to an audience's mind, with a consequent risk of royal punishment for such promiscuous deployment of royal titles without royal permission. *King Lear* was written soon after the suppression of *The Tragedy of Gowrie*, and probably overlapped with Jonson's imprisonment. So Shakespeare used those names with James's permission: division of Lear's Britain into Albany and Cornwall could point a moral warning to opponents of the proposed Great British union. Not only did this necessitate James's approval, it looks like James's suggestion (or command), so that 'Albany' should now take its place among the first British dukedoms easing into public awareness alongside so many other Scots usages, persons and patronage. Albany had pride of place in the Scottish peerage, having been bestowed on younger sons of King Robert II and King James II, and then on James's father Henry Lord Darnley, on James himself, and subsequently on his own younger son 'baby Charles' (later crowned and executed). The Dukedom of Cornwall was first bestowed on Edward the Black Prince son of Edward III, and has been automatically given to the eldest son of the sovereign either at his birth or at his parent's accession. Shakespeare would need to consult James on *Lear*. The antiquity of the original story and hence its timespan encouraged for the next play the choice of a Scottish tale from long ago. Macaulay's complaint that James behaved like a professor would perhaps have been valid here. With *Lear* finished and *Macbeth* begun, Shakespeare would have received the state of the art in Scottish history as then determined, and received it from the scholarly Scot who meant most in his life, King James himself.

Shakespeare was already learning the lesson that 'Britain' must replace 'England': it would take many of his countrymen four centuries. Professor James Shapiro notes in his *1606: Shakespeare and the Year of Lear* that Shakespeare never used the word 'British' in his plays before James became king, and 'Britain' only twice, where 'England' had appeared 224 times, and 'English' 132 times in the plays he wrote before Elizabeth's death. Professor Shapiro reports Shakespeare using the word 'British' in a play for the first time in *King Lear*. 'England' appeared only 21 times in what he wrote under James, 'English' 18 times, 'Britain' 29 times. In creating his Great Britain, James recruited the supreme English artistic creator of his time, henceforth to be British himself. But James had a natural wisdom, and in Shakespeare's case he dealt with another intellect far above the common. Insofar as they understood one another, they may have done so instinctively. Shakespeare made his English be British painlessly. He worked in more subtle forms of persuasion, beginning with lines three and four of *Lear* after Kent recalled having thought Lear preferred the Duke of Albany over Cornwall:

> [Earl of] GLOSTER: It did always seem so to us: but
> now, in the division of the kingdom, it appears not
> which of the dukes he values most; for equalities
> are so weigh'd, that curiosity in neither can make
> choice of either's moiety.

It was double-barrelled propaganda: taken in itself and momentarily ignoring the rest of the plea it sang the virtues of equality between dukedoms, symbolising the kingdoms of England and Scotland in 1605–6, the wealthier not being reckoned the superior of the less wealthy; but Gloster's speech also introduces the idea that a kingdom when divided after unity under a single king will soon show its evil effects, including himself being blinded on stage. The play in its entirety ends on a note of unity controlled by three men consistently undervalued during most of the action – Albany, Edgar and Kent – with the strong and winsome – Goneril, Regan, Cornwall and Edmund – struck down in their pride. James's apparently unheroic exterior may be faintly indicated in Albany proving the wise and just architect of future peace in a united Britain. There may have been a hint that persons who mocked James for his antic disposition would find he was the sane person, like Edgar. And the thrawn, undiplomatic Kent is a true hero driven by love for his King: James so much wanted to gain loyalty, devotion and love from servants in his entourage.

Mac Bethad, or, a truly scottish play

The real 'Macbeth,' otherwise Mac Bethad, was son of Findlaech the *mormaer* of Moray who was murdered by his nephews in 1020.

Moray at this time extended from what is now Caithness to eastern Aberdeenshire under threat from Scandinavians in the north perhaps even more than from Alba in the south. One of the homicidal nephews Gilla Comgain ruled as *mormaer* of Moray, was married to Gruoch, had a son Lulach by her, and was burnt to death with 50 of his followers in 1032. Mac Bethad could have killed his father's killer in fulfilment of blood-feud, as some historians have supposed, but there is no actual evidence tying him to the crime and what may militate against it is that he married Gruoch in a partnership remaining united until his death. He thereby became Lulach's foster-father or guardian, apparently becoming King of Scotland in 1040 as a sort of regent on behalf of Lulach (who was called 'the Simple' and was presumably a child in need of championship). Lulach was at least 25 when Mac Bethad was killed in Lumphanan in 1057 by Malcolm III. He became King of Scotland and was killed in turn by Malcolm in 1058. Lulach had a son succeeding him as *mormaer* of Moray, Mael Snechta, and a daughter whose son Oengus succeeded Mael Snechta and was killed by the troops of Malcolm's youngest son King David I in 1130.

King Malcolm II of Scotland died in 1034, bequeathing the Scottish crown on his grandson Duncan I. Duncan was young and rash, probably in his early 20s, and was defeated in attacks on Scandinavian lordships in north-east England. Malcolm II had greatly extended the power of the Scottish kings by gaining control of the Lothians and Strathclyde, and Duncan presumably with a view to showing himself as good a man as his grandfather turned his attention to the Scottish north-east in 1040 and was killed by Mac Bethad's soldiers probably in battle. Mac Bethad took over the kingdom of Scotland almost by default since neither his experience nor his ambitions had prepared him for the complexities of southern Scotland and its English and Scandinavian frontiers. His main antagonist was Duncan's father, Crinan the Abbot of Dunkeld, far more dangerous than his son and only killed in a formidable pitched battle at Dunkeld in 1045. Mac Bethad was so successful in pacifying Scotland that he could go on pilgrimage in 1050 to the reforming Pope St Leo IX. As a pilgrim Mac Bethad was a great success, memorable for the profusion of his charity to beggars. His absence may have given ideas to his rivals, and Duncan's brother-in-law the Scandinavian Siward of Northumbria invaded Scotland in 1054, defeating Mac Bethad near his Scottish fortress at Dunsinane in Perthshire and driving him back on Moray. We have no proof that Duncan's son Malcolm III was present, but apparently Siward's son was killed and Siward was satisfied on hearing his wounds were all in front. Siward himself died in 1055 and young Malcolm killed Mac Bethad at Lumphanan.

Mac Bethad seems to have been a rather unambitious man, apparently not claiming to be *mormaer* of Moray until (perhaps on Lulach's behalf) he discharged the duties of the office and may have assumed the title when facing Duncan's invasion; similarly he succeeded Duncan as king in a power vacuum rather than in a power play. The other two major characters in Shakespeare's *Macbeth* – Banquo and Macduff – are fictional, though a pale shade of possibility clings around Macduff. Nobody of that name surfaces in Mac Bethad's reign, and as a title it may be one of the hereditary honours borne by Gruoch. Malcolm III's descendants show a close relationship to the house of Macduff when it becomes visible: in particular their chieftain had the distinction of proclaiming each successive King of Scotland. *Macbeth*'s Macduff does this with almost professional formality, consistently with his personal Scottish nationalism:

> MACDUFF. [*entering with* MACBETH's *head*]:
>   Hail, King! For so thou art. Behold where stands
>   Th' usurper's cursèd head: the time is free.
>   I see thee compassed with thy kingdom's pearl,
>   That speak my salutation in their minds;
>   Whose voices I desire aloud with mine, –
>   Hail, King of Scotland!
> ALL. Hail, King of Scotland!

The mixture of exultation and ceremonial transmitted to Shakespeare by someone mingling antiquarian scholarship and monarchical pride makes James his most likely informant: aware of the tradition from reading and listening to court folklore. James's title to Scotland and England depended on his descent from Malcolm III who concludes

Shakespeare's *Macbeth* by accepting Macduff's salutation. Scholars imagining James's principal concern was with an alleged ancestor appearing in that play, Banquo, forget that there was no problem about James's royal descent, which remained undisputed for Scotland from his infant succession in place of his mother Mary Queen of Scots, and for England in place of his cousin Elizabeth. His proclamation as King of England by the most powerful of Elizabeth's surviving courtiers, Robert Cecil, was not concerned with the right of Stuart Succession in 1603 but that of Tudor Succession in 1485. Cecil was intimating the only question that could be raised against James's succession was the title of his ancestor King Henry VII and therefore the title of Henry's daughter Margaret, wife of James IV of Scotland, mother of James V and hence great-grandmother of James VI and I.

Banquo, the supposed ancestor of James, never existed and would have been irrelevant to James's titles as King of Scotland and as King of England if he had existed. Banquo surfaced in the reigns of James IV and V as a literary concoction, whose author or collector Hector Boece, first Principal of the University of Aberdeen, produced an engaging fable for his somewhat lecherous royal masters in which Macbeth encompasses the death of his dangerous rival Banquo whose son Fleance escapes and flees to Wales where he impregnates the daughter of his Welsh host who therefore kills him but the resultant offspring when reaching adolescence kills a companion who taunts him with his bastardy in his turn when reaching adolescence and is obliged to flee back to Scotland, procreating the Stuarts. Holinshed included much of this, with variations. Neither of them gave a ghostly role to Banquo nor an encore in the witches' cavern which doesn't exist: Macbeth has heard of his invulnerability save to man not of woman born and to Birnam Wood when come to Dunsinane, from a witch of old acquaintance, unconnected with the weird sisters. James VI would have recognised the story for elegant fraud, in the finest fairy-tale traditions, and was unlikely to be titillated by these alleged ancestral despoilers of female virginity, being himself a scholar who preferred gentlemen.

This gun for hire

James and Shakespeare had strong common ground for mutual diagnosis. They were both poets, both wrote sonnets, preferring their rhyme-scheme to the Petrarchan octet and sestet. Some of Shakespeare's were already in circulation, and James may have studied them. James could have learned from them, or had his inspiration prompted in some cases by the first words. For instance, Shakespeare's Sonnet 33 (perhaps written in 1598) began:

> Full many a glorious morning have I seen
> Flatter the mountain-tops with sovereign eye...

And a sonnet from James in 1604 began:

> Full many ane time the archier shakkis his bow
> That afterhend it may the stronger be: ...

Sonneteers' relationships with one another have bases beyond patron and poet. James and Shakespeare were bisexual and as exceptionally intelligent men much preoccupied with writing about love and being swayed by it, they could have recognised in one another a common pleasure in same-sex contemplation. We need not trouble about possible physical expression of it: we know Shakespeare wrote gay sonnets but we have no proof he ever had sexual relations with another man. They might readily have seen in one another a similar pleasure and pain to that which an older creative man gains from an admired younger. It might be that they recognised it in one another and knew they did not even need to talk about it, although they were likely to write about it with suitable precautions.

The word 'phoenix' as poetic symbol was common to both, in Shakespeare's 'The Phoenix and Turtle' was first published in 1601, a poem so beautiful that it is impertinence to praise it, and so obscure that it is hopeless to construe it, except that it mourns the phoenix. It was included in a book consisting mostly of a poem *Love's Martyr* by Robert Chester otherwise unknown but evidently held in such high regard by the greatest English poets of the time that he appended poems by Shakespeare, Ben Jonson, and George Chapman, amongst others. If King James saw that, it gave him a shock of recognition. In 1584 he had written 'Phoenix' in memory of his cousin Esmé Stuart, Duke of Lennox, who may have been the person he loved best in all the world. In his horrible childhood surrounded by tutorial sadism, competitive malice, sectarian bigotry, courtier intrigue, chieftain rivalry, potential assassins, and permanent threats of eternal damnation, with his mother imprisoned in England perpetually accused of his father's murder in tirades drummed into the boy's ears, the young teenager James found solace in Esmé's arms. His own abduction and imprisonment by the first Earl of Gowrie forced him to exile Esmé who died in Paris in 1583, James avenging him by executing that Gowrie in 1584, and perhaps also in the killing of that Gowrie's sons in 1600. James yearned for love more than vengeance, and long and deeply he mourned his dead love in his poem 'Phoenix'. We have to consider James not as an alien patron of the King's Men requiring smarmy flatterings in the *Macbeth* text, but a poet gently seeking collaboration with a poetic playwright. The very intellectual stature of these two enabled mutual admiration to spring up: each could see in the other the absurdities productive of contemporary backbiting, and the courage of minds reaching for the stars. Shakespeare could bring to life the English history James needed to know; James could conceive a Bible to transform the English language, as well as a transposition of a protective frontier which Scotland no longer needed to an Ireland needing Protestant people rather than profiteers, and a Union of Great Britain embedded in its own nationalism. Both in their way were social architects making huge arks they intended to conquer seas of ignorance. We have caught glimpses of their collaboration. The first lines of *King Lear* had been created in accordance with James's requirements. The first lines of *Macbeth* raise the serious possibility that James pushed an area of his own expertise – witchcraft – from the start, prompted by a recent pageant production in his honour, and that of his union project: the episode of the three boy nymphs at the gate of St John's College Oxford on 27 August 1605. It has been surmised with no proof that Shakespeare must have witnessed that pageant, but whether he was there or not, James was. A physician named Matthew Gwinne got up

Holinshed's version of the Macbeth legend and made it the basis of what James, his wife, and son Henry beheld.

Raphael Holinshed, *The Second Volume of Chronicles: The History of Scotland* (1587):

Shortlie after happened a strange and vncouth woonder, which afterward was the cause of much trouble in the realme of Scotland, as ye shall after heare. It fortuned, as Makbeth and Banquho iournied towards Fores where the King then lay, they went sporting by the waie togither without other company, saue onelie themselues, passing through the woods and fields, when suddenlie, in the middest of a laund, there met them three women in strange and wild apparell, resembling creatures of elder world, whome when they attentiuely beheld, woondering much at the sight, the first of them spake and said, 'All haile Makbeth, thane of Glammis' (for he had latelie entered into that dignitie and office by the death of his father Sinell). The second of them said, 'Haile, Makbeth thane of Cawder.' But the third said: 'All haile Makbeth that heereafter shalt be King of Scotland'.

Then Banquho: 'What manner of women' (saith he) 'are you, that seeme so little fauourable vnto me, whereas to my fellow heere, besides high offices, ye assigne also the kingdome appointing foorth nothing for me at all?' 'Yes' (saith the first of them) 'we promise greater benefits vnto thee, than vnto him, for he shall reigne indeed, but with an vnlucky end; neither shall he leaue anie issue behind him to succeed in his place, where contrarilie, thou in deed shalt not reigne at all, but of thee those shall be borne which shall gouern the Scotish kingdom by long order of continuall descent.' Herewith the foresaid women vanished immediatelie out of their sight. This was reputed at the first but some vaine fantasticall illusion by Mackbeth and Banquho, inasmuch that Banquho would call Mackbeth, in iest, king of Scotland;

and Mackbeth againe would call him in sport likewise, the father of manie kings. But afterwards the common opinion was, that these women were either the weird sisters, that is (as ye would say), the goddesses of destinie, or else some nymphs or feiries indued with knowledge of prophesie by their necromanticall science, because euerie thing came to passe as they had spoken. For shortlie after, the Thane of Cawdor being condemned at Fores of treason against the king committed; his lands, liuings, and offices were giuen of the King's liberalitie to Mackbeth.

Witches recycled to make Britain Great

Witches are usually imagined as ugly except, as Robert Burns pointed out in 'Tam O' Shanter' in 1791, the most dangerous are the most beautiful, especially when descended from the most pious grandmother. The play *Macbeth* created its own shorthand conventions down the centuries: neither 'Lady Macbeth' nor 'Lady Macduff' are so styled in the text, nor are the witches ever called witches but 'weird sisters'. The play also implies their ugliness even to senile masculinity, having beards. As first performed by the King's Men, the witches must have been boys accustomed to perform as women, sometimes beautiful women. James's visit to Oxford on 27–30 August 1605 included viewing the pageant outside St John's College where three beautiful boys appeared clad as nymphs. They described themselves as prophetic sibyls speaking in Latin not merely from academic snobbery but because prophetic sibyls emerged from very ancient Roman legend. The so-called sibyls addressed him with the information that they had told Banquo he would father a long line of Scottish kings culminating in James, whom they now informed that he also would have an endless line of descendant monarchs. Sibyl no 1 then said '*Salve, cui Scotia servit*', or 'Welcome, to whom Scotland does homage', easily rendered as 'Hail, King of Scotland', sibyl no 2's thus becoming 'Hail, King of England', and the third sibyl's 'Hail, King of Ireland' followed by a final hail to James 'who divided Britain joins into one'. It was reported that His British Majesty 'did very much applaud'. The theatre campaign for the making of Great Britain had got off the ground at last, but more would be needed than Oxonian Latin. He must have discussed the implications with Shakespeare at an early stage, and now could suggest that the scholarly and courtier worlds would expect a witchcraft theme and an opening scene for a play, *Macbeth*, as the natural sequel to the Oxford pageant. And those nymphs or sibyls could be altered from supposed benevolent half-supernatural beings to creatures on whom James, author of *Demonologie*, was the greatest living British expert, though not because of obsessions such as would inflame witch-hunters in general. In fact, he was an academic authority, and the *Macbeth* witches are presented with much more emphasis on getting them right than on frightening the audience.

James's motives when reigning in Scotland, as with many other matters, were self-protective with scant mercy for those he would sacrifice as his tactics demanded. Throughout his life he knew that if matters went wrong he might be secretly murdered, like his father, or judicially murdered, like his mother. His attempts to find another Esmé could endanger him, and leave him open to accusations of sodomy inviting divine retribution carried out by self-appointed angels of death. If James could convince resentful subjects that the Devil regarded him as his greatest enemy and was seeking his death through witchcraft, then those who were against James must be on the Devil's side. The divine right of kings naturally fell into place in keeping with that.

The witches' presence in the play derives from James himself, not simply a theatrical compliment. The story of *Macbeth* told of the vicious spirals awaiting the regicide. Shakespeare had done so in *Richard II* and sequel plays about Henry IV, in *Richard III* as sequel to *Henry VI Part III* (where the future Richard III murders Henry VI), in *Julius Caesar*, and in *Hamlet*. The play *Macbeth* also fits in with James's political hostility against warmongers such as Sir Walter Raleigh. A believer in peace as policy, James diagnosed the ensuing 17th century shrewdly enough, as we can see from its warlords Mansfeld, Wallenstein, Gustav Adolf, Condé, Cromwell, Marlborough. A military hero of that kind liable to seek kingship by murder and treason was a good object-lesson to teach from the stage. James's Great British nationalism had an eye to many details. As for Banquo, James probably knew he had never existed, merely having been invented as a court historian's compliment to James V. Grandson was wiser than grandfather: James VI was King of Scotland and therefore of England not because of his descent from an imaginary ancestor but from real ones, such as Duncan I, his son Malcolm III, *his* son David I, and so on down the line through the male Bruces and their descendants the Royal Stewarts. Holinshed's version, on which Gwinne had drawn, firmly implied that Banquo had supported Macbeth in his decision to kill King Duncan. Naturally Gwinne had excluded that in honouring Banquo's supposed descendant. It has been widely assumed that Shakespeare, in fear or flattery of James, altered Banquo's role from Holinshed's co-conspirator killed when rogues fell out, to an innocent victim. What Shakespeare actually did was to make Banquo a much more interesting character than an unsuccessful blackguard, or a virtuous patsy.

Andrew Cecil Bradley, *Shakespearean Tragedy* (1904) Lecture X:

Duncan is murdered. In the scene of discovery Banquo of course appears, and his behaviour is significant. When he enters, and Macduff cries out to him, 'O Banquo, Banquo, Our royal master's murdered'.

And Lady Macbeth, who has entered a moment before, exclaims, 'Woe, alas! What, in our house?'

His answer, 'Too cruel anywhere', shows, as I have pointed out, repulsion, and we may be pretty sure that he suspects the truth at once. After a few words to Macduff he remains absolutely silent while the scene is continued for nearly forty lines. He is watching Macbeth and listening as he tells how he put the chamberlains to death in a frenzy of loyal rage. At last Banquo

---

appears to have made up his mind. On Lady Macbeth's fainting he proposes that they shall all retire, and that they shall afterwards meet,

> And question this most bloody piece of work,
> To know it further. Fears and scruples shake us.
> In the great hand of God I stand, and thence
> Against the undivulged pretence I fight
> Of treasonous malice.

His solemn language here reminds us of his grave words about 'the *instruments* of darkness', and of his later prayer to the 'merciful powers'. He is profoundly shocked, full of indignation, and determined to play the part of a brave and honest man.

But he plays no such part. When next we see him, on the last day of his life, we find that he has yielded to evil. The Witches and his own ambition have conquered him. He alone of the lords knew of the prophecies, but he has said nothing of them. He has acquiesced in Macbeth's accession, and in the official theory that Duncan's sons had suborned the chamberlains to murder him. Doubtless, unlike Macduff, he was present at Scone to see the new king invested. He has, not formally but in effect, 'cloven to' Macbeth's 'consent'; he is knit to him by 'a most indissoluble tie'; his advice in council, has been 'most grave and prosperous'; he is to be the 'chief guest' at that night's supper. And his soliloquy tells us why:

> Thou hast it now: king, Cawdor, Glamis, all,
> As the weird women promised, and, I fear,
> Thou playd'st most foully for't. Yet it was said
> It should not stand in thy posterity,
> But that myself should be the root and father
> Of many kings. If there come truth from them –
> As upon thee, Macbeth, their speeches shine –
> Why, by the verities on thee made good,
> May they not be my oracles as well,
> And set me up in hope.

Give the public what they want

After the success and widespread retelling of Gwinne's Oxford nymphs, the prophesies for Banquo were an indispensable part of a production before the King, but James was too intelligent to sanitize the role of a non-existent ancestor. Had Banquo uttered his lines in ludicrous braid Scots, the equivalent of the royal blue pencil might have had some exercise, but a brilliant reworking of the character was another matter. Moreover, James himself for reasons of art and science might welcome depiction of dangerous neutrals in assassination plots. Shakespeare might dismiss Holinshed's indictment of Banquo as one of several accessories before the fact of Duncan's regicide, but substituted Banquo's slow accession to temptation of profit from the murder of Duncan, partly in dropping the murder investigation he had promised, partly in an apparent thought of assassinating Macbeth to facilitate kingship takeover by Banquo's progeny. The appearance of Banquo's ghost at the royal banquet and his presence in the witches' cavern are Shakespeare's interpolations, as is Duncan's being a murder under trust. Gwinne having tied theatricals for James to Banquo and his line of kingly descendants, it made sense for Shakespeare's show to make it a stage device, continuing Gwinne's pageant-work like the appearance of Hymen in *As You Like It* or the omnipresence of the fairies in *A Midsummer Night's Dream* or Hamlet using *The Murder of Gonzago* for detection. It no more meant that James was descended from Banquo than that the late Queen Elizabeth was a faerie queene as designed by Edmund Spenser. It was entertainment, enhancing the popular appeal of the play, where a vulgar porter relaxed the tension before the discovery of King Duncan's body; and the horror of little Macduff's and Lady Macduff's deaths might be deepened by their jokes before being killed. But James knew that witch-hunts could be endangered if the witches became figures of fun. There would be much about which to talk to Shakespeare concerning the dramatic progress to be made before they would reach that finale where England rescues Scotland, symbolically anglicises the Scots by having thanes rebranded as earls, and thereby would inspire the English to accept union with Scotland as their historical duty. And *Macbeth* ends absolutely firmly with James's real ancestor Malcolm III installed by the benevolent English as King of Scotland from whom all future descendants will be born, down to the present day.

Macbeth, Macbeth, Macbeth, beware the bard(s)!

Macbeth is not a play crawling with Shakespeare's attempts to please King James: it is a play which James had ensured would please himself, by teaching Great British nationalism to his subjects. Personal meetings of the king and his playwright were presumably few, but would have required thorough discussion on various stages of the script since Shakespeare wanted to please James and James wanted to please the English and both wanted a successful play, teaching a meaning for Great Britain. Shakespeare had to have a source and critic who knew Scotland: he himself could cheerfully create plays set anywhere from Troy to Denmark, in medieval England or contemporary Venice, but surrounded by the Scottish-ruled, English-staffed court he could not risk hilarious blunders.

We may never know what they said to one another, but we have the same situation as with Homer – we have a strong clue to how they said it. James enjoyed instructing by Platonic dialogue, as he did in his *Daemonologie*. As to the resultant play-script, it is not a matter of details thrown in amongst hopes of hitting James's approval: what was included was what James had made clear he wanted. It was the English rather than the king who had to be flattered enough to conceal that they were being taught, and to be entertained so that the play would become popular. The play *Macbeth* would be the thing wherein the king would catch the conscience of the English, but Hamlet uses *Gonzago* to 'catch the conscience of the king', his uncle Claudius, who is startled into revealing himself as his brother's murderer and then uses solitude to wrestle with his own conscience with a frankness never otherwise shown by him. King James gave much reflection to conscience, telling Prince Henry in *Basilikon Doron*:

> As for Conscience (which I called the conserver of Religion) it is nothing els but the light of knowledge that God

hath planted in man, which choppeth him with a feeling that hee hath done wrong when ever he committeth any sinne, & surely, althou this conscience be a greater torture to the wicked yet it is as a great comfort to the goodlie if wee will consider it rightly.

Shakespeare had also staged confrontations of conscience directly in Brutus (before murdering Caesar), Othello (before killing himself), Lear (when sane once more), and Angelo in *Measure for Measure*. Whether Shakespeare read *Basilicon Doron* by his own impulse or did so impelled by James we don't know, but conscience plays more complex roles in *Macbeth* than in the previous plays. The wicked in *Othello* and *King Lear* seem untroubled by conscience: Iago, Goneril, Cornwall and Reagan do not show a flicker, Edmund in his hour of death seems to, but having promised repentance he does nothing to save those he has doomed until Cordelia is dead. Macbeth agonises with his conscience before murdering Duncan, most of all in contemplating the one crime actually added by Shakespeare to those previously alleged against the real Macbeth (Mac Bethad) by late chroniclers (I.VII.12–16):

> He's here in double trust:
> First, as I am his kinsman and his subject
> Strong both against the deed; then, as his host,
> Who should against the murderer shut the door
> Not bear the knife myself.

Shakespeare's addition of murder under trust accords ominously well with the attempt at murder under trust James VI had alleged against the Ruthven brothers at Gowrie in 1600, and could have suggested to Shakespeare, so that *The Tragedy of Gowrie* may have had a stage afterlife after all. Macbeth's conscience goes on to make a more positive reproach, the greatest vindication of Duncan in the play canonising him for his virtuous life, so that Macbeth himself seems almost bullied into his murder against his will by his wife. She shows no sign of conscience then, but later when sleepwalking shows conscience has taken her over, proof that she has stifled but knew its reproaches while haranguing Macbeth into killing Duncan. In the last act Macbeth himself, while ready to fight to the death, is drained of belief in anything other than the witches' promises. Shakespeare has progressed so far in staging conscience to show the effects of its operations while keeping them invisible: neither of the Macbeths has the momentary hope of release by repentance seen and lost by King Claudius. The ruins of the conscience-haunted Macbeths became the most visible sign of the play's immortality, actresses judged by their sleep-walking, actors by Macbeth's sublime expression of his inability to mourn his dead wife, so that if the play has been done well the audience should recoil from Malcolm's bleak concluding epitaph on them – 'this dead butcher and his fiend-like queen' – as something not so much unjust as unfair.

They are a marriage of mutual trust, perhaps the only one among Shakespeare's major characters, ironically drawing them to murder *under* trust. When Shakespeare wrote the play under James's guidance, the conclusion had more practical audience reactions in mind. England would be knights in shining armour come to save captive Scotland from Macbeth in the play, and from penury, faction, sectarianism, and disloyalty in the near future, scarcely aware that it was doing what its Scottish king directed. *Macbeth*'s apparently irrelevant discussion of the virtues of the English King, St Edward the Confessor, was a means of teaching ideal kingship to the sabre-rattling English. The Confessor had won admiration and canonisation, in 1161, by being a man of peace while occasionally permitting expeditions to dispose of troubles on the frontier.

Macbeth didn't demand that a king must touch for the king's evil: it was simply saying that a very good English king did. There was Hecate unexpectedly bursting into III.5 and IV.1. Professor Nicholas Brooke of East Anglia in his introduction to *Macbeth* (1990) in *The Oxford Shakespeare* declared it 'extremely probable' that 'Shakespeare accepted the Hecate material even if he did not write it' (without identifying James as the alternative writer). If James demanded or even drafted the scenes with the superwitch Hecate it probably followed the draft *Macbeth* having hardened the three sibyls and Holinshed's three prophetesses into English-speaking hags, but on reflection the witches – notwithstanding their ability to fly – should be seen as human, like the witches James had diagnosed in his time: to devise damnation for a hero king needs some supervision from the Royal Family of Devils. Hecate shares with the three witches a somewhat professorial anxiety to show academic reliability: even in Act I Scene I where beyond mention of a date with Macbeth nothing is actually done, the audience is firmly told that witches have familiars with names like Greymalkin and Paddock.

A son avenges his long-lost mother

Macbeth also enabled James to settle a few personal scores against his predecessor in England, avenging his predecessor in Scotland. James had been made king at 13 months old. His 24-year-old mother Mary had been forced to abdicate, never saw her son the 'cradle king' again, fled to her cousin Queen Elizabeth of England who imprisoned her for 19 years and finally had her beheaded. Mary's partisans had declared their intention of having her restored to the Scottish throne and installed on the English one. Elizabeth let James have a pension whose loss James feared if he protested too strongly at his mother's death, while herself denied she had ordered Mary's death, imprisoned her secretary who had carried out her instructions, dismissed her chief adviser while actually retaining him, and in her childlessness treated James with the ambiguity of a stepmother. He thirsted for the English throne but dared not alienate Elizabeth or her ministers whom he would need to ensure his succession. Mary had died with Catholic piety and womanly dignity while Elizabeth and James had both behaved contemptibly, both knew it, and both denied it. As King of England, James evicted Elizabeth's corpse from her sumptuous grave in Westminster Abbey into which he installed his mother: Elizabeth found a slightly humbler grave in the Abbey. He turned his own guilt (for failure to rescue or avenge his mother) against Elizabeth but was obliged to speak respectfully of her in public while suspecting that most of her subjects thought him inferior to her.

Posterity has pigeon-holed Shakespeare among the Elizabethan dramatists but most of his ten plays in James's reign showed a level of genius evident in only a few of his 25 in Elizabeth's, and despite posthumous literary fictions assuming gratifying if brief encounters between playwright and queen, James honoured Shakespeare well beyond any notice she had accorded. The spectacle of Banquo's hyperactive ghost appearing in a witch-created vision of his future kingly descendants witnessed by Macbeth was heightened for its Jacobean audiences by an unspoken parallel in very recent British history. Elizabeth might have spoken the lines after hearing that Mary had been killed following her orders:

> Which of you have done this?...
> Thou canst not say I did it.
> Never shake thy gory locks at me!

Any surviving reports of Mary's execution seem to single out the blood in her hair. Again, the Confessor's peaceful reign contrasting with Macbeth's slaughterhouse added a turn of the screw whereby the English were invited to rejoice in James's peaceful policies as against Elizabeth's enthusiasm for her own (inadequate) aid to the Dutch rebels and for her petty pirates picking peninsular pockets. Perhaps not a word needed to be said on the matter by playwright or patron, yet the play offered rich retribution for the ancient grudge, and expiation for the uncleansed shame. James's closest advisers in England had been hers, but if she had called him a 'false Scots urchin', she had addressed crook-backed Robert Cecil as 'my pigmy' and 'Little Man'. Did these undertones transmitted from James account for Shakespeare's ruthless further blackening of Macbeth's reputation beyond Holinshed's indictment by turning the real rash youthful Duncan into the saintly figure whose virtues proved Macbeth's greatest obstacle in accepting the role of regicide, and making his killing of Duncan slaughter of his own guest – a crime traditionally abominated far beyond normal homicide or even regicide?

Elizabeth's killing of Mary was also murder of a guest. Macaulay in his early essay on Henry Hallam's *Constitutional History of England* while justly reverencing Protestant martyrs under Mary Tudor, said of the Protestant Reformation in England:

The work which had begun with Henry, the murderer of his wives, was continued by Somerset, the murderer of his brother, and completed by Elizabeth, the murderer of her guest.

In contrast to lands where it was 'from Luther, from Calvin, from Knox, that the Reformation took its character'. James knew well, no man better, how political and homicidal the Reformation had been in Scotland, and he knew it was not the work of the king. Was the killing of Macduff's wife and children on stage a deliberate analogy to the Elizabethan near-genocide of the Irish Catholic peasantry in Munster under such men as Walter Raleigh? James was the recipient of countless Irish-Gaelic poems in his honour while Elizabeth's Irish wars were devastating the country. Was posterity invited to forget the golden days of Good Queen Bess much as Shakespeare obliterated Holinshed's justifiable credit to Macbeth for ten years of benign rule? Shakespeare's highly mythical Macbeth actually commits no crime as unnatural as Elizabeth's execution of her former beloved Robert Devereux 2nd Earl of Essex (no critic or producer seems to have so far suggested that Macbeth and Banquo were lovers). Elizabeth had also sought death-sentence reluctantly commuted to imprisonment of Henry Wriothesly 3rd Earl of Southampton the patron of Shakespeare's youthful poems, whom James freed and made a valued courtier probably enhancing collaboration with Shakespeare.

James may have made additional Scottish historical sources available to Shakespeare, or spoke their content, and may indeed have known folk traditions: for all of his skill in written scholarship he had been an observing, vigilant boy who should have heard and remembered folk stories of Scots rulers. The play as we have it ruthlessly removes the years of Mac Bethad's wise, pious, and prosperous government acknowledged by many different chroniclers with different judgments on him. But the role of Mac Bethad's wife may have been conveyed to James and thence to Shakespeare as much more important in the story than the chroniclers indicated: Mac Bethad may have made himself king in 1040 to protect the claims on the crown of Gruoch and Lulach. Shakespeare turned Gruoch's ancestral claim into Lady Macbeth's being the personal pressure on her husband to kill King Duncan, far more effectively than the weird sisters. Shakespeare had staged women involved with witchcraft from Joan of Arc in *Henry VI Part One* and the Duchess of Gloucester in *Henry VI Part Two,* but in *Macbeth* he sundered all links spiritual or temporal between wife and witches.

Living today after a century haunted by the World War 1 as Paul Fussell demonstrated so magnificently in *The Great War and Modern Memory,* and in the years after Sir Sam Mendes released his all too credible movie *1917,* we may wonder how far *Macbeth* is a play about a traumatised soldier. You might also ask whether *Julius Caesar, Hamlet, Othello, King Lear, Antony and Cleopatra, Coriolanus,* and *Cymbeline* are all anti-war plays. *Macbeth*'s second scene is a peculiarly brutal description of Macbeth's near-crucifixions of Duncan's enemies which suggests that for a man with such slaughter as his chief resort, is not regicide a reasonably predictable next step? Should it be produced with the witches played by equally trustworthy television pundits such as Andrew Neil or Piers Morgan? And if Shakespeare and the King could not make the English believe in the Union of Great Britain, could anyone? *Macbeth,* however unfair to Mac Bethad, was one of the great cultural triumphs in the history of the world, achieved by one of its greatest playwrights, godfathered by a king of unrivalled royal intellect in the name of a Union of Great Britain whose parliaments would not permit it to exist. James was prepared to impose that union on his Scottish subjects: William Ferguson summed it up in his fascinating *Scotland's Relations with England: a Survey to 1707* 'Certainly, as James put it, "he knew the stomach of that people", and in his dealings with his ancient kingdom he undoubtedly succeeded better than with his new subjects in the south, the workings of whose digestions were clearly beyond him'.

CHAPTER SEVEN

From Ireland to Scotland: The Nationalisms of War and Peace

MACBETH. We have scotch't the snake, not kill'd it

William Shakespeare, *Macbeth*, III.2.13

History is now

UNTIL I WAS six we lived in what I learned to write as 25 Seafield Avenue, Clontarf, Dublin, Ireland, Europe, the World. It was a house with a large number of books and I saw that one of these was called *Wales* and was apparently by me, since its author's name was given as 'Owen Edwards'. I had no memory of writing it, and could not work out how I could write any book. I knew about Wales because my Uncle James, who was a school inspector, used to tell me that if I finished my porridge I would be the best boy in Ireland, England, Scotland, and Wales, and thanks to Uncle I thought I belonged to all four. I realised I had not written *Wales* when I saw that the author had a middle initial 'M' which belonged to my elder sister Mary, not to me. When I showed it to my father he said the author was Owen Morgan Edwards, that he had been chief inspector of schools in Wales, that he worked hard to keep Welsh taught in schools, and that he was dead.

Wales was published in 1901 which I knew was when Queen Victoria died, and it was in one of 'Stories of the Nations' which I saw included *Ireland* by the Hon Emily Lawless. We didn't have its two volumes on *Modern England* by Justin McCarthy but an Irish name would have told me the Irish sometimes wrote about England although I didn't know then that he had been deputy leader of the

Irish Home Rulers under Parnell in Parliament. Was Lawless an Irish name? To be 'the Hon' didn't seem very Irish since lords and ladies were usually English. But my mother taught me exciting poems the Hon Emily Lawless wrote about Irish soldiers winning the battle of Fontenoy, Belgium, in 1745 fighting for France and defeating the English. There was one poem about a ghost ship carrying dead soldiers from Fontenoy to the coast of county Clare where they were born. That gave a special thrill to history, in fact the ghosts seemed more real than the living soldiers.

My father wrote history, and I could see near *Wales* my father's book *Church and State in Tudor Ireland* with the name Robert Dudley Edwards along the spine published three years before I was born. He taught me the kings of England and their dates since 1066 which I found very useful (and still do). It always helped knowing what happened when. We knew about Scotland because he used to read to us from history books for children by Scottish women writers like FA Forbes (a Sacred Heart nun) or by Sister Anne Cecil Kerr where we learned about saints linking Ireland and Scotland such as 'The Story of the Boy who was Stolen by Pirates' who proved to be St Patrick and the pirates Irish, so that while many Irish writers told how badly the Irish had been treated, they had treated other people badly too. We were Catholics as well as Irish. Sister Anne taught us a different kind of nationalism, where Scottish queens were good like St Margaret married to Malcolm III Canmore or like poor Mary Queen of Scots, and so were some English kings like her grandson Charles I murdered by England and his son James II unfairly driven from the English throne. But some kings were bad like Henry II whose knights killed the good English archbishop St Thomas Beckett, and Henry VIII who killed his good and wise friend St Thomas More for telling the truth that the Pope is head of the Church. I felt a bit sorry for Henry II who had said he was sorry, but I called Henry VIII 'Fatface' which was brave because I knew he would kill me if he found out I had said that. History was very real, but although we were told how people in it had died, it would not be surprising if you met them: though it might be dangerous. So we had four nations and knew they had different histories but they ought all be Catholic, but the ones in Britain were not. Irish history might also be now. When we were staying in my grandmother's house in rural north Cork and I was ill as usual, Mother came up to tell me Parnell was downstairs, she meaning an uncle of hers hitherto unknown to me, but I, excited but not surprised, asked 'And is Michael Davitt with him?' This may have been in 1946 when their centenaries were noted on a stamp commemorating both the great parliamentary leader and the founder of the Land League whose joint work overturned an iniquitous land system.

History is elsewhere

History was happening in Great Britain, the island next door, and in Northern Ireland which the English (as we told ourselves) had kept when we became independent, and a bit of it had happened in Dublin. You could see when the bus from Clontarf got to the North Strand opposite the Strand Cinema, and you could see a large empty waste ground with nobody walking on it and this was where the Germans had bombed Dublin and our house had 'shook'. We thought bombing was terrible and didn't like anybody doing it and were frightened to be told that an atomic bomb had nearly wiped out Japan and wondered if that would happen to us. Our cousin Jimmy O'Sullivan was sent from England to live with our grandmother in Cork, and he talked a little about houses being bombed and people being killed. A Cork aunt, May Kennedy, told us that in London people didn't talk about the war, they talked about the Blitz. That told us a lot, but we children didn't realise it yet.

The Cork countryside seemed more aware of the war going on in London while Dublin talked about it as having happened though, in reality, it was still going on when we moved from Seafield Avenue to 31 Castle Avenue in December 1944. We knew Belfast was bombed in the spring of 1941 because our Taoiseach Eamon de Valera sent fire engines from Dundalk, Drogheda, Dublin and Dun Laoghaire to fight the fires caused by the German bombs. There must have been many child evacuees in rural Ireland influencing their hosts and neighbours, though apart from Jimmy we weren't aware of them. Dublin may have been more conscious of the war than Cork, I suspect partly because Dublin was the self-assured centre of news, and the news was censored absurdly yet successfully so that the war loomed much less immediate. We children knew that the war was between Churchill and Hitler and we didn't want Hitler to win, but both of them seemed self-important grown-ups. We were much less aware of the Americans. The first time I remember hearing about President Franklin D Roosevelt was on the news of his death in early 1945, though many Yanks were kept in Northern Ireland but then apart from the fire brigades of 1941 you didn't go to Northern Ireland. Even the trains going there seemed somehow darker, though trains going to Cork were bright but slow and sometimes went backwards for quite a time.

The definition of Irishness during the war was one of unspoken pride on being at peace while the world was at war. Censorship meant you were never to talk about the IRA because they wanted Hitler to win. IRA and Fianna Fail had both fought against the new Irish Free State in 1922–23, but split in 1926 on the issue of entering the new legislature, which was calling itself Dail Eireann in memory of its first existence in 1919 as an illegal organisation consisting of Sinn Féin MPs elected in the 1918 UK election. De Valera had won the election of 1932 and was continually re-elected until 1948 but few people realised that for a political leader in arms against the state in 1922–23 to be the head of its government ten years later was very unusual. De Valera had distanced Eire (as Ireland's 26 counties were now called) from the UK whose inclusion of Northern Ireland he denied in his Constitution passed in 1937. His newspaper the *Irish Press* poured out a lot of Anglophobia in the 1930s. It was obvious that much of it was nonsense but it may have prevented fascism getting much ground in the 1930s: with so much hatred against England there wasn't enough to go anywhere else. De Valera was giving a terrible hostage to fortune because his *Irish Press* kept up denunciations of England for keeping 'our lost six counties' (you weren't supposed to call them 'Northern Ireland') and once World War II broke out in September 1939 the IRA could make use of the hatred of England in whispers which now could no longer be expressed in print in case it annoyed the English and they invaded us.

What British people actually resented, we later found out, was Irish neutrality instead of alliance with the UK but Eire could not enter World War II because Hitler would probably have captured it within the week and the UK could not have spared weapons and soldiers to help. If Hitler had taken Ireland, the UK from July 1940 would have been trapped in a pincer squeeze from the west as well as from Nazi-occupied Europe. De Valera wanted the UK to win but was well aware that those like him, who had opposed the Treaty of 1922 with the UK, included several of his Fianna Fail colleagues who had fought against the UK and then against the Irish Free State whose rulers were those of their Sinn Féin party comrades who had accepted the Treaty. There was a small but dangerous pro-German element in Eire, and there may have been more among the Catholics of Northern Ireland bitterly resenting the second-class citizenship to which the Ulster Unionist government condemned them. Almost certainly, Hitler would have found Quislings north and south of the border. De Valera was actually breaking neutrality in favour of the UK, and, after 7 December 1941, the USA. Allied military personnel accidentally landed in Eire were secretly zoomed across the border, lights on Atlantic seaports dowsed whenever the UK asked, and 18 other respects gratefully but silently noted by the UK.

The last head of the IRA to down arms in 1923 thus ending the Civil War had been Frank Aiken born in 1898 in Camlough, close to the border but firmly on what became the Northern Ireland side, where his fellow-Catholics (a majority there) were left at the mercy of Protestant authorities and paramilitaries under the Treaty settlement. Aiken may well have been de Valera's closest friend and enabled him to enter Dail Eireann in 1927 by promising to follow his lead, but his surviving common ideology with the IRA meant that he probably preferred the Germans in World War II when de Valera gave him a grandiloquent cabinet post as co-ordinator of defensive measures with responsibility for wartime censorship, while keeping the real work of defence in the hands of an even less intellectual old IRA chief Oscar Traynor whose command in 1922 had been in Dublin. Censorship is an intoxicating weapon and, given its existence to ban supposedly indecent literature, the powers were simply extended to cover considerations of neutrality. This kept Aiken glued to the Unionist Protestant-owned pro-UK *Irish Times* in hopes of detecting insufficiently neutral solecisms, while its editorial staff girded up their loins to maintain benevolence concealing bias. Both parties were activated by devout nationalisms, Aiken dreaming of a 32-county Ireland cleansed from all taint of Britishness, and the *Irish Times* yearning for UK victory supported as much as possible by a sympathetic Ireland south as well as north, edited for 20 years by the Glasgow-born Sligonian Robert Smyllie who had spent World War I interned in a German concentration camp.

The passionate, if non-violent, duel of the two men both born outside the actual jurisdiction of Eire brought out Irish nationalism's capacity for enlisting God knows how many outsiders for God knows what Irish identity. Each caricatured the other as their polar opposite but each opposite existed in innumerable variations. Smyllie's role might seem conservative since it was Unionist, but the *Irish Times* was a ferociously liberal enemy of censorship long before the war. The Irish Censorship Board decreed that Irish innocence must not be violated by works as objectionable, obscene and possibly liable to advocate the prevention of birth by artificial means as Sinclair Lewis's *Elmer Gantry*, Ernest Hemingway's *A Farewell to Arms*, Aldous Huxley's *Brave New World*, George Bernard Shaw's *The Adventures of the Black Girl in Her Search for God*, Liam O'Flaherty's *The Martyr*, Sean O'Casey's *I Knock at the Door*, Frank O'Connor's *Dutch Interior*, Eric Cross's *The Tailor and Ansty*, and every known translation of Brian Merriman's 18th century *Cuirt an Mhean-Oidhche* but never the original since obscenity was deemed impossible in the Irish language. The book censorship may in any case have been close enough to Aiken's cultural sentiments, but what was really at stake was a nationalism intent on denying a voice in Ireland for courageous Irish literary genius, as well as against cultural emancipation from overseas, since it represented a more alien corruption, akin to Hollywood. This was not what Orwell might call 'political Catholicism': *Brave New World* was constructive support for Catholic doubts about wholesale capitulation to science, Hemingway became a Roman Catholic and his *Farewell* has a likeable priest, *Elmer Gantry* would have been enjoyed by Catholic clerics critical of American hot-gospel. But O'Flaherty and O'Connor were hailed across the world as unrivalled short-story writers, Shaw and O'Casey as two of the greatest playwrights in the English languages: jealousy was clearly a sufficient reason to ban them. *The Tailor and Ansty* was the worst case: it was an engaging articulation of folk stories and customs even more hostile to the imaginary rural paradise demanded by bourgeois Dubliners to qualify as landscape for their possible ancestors, and after it had been banned three priests called on the tailor and made him burn his own book in his own hearth. These sadists should never have been admitted to the priesthood. Irish cultural nationalism had emerged in the late 19th and early 20th centuries in full literary flower, and independence produced the time to wither it, leaving a miserable diet of pre-digested Irish nationalism as WB Yeats had warned.

Ireland in the orient express

Agatha Christie's *Murder on the Orient Express*, magnificently filmed under the direction of Sidney Lumet and botched in other hands, turns on Hercule Poirot's investigation of the murder of a gangster who has kidnapped and killed a small child, and who proves to have been killed by all of the suspects in the snowbound carriage. Its chief rival as choice for the best Christie now known as *And Then There Were None* ended with ten corpses one of whom has killed the others and then suicided, all of whom are murderers before reaching the fatal island (apart from the one who murders the rest, but obviously qualifies by those murders). Christie had a kindness for the Irish, including a sympathetic mid-war portrait of the IRA family of an executed Irish patriot in *N or M*. Nationalism in Irish history resembles these quests. Everyone has their nationalism. Everyone is doomed. Everyone may denounce everyone else for being insufficiently Irish or for being too Irish. The entire island as I was growing up teemed with nationalisms. We were all very historically conscious on both sides of the border, though it gave us very different answers. If our history meant grievance, or tragedy, or lament, it might direct us towards an ideal conclusion quite opposed to our immediate conclusions. I remember returning to Dublin from Edinburgh in the 1970s and playing the old but still fruitful journalistic game of asking the taxi-driver if he thought the island of Ireland ought to be united:

> 'Of course it should be united. Isn't Ireland an Island? and an island should always be united.'
> 'Well, not everyone in Britain might agree with that. But would you like to have Ireland united tomorrow?'
> 'Are you out of your mind? And have all them murderers comin' down here fightin' and killin'?'

He refrained from stating to which murderers he referred, and I saw no need for such a disclosure. It was clear that as far as he was concerned, any side would produce murderers, Catholic, Protestant, IRA, UVF, Orange, Green, Bannside or Bogside. He wasn't concerned with the majority of the Northern Ireland population who were averse to violence from anyone. 'Pick up a gun and you shake hands with the devil', says an early 20th century Irishism. True enough, but there are many who don't. The constitutionalist nationalist who may even be an absolute opponent of the use of violence in all circumstances has made remarkable appearances in Irish history, Daniel O'Connell as the most obvious, Michael Davitt another, both rejecting violence after early involvement in it. In O'Connell's case early 19th century Dublin and London society rejoiced in duelling, and those who rejected the barbarism were denounced publicly as cowards. When O'Connell entered Parliament the Prime Minister, Arthur Wellesley first Duke of Wellington had recently fought a duel with George Finch-Hatton 10th Earl of Winchelsea and 5th Earl of Nottingham on 29 March 1829. Sir Robert Peel, when Chief Secretary for Ireland, tried to fight a duel against O'Connell and so did other pillars of government. By any sane measurement, O'Connell belonged to a superior civilisation than Wellington and Peel but historians seem to have difficulty grasping the point.

Technological superiority, industrialisation, accumulation of landed property, successful finance manipulation, and unpunished gigantic swindles rule the social and moral standards by which enduring value judgments are made: sometimes they buy or at least bully the historians. Non-violence in an opponent is either despised, or denied even when the arbiter is supposedly a symbol of peace. David Lord Trimble won the Nobel Prize for Peace, but when the referendum on Scottish independence in 2014 was nearing polling day, he stated that 'we' had beaten the nationalists in Northern Ireland and would beat them again in Scotland. Lord Trimble knew was he was doing. He was a distinguished academic in former life, and is probably among the brighter Lords. His audience would naturally assume that by Northern Ireland nationalists he meant above all Sinn Féin, the largest Catholic or nationalist political party in Northern Ireland, and the political arm of the IRA. To imply that Scottish nationalism was the equivalent of paramilitaries was to announce that chalk was cheese. Alas, to be an Orangeman with its militaristic trappings on public display was to assume that violence is the superior form of political ethics, just as did the Dublin ceremonies honouring violent insurgents in 1798, 1803, 1848, 1867 and 1916. The soldier however squalid is always ready to profit by politicians trying to ingratiate themselves with public favour by implying or stating that violence has a sacred superiority to non-violent politics, the soldier spiritually clean and the politician grimy.

To grow up in Ireland after the war was to swim as best you could in a sea of militarism, with your own preferred variety of nationalism on offer. Understandably, with the war over, many Unionists north or south of the border wanted to sing their victory hymns. Some were direct English or British nationalists hoping to make the earliest return to the mother country, however long their families might have lived in Ireland. Some were English or British nationalists drawing perfectly good salaries in the Republic of Ireland with no intention of leaving it. Some were English or British nationalists intent on ruling Northern Ireland as Ulster Unionists. Some called themselves Irish nationalists while having no desire to live in the Republic especially as age necessitated more visits to doctors who become expensive without a National Health Service. Some were Irish telling themselves nobody else was Irish, perhaps the most extreme nationalism of all, and there was a lot of it about.

The new Christ

The most obvious common identity between these endlessly adverse Irish nationalists was that almost all of them were Christian, nominally, spiritually or filiopietistically; usually very conscious that it had begun in their infancy. The most obvious exception was Bob Briscoe, the Jewish Lord Mayor of Dublin in 1956 and again in 1961, who proved the best unofficial ambassador to the USA Ireland ever had, successfully fighting Irish anti-Semitism by denying its existence. His *For the Life of Me* is one of the funniest, warmest and most generous political autobiographies ever written and admirably proved the kinship of Catholic and Jewish humour, at least when both are Irish. The historian Desmond Ryan, pupil, secretary, and editor of Patrick Pearse, wrote in his review 'O rare Bob Briscoe!' Another quality shared between Ireland's Jews and Catholics – and Protestants – was that around 1951 on both sides of the border their religious observance on Sabbaths and Sundays may have been the highest percentage for their faiths in the world, all the more because their Irish rivals were so obviously devout in practice. Briscoe enjoyed proving that his Irish nationalism (with utter devotion to de Valera), Zionism and Judaism, had no trouble in declaring all naturally and happily coexistent. He didn't disguise the surprise caused by his simultaneous zealotry in all three identities, and the hilarious confusion it sometimes caused. Its breadth of loyalties was equally true of many Christian nationalists: the notion of nationalism as monomaniacal is as mythical as anything nationalism has produced. But the chief paradox is Christian. Jesus Christ's instructions to His followers to love their enemies and forgive injuries were perpetually violated by all forms of Protestantism and Catholicism alike (apart from the Quakers). They found identity in their hatred of one another, whether or not they limited it to anti-social distance. If anything, their clerics were frequently worse than the laity.

From the late 1950s onwards, Protestants and Catholics on
both sides of the border told themselves and their auditors how
bigoted and how unlike themselves was the Reverend Dr Ian Paisley, who certainly rose to wide notice by deliberately offensive
ridicule of the Roman Catholic faith. But when Bernadette Devlin
MP, a Catholic civil rights leader (then non-violent though later,
variously, IRA, INLA, etc), announced in 1971 she was pregnant
out of wedlock and the press called on Paisley for denunciation,
he looked contemptuously at them and in the words of Jesus
Christ commanded 'he that is without sin among you, let him
first cast a stone at her'. Any Christian minister or priest should
have taken pride in saying that, but it was Paisley, their scapegoat,
who said it. The conflict of nationalisms in Ireland arose from
their kinship to the various divisions of Christianity, so like one
another and therefore so vehement in their mutual hostilities from
the days when they ordered or blessed the killings of one another
in their own self-righteous self-preservation whether their special status was Catholic or Protestant. On 28 September 1912 the
Moderator of the General Assembly of the Presbyterian Church
in Ireland, and every Church of Ireland bishop with bishoprics
inside or straddling Ulster, signed the Ulster Covenant alongside
nearly half a million co-signatories pledging to resist the threatened Third Irish Home Rule Bill 'using all means which may be
found necessary' which gave all of them a door to violence if
they chose, or if Sir Edward Carson chose, an interesting case of
spiritual enlistment following a secular leader but with comparable cases to ensue all over the world from August 1914. Patrick
Pearse responded to the Ulster Covenant with a natural corollary
to the Protestant sacerdotal fellowship sealed in the Covenant, in
a reply 'The Coming Revolution' developed in November:

> The Gaelic League was no reed shaken by the wind, no
> mere *vox clamantis*: it was a prophet and more than a
> prophet. But it was not the Messiah. I do not know if the
> Messiah has yet come, and I am not sure that there will be
> any visible and personal Messiah in this redemption: the

people itself will perhaps be its own Messiah, the people labouring, scourged, crowned with thorns, agonising and dying, to rise again immortal and impassible. For peoples are divine and are the only things that can properly be spoken of under figures drawn from the divine epos.

I am glad, then that the North has 'begun'. I am glad that the Orangemen have armed, for it is a goodly thing to see arms in Irish hands.... I should like to see any and every body of Irish citizens armed. We must accustom ourselves to the thought of arms, to the sight of arms, to the use of arms. We may make mistakes in the beginning and shoot the wrong people; but bloodshed is a cleansing and a sanctifying thing, and the nation which regards it as the final horror has lost its manhood. There are many things more horrible than bloodshed; and slavery is one of them.

The answer to that is that war is slavery, a slavery into which he drove Irish nationalism for almost the rest of the century in place of the effective constitutional nationalism of O'Connell, Parnell, William O'Brien, and John Redmond. In his demand for the Irish people, Pearse was in fact walking in their footsteps which had beaten out the advances in democracy they forced on the Union for the entire archipelago. For all of his Anglophobia, Pearse was a prisoner of English fashions such as flourishing the yardstick of 'manhood', which however virtuous his intentions, was the language of the playground bully: fight, or you are a cowardy custard. He was absolutely typical of the world's youth panting for war in 1913, from Charles Peguy to Rupert Brooke. Vladimir Dedijer, Tito's comrade in arms, investigated the South Slavic nationalist roots of the assassination of the Archduke Franz Ferdinand which started World War 1, and closed his authoritative *The Road to Sarajevo* in 1968 by seeing the similarity of the Archduke's assassin Gavrilo Princip to Pearse and James Connolly. Pearse was a profound analyst however absurd his polemics. He clearly saw the confluence, the family resemblance, the comparable destinies of Ireland's war-worshipping nationalisms,

Ulster Unionists and their UK Tory allies as well as the nationalist varieties. As Yeats wrote in 'Easter 1916', he 'rode our winged horse' (meaning the Irish-Gaelic language) but here he was standing on it, surveying its equally spirited neighbours as they thundered on to doom apparently in glorious imitation of Tennyson's 'Charge of the Light Brigade', a prime favourite in school concerts throughout the UK. But 'The Coming Revolution' was also giving a perfect illustration of the press-ganging of Christianity by secular nationalism, on lines professionalised by Britannia to maintain her rule of the waves. Pearse was being more honest than the belligerent Ulster Protestant Bishops whose rhetoric seems to have inspired him, notably the Rt Reverend Charles D'Arcy, Bishop of Down, Dromore and Connor in whose diocese the Covenant was first signed with himself as the fourth signatory, stating:

> We must face the fact that there are worse things than
> war. Our trust is in God.

Pearse simply usurped Christ's place for Irish nationalism. The persecution of both Protestants and Catholics naturally led to an identification of their martyrs' suffering with the passion and death of Christ, but Pearse substituted the Irish Gaelic-speaking people implying they would now take His place, and had in their history suffered all His torments. Here he was less sectarian than the Ulster Covenant. While he was ruthlessly politicising the Gaelic League, and declaring its work reviving the Irish language was now secondary to that politicisation, its founder Douglas Hyde was a Protestant and Pearse was still calling him 'my leader', and honouring his League as the latter-day John the Baptist. For all of his idealism, Pearse could be a clever, devious Irish politician in intellectual architecture, so that if he called the Gaelic League John the Baptist readers would naturally know that in Ireland we tend to talk in personalities rather than institutions so that what he was really saying was that Douglas Hyde was the real John the Baptist, and therefore if Pearse called the Irish people Jesus Christ this meant that he was the real Christ but with his martyrdom ahead of him, not simply a historical interpretation. Christianity had claimed to be the new faith, as its particular Scriptures show in being called the New Testament. Pearse might appear to have been conservative in his zeal for Gaelic revival (and for bloodshed) but as his essay-title claimed he was preaching revolution in which Christianity no less than the Gaelic League were to take honoured places with the respect due to the retired. Desmond Ryan, great historian and memorialist (in one of the most valuable memoirs of Irish nationalism and its times, *Remembering Sion*) devoted to Pearse, called the Easter Rising 'the triumph of failure'. This was later adopted by my sister, Ruth Dudley Edwards, for her *Patrick Pearse: The Triumph of Failure* in 1974: the first assessment of Pearse by scientific professional standards of historiography. Insofar as Pearse planned the Easter Rising, however active in preparations with his six fellow-signatories of the Proclamation of the Irish Republic which officially began it and which would doom the seven in the UK military tribunals after the Rising – what he really imagined was his own suffering and death, and the resurrection of his cause – of himself – in the triumph of that failure. Some of his visionary poems – for instance '*Fornocht do Chonnac thu*' – envisioned that proposed pilgrimage in simple and even modest terns. Translated, it reads:

> Naked I saw you.
> O beauty of beauties,
> And I blinded my eyes
> For fear I should stare.
>
> I heard your music,
> O melody of melodies,
> And I closed my ears
> For fear I should hear.
>
> I tasted your mouth,
> O sweetness of sweetness,
> And I hardened my heart
> For fear of my spoiling.

I blinded my eyes
And I closed my ears,
And I hardened my heart
And I smothered my lust.

I turned my back
On the dream-vision I shaped,
And on the road before me
I set my face.

I have turned my face
To this road before me,
To the deed that I see
And the death I shall die.

It is finer in the original. It is unusually representative of all the Irish
people in its virtual love of asceticism, in readiness for self-sacrifice
for its own sake, in our assumptions (mistakenly) of our unique-
ness in wallowing in this austerity. It evolves in part from devotion
to Roman Catholicism in its days of persecution, as expressed by
Thomas Moore in lines still deeply cherished in Pearse's time. Pearse's
'Irish People' being the new Christ had a logical antecedent in verses
well known to Irish Catholic schoolchildren of his own day, Moore's
personification of the Irish Catholic church in 'The Irish Peasant to
his Mistress':

Through grief and through danger thy smile hath cheered
my way,
Till hope seemed to bud from each thorn that round me
lay;
The darker our fortune the brighter our pure love burned,
Till shame into glory, till fear into zeal was turned;
Yes, slave as I was, in thy arms my spirit felt free,
And blessed even the sorrows that made me more dear
to thee.

Thy rival was honoured while thou were wronged and
scorned,
Thy crown was of briars, while gold her brow adorned,
She wooed me to temples whilst thou layest hid in caves,
Her friends were all masters while thine alas were slaves;
Yet cold in the earth, at thy feet, I would rather be,
Then wed what I loved not, or turn one thought from
thee.

They slander thee sorely who say that thy vows are frail –
Hadst thou been a false one thy cheek had looked less
pale,
They say, too, so long hast thou worn those lingering
chains,
That deep in thy heart they have printed their servile
stains –
Oh, foul is the slander, – no chains could thy soul subdue –
Where shineth thy spirit, there liberty shineth, too.

It is noble, and gains rather than loses when we realise that with
small variation these could be the sentiments of Jews persecuted by
Christians for two millennia, Protestants persecuted by Catholics
across southern Europe, the Scottish Covenanters under Charles II,
and (as Byron would put it), the Devil can tell.

The new Christians

But Pearse triumphed in his failure, as Ruth Dudley Edwards finished her book by quoting:

I care not though I were to live but one day and one night
provided my name and my deeds live after me.

This process meant that he was canonised where he was not deified, but posterity prettified his grand vision as an educationist,
shop-windowed and carefully museumed it while renewing the
vampire existence of tatty Victorian snobocratic teaching, painting

it green, and hammered it into ensuing Irish generations. Shaw's Preface in 1915 to *Androcles and the Lion* is one of the best discussions of Jesus, Whom Shaw clearly liked and admired once he studied Him, but thought that Jesus went mad and thought He was God, whereas I think that (in most respects) the rest of us went mad and Jesus is God. But the Preface was deeply affected by World War 1 which had commenced midway between production of the play and creation of the Preface, with additional words following the play:

> ... the most striking aspect of the play at this moment is the terrible topicality given it by the war. We were at peace when I pointed out, by the mouth of Ferrovius, the path of an honest man who finds out, when the trumpet sounds, that he cannot follow Jesus. ... Great numbers of our clergy have found themselves of late in the position of Ferrovius.... They have discovered that they hate not only their enemies but everyone who does not share their hatred, and that they want to fight and to force other people to fight. They have turned their churches into recruiting stations and their vestries into munition workshops. But it has never occurred to them to take off their black coat and say quite simply, 'I find in the hour of trial that the Sermon on the Mount is tosh, and that I am not a Christian. I apologise for all the unpatriotic nonsense I have been preaching all these years. Have the goodness to give me a revolver and a commission in a regiment which has for its chaplain a priest of the god Mars: *my* God.' Not a bit of it. They have stuck to their livings and served Mars in the name of Christ, to the scandal of all religious mankind. ... apparently it seemed to the bishops as natural that the House of God should be looted when He allowed German to be spoken in it as that a baker's shop with a German name over the door should be pillaged. Their verdict was, in effect, 'Serve God right, for creating the Germans!'

Shaw, whether or not he knew it, had succeeded in diagnosing Pearse's propinquity to the very forces against whom he was seeking to lead the Irish. The beginning of the Preface insisted that Barabbas had stolen the name of Jesus 'and taken his cross as a standard'. Barabbas as a Zealot, a violent Jewish nationalist insurgent, had natural affinities with Pearse and with the UK war-lords, including General Sir John Maxwell who had him shot. Christianity was an empty formula for use when required and thereafter returned to the closet. Pearse had brought it to a finer art, admittedly, by the more direct identification with Jesus Christ, and its exploitation so that the cult of Pearse became a more rigorous martyr than ordinary Christianity. It went far beyond ordinary nationalism. No other Irish nationalist hero enjoyed such veneration. Nationalism among the Catholics liked to insist it was non-sectarian but there was an undertow of ecclesiastical cooler temperature for the names of Protestant leaders such as Wolfe Tone (suicide), Robert Emmet (Freemason?), Parnell (divorce), while O'Connell was blackguarded by republican ranks for being opposed to violence.

The Pearse cult had been carefully fostered by de Valera, with Pearse's mother and sister prominent on occasions appropriate to draw on reverent emotions. It carried a devotion to self-sacrifice: Pearse like Christ, but in our century, remembered publicly by a judiciously selected few, superior to the sacrosanct sacrificial soldiers Theobald Wolfe Tone, Lord Edward Fitzgerald, and Robert Emmet of the era of Revolution and Napoleon when the Union had been carried by treachery and corruption, superior also to the Young Irelanders and Fenians for all of their fine polemics and grand speeches from the dock, superior to the politics of O'Connell and Parnell and Redmond who only talked without reaching the stature of soldiers. It also appealed first of all to children: Pearse wrote little stories in Irish-Gaelic about Christ-like children redeeming old non-practising Catholics, or pretending to be priests saying Mass, or being saved from death by faithful dolls, or loving little birds and dying with soul flying away with them. The most obvious influence on them was Oscar Wilde, but they could not be suspected of plagiarism since Wilde's name could not be mentioned in polite early 20th century Irish society consecrated to Irish freedom.

The main fighting in the Easter Rising had been around the General Post Office in the centre of Dublin which had been the insurgents' headquarters, rather than being a shrine a sacred place through which everyone went and could see the heroic statue of Cuchulain by Oliver Sheppard, with the hero dying tied to the pillar to which he had tied his dying frame so that it would still intimidate his hateful fellow-Irish enemies: Sheppard, a sympathetic Irish Protestant from county Tyrone whose province Cuchulain had defended commemorated in plays by WB Yeats at the Abbey Theatre, but the statue itself made in 1911, inspiring Pearse and his brother Willie was placed in the Post Office by order of de Valera as head of Government in 1935. Irish iconoclastic wit could build its own armour, and nobody thought it funny that 'the Post Office' was a sacred allusion. Cuchulain's dying sigh broke the pillar to which he was tied, and made Nelson's Pillar outside in O'Connell Street irrelevant while silently also honouring a hero who gave his life for his country in any case blown up early in 1966, rumour said by a Breton nationalist on sabbatical leave then in communion with the IRA (who later put him on the run). Yeats's 'The Statues' written in 1938 concluded:

> When Pearse summoned Cuchulain to his side,
> What stalked through the Post Office? What intellect,
> What calculation, number, measurement, replied?
> We Irish, born into that ancient sect
> But thrown upon this filthy modern tide
> And by its formless spawning fury wrecked,
> Climb to our proper dark, that we may trace
> The lineaments of a plummet-measured face.

There you were. That said it all, even if you didn't know what it meant, for however anti-Catholic Yeats may have been or may have seemed from time to time, he spoke for Ireland now creating his mysteries like those in which Irish Catholic popular worship steeped itself contemplating Christ's passion and self-sacrifice as we said the Rosary and remembering Cuchulain's own cry that he wanted a life of great deeds and fame instead of living long, safe and happy. Two great figures seemed to echo that pagan prayer, neither of them Irish.

One was the great-grandson of Irish Catholic emigrants to the USA. John Fitzgerald Kennedy's election as US President in 1960 meant that Irish Catholic identity could declare itself a success at last, not merely claim some celebrity's grandmother as Irish: and when he was killed at the age of 45 my mother heard a man on a bus say 'Our little bit of grandeur is gone'. Pope St John XXIII became known to have been warned by a doctor when he had become Pope in 1958 that he could only live long with a quiet life and he transformed the Roman Catholic Church by summoning the Second Vatican Council telling us the Protestants we had repudiated as heretics damned in all senses of the world were our separated brethren whom we must love and among whom we must pray, just as we must love Christ's own people the Jews and expel all anti-Semitic beliefs from our minds and prayers. He also died in 1963.

A child is crying

Nevertheless, in 1966 the Republic of Ireland headed by its President Eamon de Valera commemorated the Easter Rising for its Golden Jubilee which meant six successive days of long essays revering Pearse in de Valera's own *Irish Press*. The *Irish Times* carried a massive supplement later edited as *1916: The Easter Rising* by the Features Editor Fergus Pyle and myself. Its star contribution was Conor Cruise O'Brien's 'The Embers of Easter' assessing where we were now in the light of what the insurgents of 1916 had sought. It also included Major Henry Harris's essay on the Irish Catholics and Protestants serving in the UK Army during World War I who were never mentioned on Catholic nationalist occasions, while in Northern Ireland the Protestant Ulstermen who died, especially at the Somme, were continually honoured in rhetoric as fulsome and unquestioning as that perpetually deluged around Pearse. The Catholic Irish who served, and many of whom died, in the UK forces were ignored on both sides of the border. The nationalism of the Republic, and the nationalism of Protestant Northern Ireland, found a common chord. In 1970 Reverend Professor Francis Shaw died in Dublin, for many years holder of the Chair of Early Irish in University College Dublin, leaving his Jesuit brethren to publish in their journal *Studies* 'The Canon of Irish History: A Challenge', in which he had written:

> In the commonly accepted view of Irish history the Irishman of today is asked to disown his own past. He is expected to censure as unpatriotic the common Irishmen who were not attracted by the new revolutionary ideas, but who adhered to an ancient tradition. Irishmen of today are invited at least implicitly to apologise for their fellow-countrymen who accepted loyally the serious guidance of the Church to which they belonged. Irishmen of today must despise as unmanly those of their own country who preferred to solve problems, if possible, by peaceful rather than by violent means.

My sister Ruth, quoting this in the last paragraphs of her Pearse biography, thought that Shaw

> made the same mistake as the propagandists he was attacking. No doubt intending to correct the balance, he painted Pearse in dark colours, contrasting starkly with the bright unsullied tints in which he had hitherto appeared: he too forgot the human being. Pearse can only be assessed accurately in the light of his own experiences and attitudes.

She then chose the best of all sources from whom to seek a reply, quoting extensively from 'Desmond Ryan, who loved him' in his *Remembering Sion* including:

> No honest portrait can hide certain shadows: a Napoleonic complex which expressed itself in a fanatical glorification of war for its own sake, an excess of sentiment which almost intoxicated him both on the platform and in private ventures ...

I loved Desmond Ryan, one of the most beautiful souls I have ever known, and if he loved Pearse, Pearse was worth loving. I did not love Frank Shaw, though at least one person I loved, did. What Shaw was really attacking was the deification of Pearse: that which presumed the Catholicism of Pearse's votaries but clearly placed him above Jesus Christ. Desmond Ryan himself was horrified at the continuation of the IRA. He might have agreed with me that Pearse could have been upset by the frighteningly prophetic cartoon in 1919 from Will Dyson in the Socialist *Daily Herald* showing David Lloyd George, Vittorio Emmanuele Orlando, Georges Clemenceau, and Woodrow Wilson leaving the Versailles Conference presumably after the last meeting of the all-powerful Council of Four. Clemenceau is depicted looking uneasily around at one of the classical pillars, captioned: '*THE TIGER: 'Curious! I seem to hear a child weeping!'* but failing to see a naked baby with its hand to its eyes, above whom appears: '1940 CLASS', and at its foot a discarded paper headed 'PEACE TREATY'. How would Pearse have felt were he to know that 2016's best-seller book in Dublin would be about the children killed in Dublin during the Easter Rising? Or that within four years of the Golden Jubilee in which he was still given top billing, and an eight-day full-dress serial television historical soap-opera flanked by television, radio, stage, pageant, and press commemorations, reaped their harvest in the 30 years' war in Northern Ireland?

The realism preached by Conor Cruse O'Brien with wit and imagination also took effect rapidly and the politics of social justice began to displace monotonous anti-partition regurgitations. Serious historical questions began to be asked about figures other than Pearse, most notably his ultimate comrade in arms James Connolly whose socialist ideas began to win much wider celebration in their own right instead of merely pigeon-holed as funny things happening on the way to the Rising. The Rising itself cast socialist shadows, as Fergus Pyle and I discovered two years later when our publisher, Timothy O'Keeffe of MacGibbon & Kee sent a copy of our *1916: The Easter Rising* to Ho Chi Minh in Hanoi. Being a pacifist I didn't support any fighting by anyone. I had been a part of the protest against the war in Vietnam, most of whose number were for peace, not for any side. David Aberle, Professor of Anthropology, at the University of Oregon, who led our Faculty-Student group against the

War in Vietnam where I taught from 1963 to 1965, would say 'I do not propose to weigh the corpses'.

We found it particularly tragic in that everyone had voted for or (if like me a non-voter) supported President Lyndon Johnson in the Presidential Election of 1964 and admired his utter dedication (superior to that of any previous President) to integrate all persons of race, colour, previous condition of servitude etc. LBJ had felt so passionately against segregation that he deliberately made a speech at New Orleans near the end of his campaign denouncing the destruction of southern politics from the white population's obsession with maintaining segregation: he knew it would cost him the Deep South, and it lost him Alabama, Georgia, Louisiana, Mississippi, and South Carolina, Georgia voting Republican for the first time in its existence. Johnson had absolutely no interest in foreign affairs, in which he was unlike many white southern politicians, notably Senator William Fulbright of Arkansas, rapidly becoming a major critic of the war in Vietnam.

The Teach-In movement on Vietnam discovered to its considerable surprise that the White House was much more ignorant of Vietnamese realities than were its academic critics across the USA. LBJ was still using Kennedy's advisers on foreign affairs, very much mired in a smart-ass recycling of conventional Cold War postures. The Teach-In movement won agreement to a debate early in 1965 between Kennedy's leading Harvard adviser McGeorge Bundy and Professor George McTurnin Kahin of Cornell. Kahin's thesis, which most of us shared, was that Ho Chi Minh was a Vietnamese nationalist, whose communism was secondary to his nationalism, and that his success arose because of Vietnamese reverence for him as the nationalist leader who had led them against the Japanese, against the French, and now against their war-time allies the Americans who had betrayed war-time promises to support Vietnam independence and instead backed the French attempt to reconquer their former empire in Indo-China. In the event, Bundy chickened out of the debate at the last moment. Ho sent a very kind message for our book in late 1968 and told us that when Lord Mayor Terence MacSwiney of Cork was on hunger-strike against his UK police custodians in Brixton Prison, from 16

August 1920 until he died on 25 October, the 30-year-old Vietnam-ese followed his suffering day-by-day. After the failure of Vietnamese nationalists to win attention from the Versailles Conference Ho Chi Minh remained in the UK and in France, and in autumn 1920 was a kitchen scullion in the Ritz hotel where he managed to get hold of newspapers describing the hunger-strike. He remembered crying his eyes out. He died in 1969. I think I had a Mass said for his soul. Ho Chi Minh had started life as a Catholic. Hunger strikes are obvi-ously contrary to God's teaching since they are suicide, but Christ's 40-day-fast in the wilderness before beginning his public life was a natural inspiration to MacSwiney and would have made sense to Ho Chi Minh.

Initially hunger-strikes were actions by non-violent prisoners, before World War 1, notably the suffragettes (some of whom did commit violent actions but not against persons) and labour agitators. After the Easter Rising, surviving insurgents went on hunger-strike and one commandant who had participated in the fighting – Thomas Ashe – died on hunger-strike in 1917. MacSwiney was not associated with violence and Ho seems to have thought of him as non-violent. Bobby Sands who led the Provisional IRA hunger-strikers in Belfast, dying in May 1981, had considerable violent experience including gun-battles against the police. The nonagenarian nationalist leader, independent communist, and novelist Peadar O'Donnell countered the waves of sympathy these martyrdoms excited by saying in the Labour History Society conference and elsewhere:

> The hunger-strikers are a pack of snobs! They say they object to being treated like ordinary criminals! What's wrong with ordinary criminals, I'd like to know? A very decent crowd I've always found them!

Scotland a nation?

My wife Bonnie Lee, a Philadelphian by birth, married me on 27 July 1966 in Dublin and we came to Aberdeen where I was to teach at the university, stayed for two years becoming parents of twin daughters before we left, and went to the University of Edinburgh where I taught history and our son was born. We have been here since then. I had known Scotland before, having been welcomed here by Robert Burns, Walter Scott, Robert Louis Stevenson, Arthur Conan Doyle, John Buchan and Hugh MacDiarmid (the last of whom I knew in person as well as in his writings), apart from infantile acquaintance with Scottish history books for children and Highland history serials in the close print of the *Adventure* comic from DC Thomson of Dundee.

Thomson did not name authors but quite exceptionally identified stories by the Scottish history author with ascription of his earlier work. His name may have been Maclean or he may have had a family connection with the clan. I found that other Irish Catholic readers of Stevenson or *Adventure* testified that there was a natural affinity between Scots characters and ourselves (Protestant youthful friends were ready to identify with Stevenson's sentiments rather than his characters, and where they didn't feel Irish they usually felt more English than Scottish). The *Adventure* tried its hand with a few Scots-Gaelic words: these often linked with Irish-Gaelic though more with Ulster than Munster or Connacht dialects.

By the time we came to Scotland, James Connolly's Scottish birth and upbringing had been established by Desmond Greaves, the great London communist historian of Irish nationalism. It was some time before I realised that the continual error in Irish reverential republicanism that Connolly was born in 1870 in Monaghan instead of in 1868 in Edinburgh, may have started with Connolly himself. Connolly worked on some projects with the xenophobic Arthur Griffith who evaded unanswerable arguments by identifying the questioner as non-Irish and therefore not permitted to speak. Nevertheless, there were Connolly admirers and to spare in the Edinburgh I met from 1968. His great-nephew Ian Bell became one of the crack reporters, analysts and essayists in Scottish journalism, and wrote one of the best books on Stevenson to have appeared in the past century: *Dreams of Exile* in 1992, worthy to put on the same shelf as the Stevenson studies by Edinburgh's foremost Jewish literary critic and historian David Daiches, by his daughter Jenny, and by GK Chesterton. Bernard Ransom, one of my students, produced a fine doctoral thesis on Connolly's Scottish years and relations with the Scottish Left, particularly establishing Connolly's syndicalism, as shown in his *Connolly's Marxism*. Connolly's great achievement was to integrate socialism and nationalism notably in his *Labour in Irish History* and *Labour, Nationality and Religion* released in 1910, *The Reconquest of Ireland* in 1915, innumerable editorials and brief notes in the various weekly and monthly newspapers he edited or contributed to in Edinburgh, Dublin, Belfast, New York, Chicago and elsewhere. His ambition was to make Irish Catholics look back through their history and see what workers were doing or what was being done to them. It was not simply an application of Marxism to Irish history, though he could come up with interesting, thitherto undiscovered results of research bringing unknown observers and theoreticians to light and chapters of unknown proletarian history. He was actually demanding total history, recognising that much of history limited itself to elites of various kinds, all holding on to their gains by whatever means.

It was, for instance, Connolly – as modern historical scholarship has recognised – who saw to the heart of the Irish Great Famine of the 1840s when pointing out it was created by the existing land system. He was impressively cosmopolitan in writing for audiences in Scotland and America, but he was trying to convert his own ethnic group to socialism, and failed sufficiently to analyse the history of the Protestant working class in Ireland. He had learned the art of mini-polemic in Scotland up to 1896. The Scots seem to have shown him how well humour could travel as an essential part of socialist education. He realised how successful anti-socialist Catholic priests could be, and how much socialists could gain by having the courage to take them on, and the learning and logic to answer them. He may have drawn this from Scottish Protestant comrades: hearing of the Presbyterians after the service discussing points of (dis)agreement with the sermon just concluded, may have spurred him on to controversy with priests in print and in lecture, since confronting the holy man after Mass was not encouraged by Catholic priests or laity.

Connolly thought that his participation in the Easter Rising would give socialism credentials for the new Irish state if it ever arrived, whereas in fact it was taken as approval of the new state to have had his own martyrdom sanctified by inclusion under Pearse's super-martyrdom. Connolly, dying (of gangrene in a wound before his execution) told his family that his old comrades surprised at his death would have forgotten that he was an Irishman; perhaps, but they hadn't forgotten that he was a Scot. John Maclean, self-discovered as his honorary disciple, testified to their joint faith and Maclean himself was honoured by Lenin in revolutionary Russia, as he was in the Silver Jubilee of his death when Hugh MacDiarmid, Sidney Goodsir Smith and Hamish Henderson gave song and poetry in his honour in Dundee.

A different legacy from Connolly struck the great Tom Johnston – who had been the editor of *Forward,* the major Scottish socialist weekly to which Maclean contributed, as did Connolly still only weeks before leading his Irish Citizen Army into the Easter Rising. Connolly's death from firing-squad bullets made Johnston feel that international socialism had lost one of its greatest sons: self-sacrificed in an absurd nationalist self-destruct. He worked thereafter to keep Scotland as much socialist as possible, and as little nationalist. Johnston's *Our Scots Noble Families* proved invaluable for the development of socialism in Scotland selling 100,000 copies. He followed it with *History of the Working Classes in Scotland* in 1920. He rose high within the Labour Party and became Secretary of State for Scotland in Churchill's wartime coalition, establishing the North of Scotland Hydro-Electric Board which proved to be a great achievement in his life's work. On the other hand, Robert Bontine Cunninghame-Graham – first President of the Scottish Labour Party in 1888 and first President of the Scottish National Party in 1934 – had been the first socialist in the House of Commons as MP for North Lanarkshire 1886–92, but he was a fanatical supporter of the UK war effort in 1914. Cunninghame-Graham was all in favour of Irish constitutional nationalism. He was cudgelled by the police when he charged the constables prohibiting a meeting for the release of the Irish Home Rule leader William O'Brien MP at Trafalgar Square on 13 November 1887 and was subsequently sentenced to imprisonment for assaulting the police.

These were but a few ways in which Irish nationalism haunted the birth of Scottish, and Hugh MacDiarmid and Compton Mackenzie – vociferous admirers of Irish literary nationalism – were but two of earliest campaigners for the National Party of Scotland founded in 1928. Its earliest history being Eric Linklater's autobiographical novel *Magnus Merriman* (1934) describing his experiences as a Scottish nationalist candidate for Fife. One of the effects of the dissolution of the UK Union of Great Britain and Ireland in 1922 was the birth of two great literary nationalist topographical fictionists when two excise officers Neil Gunn and Maurice Walsh were informed that Walsh's transfer to Scotland, where their collegiality and friendship had been consolidated, must now end with his return to his native Ireland. The great Caledonian antisyzygy – perhaps best summed up in MacDiarmid's self-location 'where extremes meet' – likes the idea of official, douce, legalised, masterful, common-sensed figures respected in law, church or state hungrily embracing folk-poetry, uncouth landscapes, contradictions, alcohol and comradeship across implacable seas. Burns as an excise officer is one perfect example (and Scott as lawyer, landowner, and sheriff another), and the parting of Gunn and Walsh one of its most ironic twists, for to stay in cultural communion they gave themselves new identities as topographical novelists of Scotland and Ireland publishing first novels in 1926. Walsh recorded the legacies of nationalism in Ireland with greatest celebrity in his short story so triumphantly filmed by John Ford as *The Quiet Man* in 1952, and Gunn opening his masterpiece *The Silver Darlings* with a husband and father seized from his fishing-boat by UK Navy pressmen in the Napoleonic wars leaving a family bereft and mystified: a grim metaphor for the potential effects of the Union on its remote subjects, crafted by a life-long Scottish nationalist. The National Party of Scotland was merged forever with the Scottish Party to become the Scottish National Party in 1934. 'King' John MacCormick, the dynamic learned lawyer building up the diplomatic – and undiplomatic – moves, recorded something of the ancillary debates in his memoir *The Flag in the Wind: The Story of the National Movement in Scotland* in which he revealed how

Ireland's vicissitudes raised questions as to what kind of an Irish nation Scotland might become:

> At last it came the turn of Angus Clark to speak in his own defence. Never have I heard a more eloquent or restrainedly impassioned statement. He was a native Gaelic speaker bred in Ballachulish and, in spite of many years in London, his voice still carried a strong Highland inflection which like some nostalgic music stirred me strangely. Nearly everything he said appealed strongly to the more romantic side of my nature. He was out and out for Scotland's independent nationhood and no compromise. Those who sought for practical means of attaining even a tithe of what he wanted were mere timeservers, careerists, traitors to the cause. With a scornful gesture he pointed to me as a young upstart who would soon find his proper place in English politics. 'Let us', he said, 'take a leaf from the pages of Ireland's recent history, and let us remember our ancient past.'

> He ended by quoting that memorable phrase from the Declartion of Arbroath:

> For as long as one hundred of us remain alive we shall never submit to the dominion of the English.

> When he sat down there was a tremendous outburst of applause from the whole assembly. Every member there was visibly moved by his impassioned sincerity and obvious good faith. I felt that the day was lost and I almost rose to move that the resolutions should be withdrawn. Instead I replied with as much coolness as could tom his charges of treachery and careerism. We in this hall, I suggested, were not the Scottish nation, however much we might be tempted so to picture ourselves. The nation was not an abstraction, an imaginary Dark Rosaleen, but a living reality composed of living individual people. It was with the people we had to contend and it was their mood

which we must seek to interpret. We could only be effective leaders of opinion so long as we did not race too far ahead of those whom we wished to follow us.

Even an effective and austere organiser, such as John Mac-Cormick, reflected the Caledonian antisyzygy – perhaps not as fully as his son Professor Neil MacCormick MEP: Scotland's master-philosopher of law and joyful celebrant of Scottish literature. The business in hand in October 1933 entailed the expulsion of Angus Clark, and the remaking of his London branch. That clash of titans as remembered by 'King John' turned on their Irish question: was Scottish nationalism's pursuit of Ireland to be renewal of the alliances between Scots crofter champions and the Irish Home Rule Party under Parnell, or was it to follow the Irish armed revolt begun in 1916?

MacCormick stated an excellent creed in rejecting the personalised Ireland for the reality of the Scottish people and it has been an SNP virtue ever since that its national idea remained the Scottish people, welcoming the world so long as it knows that in Scotland we are Scots. It was also a perfect definition of nationalism: 'not an abstraction… but a living reality composed of living individual people.' It was certainly classifiable as populist and an excellent example of populism at its best. But 'Dark Rosaleen' had another meaning which Clark and MacCormick knew. The leaf from the pages of Ireland's recent history and the memory of our ancient past meant equating Michael Collins and Robert Bruce, remote heroism conscripted into modern vendetta, destructive idealisation of the world-wide slaughter of the Great War and the cruel fratricidal campaigns of Ireland's war for independence – the UK's Black and Tans and public-school Auxiliaries, the IRA's guerrilla ambush and killer squads with consequent civil war. It was an appeal to Yeats's *Cathleen Ni Houlihan* with young men rejuvenating an ideal Ireland by the bridegroom denying his betrothal to embrace his killings and death. Was it purely Ireland? Irish romantic nationalism had owed much to the folklore and creativity of Walter Scott whose 'Pibroch of Dhonuil Dhu' had sung Cathleen's message a century before her play:

> Leave untended the herd,
> The flock without shelter,
> Leave the corpse uninterr'd,
> The bride at the altar...

Dark Rosaleen was older, MacCormick obviously remembering James Clarence Mangan's mid-19th century formalisation of a 16th century Irish-Gaelic poem '*Roisin Dubh*' culminating:

> O! the Erne shall run red
> With redundance of blood,
> The earth shall rock beneath our tread,
> And flames wrap hill and wood,
> And gun-peal, and slogan-cry,
> Wake many a glen serene,
> Ere you shall fade, ere you shall die,
> My Dark Rosaleen!
> My own Rosaleen!
> The judgment hour must first be nigh,
> Ere you can fade, ere you can die,
> My Dark Rosaleen!

Modern scholarship, at its most impish, has suggested that Dark Rosaleen really was a woman rather than Ireland, and the author a somewhat demented Irish priest enraptured by his illicit love for her. It may not have been virginal then, but Mangan restores its virginity, a remarkable achievement in any language. The 20-year-old James Joyce when a student at University College Dublin wrote that in 'Dark Rosaleen' Mangan's

> music shakes off its languor and is full of the ecstacy of combat... it does not attain to the quality of Whitman indeed, but is tremulous with all the changing harmonies of Shelley's verse.

MacCormick was genuine in his near-seduction by the idea, very conscious of his Gaelic-speaking parentage and as ready as any fundamentalist Irish-Gaelic hagiographer to denounce Normans. He may have read 'Roisin Dubh' in the original Ulster Gaelic whose apocalyptic last verse merely leaves the 80-mile River Erne with strong waves amidst raped hills but promises the Atlantic Ocean in red waves and the sky filled with blood before the little dark Rose will die. Wilde uses the Gaelic heritage in 'The Nightingale and the Rose' where the Rose becomes red when the Nightingale drives its thorn into her own heart. In any version the red meant blood and death. MacCormick's rejection of the abstraction, however beautiful, and homage to the people, however cold, meant outlawing violence from nationalism and putting humanity before dogma.

Whose war?

The Scottish National Party was born in April 1934 pledged to non-violence. It barred some of MacCormick's opponents, minutes of its first meeting specifically stating that if Mr CM Grieve (aka Hugh MacDiarmid) attempted to pay his shilling it was to be given back to him. The charter of modern Scottish Nationalism, MacDiarmid's *A Drunk Man Looks at the Thistle* quickly became the permanent reservoir of nationalist spirit, with other spirits always welcome. Yet in June 1942, the Party Convention ended with MacCormick's resignation on the issue of violence. MacCormick recalled the impact of World War II beginning on 3 September 1939 for the UK:

> When finally war broke out we adopted a strongly worded resolution pledging full support to the war effort although reserving the right to speak out for what we believed were Scotland's special interests. We realised that the impact of war would inevitably restrict our capacity for propaganda but we were determined to maintain the identity of our movement.

This was the rock on which the SNP nationalism of John MacCormick ultimately broke, and his break was not simply ideological: it was partly the anger of the most professional politician in the party. As such he was always the party Secretary, never Chairman. He fostered intellect, becoming the father of one of Scotland's greatest

intellectuals of our time in his son Neil, though his own nationalism was as crude as that of Ireland's Michael Collins in imagining
his nation's 'essential core' as 'racially unchanged through all the
centuries since Calgacus had defied the Roman legions of Agricola'
which is almost as daft as believing that Calgacus never existed. John
MacCormick's greatness of heart is evident in the generosity of his
evaluation of the 30 year old who became his Nemesis in 1942 perhaps without ever knowing it:

> Douglas Young, then a lecturer in Greek in Aberdeen, and
> a very striking figure indeed. He was over 6 feet 5 inches
> in height and wore a neatly trimmed black beard. He was
> forceful and eloquent in public speech and a most per-
> suasive talker in private conversation. He had joined the
> Party some years ago but, except in Aberdeen, he had not
> made any great impact on the movement until now. By
> refusing to accept his call-up papers to the Forces, how-
> ever, he now leapt into prominence. He pleaded before
> the Conscientious Objectors' Tribunal not that he was a
> pacifist, but that, as a Scotsman, no Government of the
> United Kingdom had power to impose conscription upon
> him. He quoted the terms of the Treaty of Union in sup-
> port of his case but, needless to say, the Tribunal rejected
> his plea. When he then indicated that he would, in any
> case, refuse call-up and suffer imprisonment rather than
> yield, he became the hero and the natural leader of the
> anti-war section of the National Party. Matters came to
> a head when, after having been sentenced in the Sheriff
> Court to one year's imprisonment and while still await-
> ing his appeal to the High Court, he was nominated for
> the Chairmanship of the Party in opposition to William
> Power, at our Annual Conference in June, 1942.

What nobody except Douglas Young and English officials seem to
have known was that Young was out of the country on research
when the war broke out and, on return to the UK, he reported to
the authorities in the Clarendon Buildings at Oxford as a volunteer

for war service and was discovered to have a heart condition which invalidated him. SNP had passed a resolution declaring conscription in Scotland was unlawful. They were not alone. Both the Labour Party and the Liberals had opposed its enactment immediately before the war. It was extended during the war but maladministered. It was never enacted for Northern Ireland, although the Northern Ireland Ulster Unionist government wanted it, and the Churchill coalition cabinet seriously discussed it (fortified by a characteristic Churchillism that they might as well introduce it since all the recruits there came from the South – close, and he already had the cigar). The following week Home Secretary Herbert Morrison, to his great credit, informed the cabinet that new information indicated he had been wrong to have advocated it, and that the UK's friend the *Irish Times* strongly opposed it. In fact, it would probably have increased local IRA recruitment to the advantage of the Nazis, and might even have led to violent revolt in Catholic districts. After all, the mere threat of conscription extended to Ireland in 1918 had enabled Sinn Féin to win the December election, with the ultimate loss of the 26 counties.

Young's motivation was in the UK's interest in that it showed that shoddy administration of Union obligations needed to be cleared up. In peace or war 'Britain Muddles Through' was frequently preferred to efficiency and taken for patriotism, and HM judges in wartime had little desire to dissent. Young was elected party chair at the June SNP Conference and MacCormick, although re-elected secretary, resigned from the office and the party. Young's appeal was dismissed on 10 July and he served eight of his 12-month sentence, although in recognition of his actual medical condition the prison Governor had him sleep in the Governor's quarters, he played the music at Church of Scotland Sunday services, and the party secretary Dr Robert McIntyre had bagpipes played in his honour outside the jail on Sundays. Young was once again prosecuted, this time for failing to report for labour duties, once more declared conscription violated the Treaty of Union, was sentenced to three months' imprisonment on 13 June 1944, his appeal dismissed on 7 October 1944. Meanwhile Young had been nominated as SNP candidate in a Kirkcaldy by-election and although defeated won 42 per cent, prison having accomplished more than with all of his professionalism MacCormick had been able to achieve for the party's various candidates. Irish history could have told him that story. MacIntyre was nominated at the Motherwell by-election in April 1945 and won. Major party wartime arrangements meant a single Unionist candidate at by-elections from the wartime coalition parties, but it was clear that Scotland had accepted Young (however secretly innocent) as having become a convict in good faith with no crypto-Nazi implication.

Old dogs with new tricks

MacCormick learned a lesson here and used the law courts to question the title of the new Queen to be officially known as Elizabeth II Queen of Scotland instead of Elizabeth I. The issue aroused excitement being a rarity. Scotland, England, Wales and Ireland had received the same number of Georges until the abdication of Edward VIII meant that Eire under de Valera and his new Constitution could accept one King's departure but decline an Irish enthronement of George VI, making Edward Ireland's last King. He was in fact only Edward II of Scotland but never being crowned was off the throne before the numbers game could be resumed. There had been criticism of Edward VII not being Edward I, but the delay in his coronation by his almost fatal illness may have muted that.

MacCormick, although out of the party, obtained two million signatures out of Scotland's five million asking for a devolutionary legislature, and for all of his suspicion of Irish precedents learning from de Valera's exploitation of the constitutional momentum created by Westminster's parochialism in 1936–7. Elizabeth's coronation inaugurated a Tory revival celebrating the return from war and its consequent austerity, and so neo-Elizabethanism dawned with English historians rejuvenating themselves and their subjects with bright studies of Good Queen Bess. Northern Ireland, initially and informally taken to be a temporary solution to shelve rather than solve the Irish question, now had an appearance of durability after the Dublin coalition against de Valera trying to outbid him in gestures of nationalism had declared a Republic in 1949, to which Clement

Attlee as Labour Prime Minister responded with a guarantee of permanent status for Northern Ireland regardless of its Unionist rule which supplied permanent support for the Tories from the MPs it sent to Westminster. So, formally acknowledging the change of union since 1922, the Proclamation of Elizabeth on 28 May 1953 for the first time substituted 'Northern Ireland' for 'Ireland' since the Proclamation of George VI had desperately cut corners necessitated by the unexpected change of king, and the even more unexpected disappearance of the king from Ireland's more Papist 26 counties. It may have been that John MacCormick was encouraged by the success of Terence Rattigan's play *The Winslow Boy* in 1946, and subsequent film with Robert Donat as Sir Robert Morton, clearly based on Sir Edward Carson who fought for the rights of the victimised naval cadet George Archer-Shee in the real-life case *Archer-Shee v Rex*. When *MacCormick and Another* was decided against the plaintiffs in the Court of Appeal, an unexpected assertion of Scottish nationalism emerged from the Lord President of the Court of Session, Lord Cooper, delivering judgment for a united judicial trio. Thomas Cooper had been a bright, perhaps brilliant, Tory MP for Edinburgh West, Solicitor-General for Scotland and Lord Advocate before becoming Lord Justice-Clerk and then Lord President. The judgment brought out the existence of legal nationalism, otherwise conservative Scots lawyers thunderously defensive of Scots law, sure of its superiority to English law, and contemptuous of the slovenly workmanship of English authorities in the creation of the circumstances which gave rise to MacCormick's action which however wrong was justifiably undertaken, costs being therefore denied to the Government with all parties paying their own. The Act of 1953 under which the Proclamation of Queen Elizabeth had been made could not have been construed had it been necessary to construe it

> because the Act is not self-contained... The Lord Advocate admitted that the Act was not self-explanatory, and offered in supplement a White Paper, which he indicated had been made available in the Vote Office prior to the consideration of the Bill. But Parliament can only speak

through the medium of a statute. A Court of Law is not entitled to investigate the Parliamentary History of a Bill whether in the pages of Hansard or their equivalent a 'white paper', and I am therefore forced to the conclusion that this act must remain incapable of being fully understood or intelligently interpreted by any Court, the legislature having withheld the material necessary for that purpose. Be that as it may. I consider that the Lord Advocate failed to show that there is or ever was, Parliamentary authority for the adoption by Her Majesty of the name and the 'numeral' which in fact were adopted on Her Majesty's Accession and have been used ever since.

Implicitly here it was the complacency of Westminster that was punctured in its parochialism. Cooper harmonised with the US Supreme Court judgment of Marshall, CJ, in *Chisholm v Georgia* in 1810 where a Georgia statute was invalidated partly on the ground that a Court may not enter into the motivations of a legislature. Lord Cooper then declared:

> The principle of the unlimited Sovereignty of Parliament is a distinctively English principle which has no counterpart in Scottish Constitutional law.

He went on to dispose of English constitutional authorities, notably Alfred Venn Dicey, whose conclusions had been passed off as scholarly but were chiefly dignified polemic. Neal Ascherson and Tom Nairn, eloquent devolutionist journalists of the 1970s and 1980s, followed this beacon in attacking the tyranny of a Thatcherite parliamentary majority elected under the anti-democratic first-past-the-post election system. They also symbolised the transformation of so many Scottish intellectuals from instinctive unionism to profound nationalism, the historians Angus Calder and Christopher Harvie being among the most distinguished. Both John MacCormick and Douglas Young reached for wider participants. The covenant two million brought no results at the time though Lord Cooper would have been aware of them while not noticing them: they did represent a potential for Scottish nationalism.

Non-violent nationalism in politics across the world meant parties of yesterday: the SNP was now the party of tomorrow. Douglas Young resigned the party chair after the war, and left the party in 1948 in protest against a decision to no longer permit members to hold members to hold simultaneous membership of other political parties (the exception being the Welsh nationalist party, Plaid Cymru). His future literary career ranged from translation of Aristophanes into Scots (including *The Burdies* at the Edinburgh International Festival in 1967) and one of the widest ranging poetic anthologies *Scottish Verse 1851–1951*: the wider Scottish nationalist landscape was visibly beckoning from Homer to Hugh MacDiarmid. Meanwhile SNP's Chair of the late 1950s, the historian Jimmy Halliday, gently permeated the party with the ideals of American democracy at their most liberal, identification with ideals of racial integration in the USA (and South Africa), hatred of witch-hunting of Joe McCarthy, courage amid upheaval. Individual SNP Chairs – MacIntyre, Arthur Donaldson, Billy Wolfe, Gordon Wilson – appealed to different souls winning very different forms of nationalism, but all vigilantly non-violent.

Ultimately SNP found its Franklin D Roosevelt in Alex Salmond whose transformation of the party in size and power in the new devolved Scotland meant a new deal. He brought back to political life FDR's genius for improvisation, for education, for exhilaration and for laughter, and like FDR it will take historians as yet unborn to face his fascination.

Yet while Scottish nationalism continues on its quest into the future seeking permanence for peace and justice nationally and internationally, it remains the nationalism declared at Arbroath in 1320 where the nobles, articulated by the clergy, told Pope John XXII having detailed the fate of the Scots under the late Edward I:

> But from these countless evils we have been set free, by
> the help of Him Who though He afflicts yet heals and
> restores, by our most tireless Prince, King and Lord, the
> Lord Robert. He, that his people and his heritage might
> be delivered out of the hands of our enemies, met toil

and fatigue, hunger and peril, like another Maccabeus or Joshua and bore them cheerfully. Divine providence, the succession to his right according to our laws and customs which we shall maintain to the death, and the due consent and assent of us all, have made him our Prince and King. We are bound to him for the maintaining of our freedom both by his right and merits, as to him by whom salvation has been wrought unto our people, and by him, come what may, we mean to stand. Yet if he should give up what he has begun, seeking to make us or our kingdom subject to the king of England or to the English, we would strive at once to drive him out as our enemy or as a subverter of his own right and ours, and we would make some other man who was able to defend us our king. For as long as a hundred of us remain alive, we will never on any conditions be subjected to the lordship of the English. For we fight not for glory nor riches nor honours, but for freedom alone, which no good man gives up except with his life....

It concluded by declaring itself directed to the Pope by the community of Scotland, and committing their cause, their cares and their continued courage to God.

Timeline of relevant events

4004BCE	God's creation of Earth as believed by most Christians before 1914
c 1200BCE	Supposed destruction of Priam's Troy
1290/1260BCE	Supposed exodus of Israelites from Egypt led by Moses
c 1000BCE	Saul King of Israel (then including Judah) followed by David
c 800BCE	Possible date in the life of Homer
753BCE	Traditional date for foundation of Rome
70BCE	Birth of Virgil
44BCE	Murder of Julius Caesar
19BCE	Death of Publius Vergilius Maro
14AD	Death of Caesar Augustus
c 33AD	Crucifixion of Jesus Christ
c 83AD	Calgacus, Caledonian general, defeated by Julius Agricola
c 98AD	Cornelius Tacitus completes *Agricola*
430AD	Death of St Augustine
c 600AD	Aneirin near Firth of Forth creates *Y Gododdin*. Taliesin in Clyde valley creates Welsh poems, songs and prophesies
1013	King Svein of Denmark conquers England
1014	King Brian Boramha of Ireland defeats Viking leaders at Clontarf
1016	Cnut son of Svein King of England
1040	MacBethad succeeds Duncen I as King of Scotland
1050	MacBethad visits Pope St Leo IX
1054	MacBethad defeated by Siward Viking ruler of Northumbria
1066	King Harold II defeats invasion led by King Harald Hardrada of Norway. William the Norman defeats and kills Harold II, usurping English throne
1155	Death of Geoffrey of Monmouth: mythologist inventor of British history
1169	Henry II authorises Norman invasion of Ireland

1175	Treaty of Windsor confirms Henry II's lordship of Ireland
1282	Llywelyn the Last, Prince of Wales, killed in Builth
1284	Wales declared annexed by Edward I in Statute of Rhuddlan
1305	Edward I executes Sir William Wallace Guardian of Scotland
1306	Robert Bruce crowned King Robert I of the Scots
1307	Death of Edward I *en route* for reinvasion of Scotland
1314	Robert I defeats Edward II at Bannockburn
1320	Declaration of Arbroath affirms perpetual independence of Scotland
1366	Statute of Kilkenny decrees segregation of native Irish from English, unsuccessfully
1415	Henry V invades France
1422	Death of Henry V
1431	Joan of Arc defeats English who have her burnt at Rouen
1485	Welsh-born Henry VII (Tudor) defeats and kills Richard III at Bosworth
1522	Death of Bishop Gavin Douglas translator of *Aeneid* into Scots
1533–36	Henry VIII nationalises Church of England rejecting Papacy
1536	Henry VIII declares himself King of Ireland and Supreme Head of its Church
1536–43	Henry VIII's Parliament enacts Union of England and Wales
1560	Reformation Parliament in Scotland breaks with Papacy
1561	Return of Mary Queen of Scots widowed Queen of France
1567	Enforced abdication of Mary Queen of Scots in favour of infant son James VI
1569	James Fitzmaurice Fitzgerald killed leading Papal invasion of Ireland
1587	Execution of Mary Queen of Scots by Elizabeth I's order
1588	Destruction of Spanish Armada
1601	Defeat of Irish chieftains and Spanish invaders at Kinsale
1603	James VI of the Scots inherits England, Ireland and Wales as James I
1604	James VI and I proclaims himself King of Great Britain and Ireland
1606	*King Lear* and *Macbeth*
1616	Death of Shakespeare
1625	Death of James VI and I

1638	National Covenant defending Scottish presbyterianism against Charles I
1649	Execution of Charles I
1652	Cromwell declares Union of England, Scotland and Ireland, ratified 1657
1658	Death of Cromwell
1660	Restoration of Charles II, Union abolished
1688	Dutch invasion of England under William of Orange ousting James II and VII
1689	William and James's daughter Mary accept Crown of England, then that of the Scots
1702–14	War of the Spanish Succession led by England against Louis XIV
1707	Union of England and Scotland
1714	George I (Hanover) inherits Great Britain and Ireland
1776	Declaration of Independence by British colonists as United States of America
1775–83	War of American Independence
1787–88	Constitution of USA drafted and ratified by required majority
1789	Eisteddfod at Corwen inaugurates festival celebrating Welsh music and poetry
1789–1815	Revolution in France followed by Napoleonic revival and empire
1796	Death of Robert Burns
1800	Union of Great Britain and Ireland enacted abolishing Irish Parliament
1801	United Kingdom of Great Britain and Ireland established retaining Irish viceroyalty
1829	Catholics admitted to UK Parliament where O'Connell becomes radical leader
1832	Death of Sir Walter Scott
1842	Young Ireland founds weekly *Nation* with unrivalled success across UK
1843–44	O'Connell convicted for non-violent monster meetings to have Union Repealed
1845–52	Irish Great Famine, 1.5 million dead, 1 million emigrating to Britain and abroad
1847	Death of O'Connell

1859	Death of Thomas Babington Macaulay
1861–65	American Civil War ending in defeat of 11 seceded slaveowner states
1869	Episcopalian state Church of Ireland disestablished and disendowed
1880	Parnell tours North America and becomes Home Rule party leader in Westminster
1884	Gaelic Athletic Association founded by Michael Cusack
1886	Gladstone's First Irish Home Rule Bill defeated in House of Commons
1891	Parnell repudiated by Irish voters after O'Shea divorce scandal, and dies
1893	Gladstone's Second Irish Home Rule Bill defeated in House of Lords
1904	Yeats and Augusta Gregory found Irish national (Abbey) Theatre
1911	House of Lords veto abolished retaining two years' delay
1912–14	Third Home Rule passed: Tories back Ulster Unionist threat of armed resistance
1916	Easter Rising allied with Germany defeated after UK bombardment of Dublin
1916–22	David Lloyd George UK Prime Minister
1918	General Elections produce Irish majority for separatist nationalists
1919	Irish republican guerrillas begin Anglo-Irish war
1920	Government of Ireland Act creates Northern Ireland as six-county substate of UK; Episcopalian state Church of Wales disestablished and disendowed
1921	George V opens Northern Ireland Parliament and demands UK peace in Ireland
1922	Establishment of Irish Free State under Government of Ireland Act 1922; Irish republican minority reject Treaty Settlement with UK, starting civil war
1926	Hugh MacDiarmid's Scots epic *A Drunk Man Looks at the Thistle*
1927	The United Kingdom of Great Britain and Northern Ireland adopted as state title
1934	Scottish National Party founded

1937	De Valera's Constitution of Eire adopted claiming 32 counties but acting for 26
1939	Death of WB Yeats
1939–45	World War II
1949	Eire becomes Republic of Ireland, leaving British Commonwealth of Nations
1950	Death of George Bernard Shaw
1955	Ireland admitted to United Nations
1970	IRA supplant Northern Ireland civil rights movement inaugurating 28 years' warfare
1978	Death of Hugh MacDiarmid
1979	Scotland passes Referendum for devolved legislature, dropped by Callaghan
1981	Death of Bobby Sands after 66 days on hunger strike
1997	Referendums demand Scottish Parliament and Welsh Assembly duly implemented
2007	Scottish National Party elected minority Scottish Government under Salmond
2011	Queen Elizabeth visits Dublin honouring graves of 1916 insurrection leaders
2014	Scottish Referendum rejects independence for Scotland by 55 per cent
	Nicola Sturgeon takes over from Alex Salmond as SNP Leader and First Minister, becoming the first woman in either position
2016	UK Referendum votes UK from European Union, Scotland votes 62 per cent to remain
2020	UK officially leaves the EU and agreed a final deal in December
2021	Alex Salmond and Laurie Flynn found an alternative nationalist and pro-independence political party, The Alba Party. Pro-independence parties, SNP and Greens, win majority in Holyrood elections.

Acknowledgments

I WROTE THIS BOOK out of gratitude to Scotland and its non-violent nationalism. I was born a Dublin Catholic in 1938. Nationalism was part of us, and people talking about it seemed showing off. Eire had a few opponents of Irish nationalism, mostly Protestants. Its violent irreconcilables the IRA allied with Hitler in World War II in hopes of his conquest of Eire. Protestant nationalisms in Eire resembled our own in unquestioning piety, still nurturing the diminished fires for its Unionist household gods with the editorial aid of the *Irish Times* (until UK repression of Cypriot nationalism in 1955). Irish nationalism as a state creed reinforced by newspaper polemics resembled English nationalism published in England for the English: much of official state Irish nationalism was based on Irish awareness of English nationalist practice. Eire showed its independence by maintaining some administrative policies where the UK had left them in 1922.

Each kind of nationalist doctrine assumed that the ultimate ethic for each was military victory. Might was right, whether in the thin red line of heroes maintaining the British Empire or in successful Irish Catholic ambushes of the Anglo-Irish war of 1919–21. For those nationalisms waxing strong on their rulers' versions of history, what had happened since 1918 was something left with thanks to God for making sure we Irish had won, just as in the next island the British thanked Him for saving them and their King. The same was true of Northern Ireland's Unionist Protestants who, unlike most English, were interested in Irish History, but thanked God that they had won and that so had the English when you could rely on them. But in the 26 counties few of us travelled in Northern Ireland: we knew the English better than we knew our fellow-Irish in the north, and they knew the English better than they knew us. Ulster Unionists were overwhelmingly Conservative but Northern Ireland's maintenance of the Union of Great Britain and Northern Ireland was ensured by the UK welfare state forced down the throats of its governing Unionists of 1945–51.

The English and the Americans in general seldom admitted English or American nationalisms, still less that the American war of independence in 1775–1783 had been the product of a clash between them. The Irish throughout Ireland commemorated 17th century warfare between British and Irish, celebrated by Ulster Protestants on 12 July (Battle of the Boyne), while Irish Gaelic poetry studied in schools remembered the Catholic version. Tudor conquest in Ireland seemed obviously between two nations, and the spirit of mutual hostility might as well be called nationalism. And when you started looking at them, expressions of nationalism drew very heavily on ancient legends surviving in various parts of our archipelago, on the Judaeo-Christian tradition, and on Homeric legend as retold by the Greeks and exploited by the Romans. So I must thank my own teachers, fellow-students, and pupils, in our archipelago or in North America. Irishwomen and Irishmen talked endlessly about our country in my hearing, greatly intermingled with religion, thus breeding confidence in the truth of what they were saying. Irish talkers were learned in various ways, and their sources were not merely Irish. Most had read or been told Biblical narratives, especially on the life of Christ. Apart from Our Lord, the teacher many knew best was Shakespeare.

Acknowledgments are thanks to our benefactors, ancestors, parents, relatives, sponsors, teachers, friends, colleagues, partners, children, pupils, students, librarians, pastors, leaders, declaring personal nationalism – what Edmund Burke called our 'little platoon', happy in our debts to those we thank, testifying that they enlarged our knowledge, and that without them we are the poorer. My own first debt is to God without Whom I certainly could not have done this, although I alone am to blame for obstinate errors. Nationalism evolved out of religion, twinned with it, partnered it, argued with it, copied it, exploited it, resented it, disgraced it, and is incomprehensible without it. I saw the omnipresence and antiquity of nationalism. I saw nationalism, however cultural and communal, breeding belief in justification by violence. African Americans taught me how nationalism did not require violence and was spoiled by it. Their non-violent demand for equality was nourished from the Bible sustaining their courage and self-respect under slavery, segregation, and racial murder, preaching the courage of the Jews under persecution, imprisonment, exile and martyrdom, crowned with the sacrifice of Jesus for the redemption of the world. From Jesus to Martin Luther King was a clear line of ideology and example, through which African Americans proved themselves a nation, and the love they returned for hatred vindicated nationalism. Journalists, soldiers, police and historians give excessive attention to violence, but non-violence drove the advocates of civil rights including Ireland's leading opponent of slavery Daniel O'Connell.

My benefactors in making this book have been many throughout over 80 years of my life. Dr Colin Affleck read an early draft and eradicated many absurdities, with characteristic care and wisdom. I have learned much from Professor David Aberle, Dr Paul Addison, Dr Osita Godfrey Agbim, Reverend Dr Robert Akroyd, Professor Anthony Aldgate, Professor Robert Anderson, Dr John Appel, John Arnott, Dr Neal Ascherson, Dr Bernard Aspinwall, Professor Bernard Bailyn, Professor Charles A Barker, Dr Nicolas Barker, Dr Thomas J Barron, Colin Bell, Professor Geoffrey Best, Dr Eberhard ('Paddy') Bort, Reverend Professor Ian Boyd, Dr John Brown, Professor Edwin R Bingham, Dr Adam Brown, Professor Stewart J Brown, Professor Thomas N Brown, Dr Noel Browne, Ms Morag Bruford, Norman Buchan, Dr George Buchanan, Professor Sir Herbert Butterfield, Professor Gilbert A Cahill, Angus Calder, Professor Ewen Cameron, Professor Ian Campbell, John Campbell, Professor Nicholas Canny, Elisabeth and Geoffrey Carnall, James and Mrs May Carty, Alastair Cherry, Joanna Cherry, Professor Aidan Clarke, Professor Frank Cogliano, Professor James V Compton, Robin Cook, Alfred Coppola, Reverend Professor Patrick J Corish, Dr Jack Cormack, Professor James Cornford, Michael Coyne, Professor Jeremy Crang, Professor Bernard Crick, Professor David Daiches, Tam Dalyell of the Binns, Dr John Davies, Professor Sir Thomas and Lady Devine, Donald Dewar, Professor Harry Dickinson, Dr Thomas Dolan, Lord

Hugh Douglas-Hamilton, Lord James Douglas-Hamilton, Revd Kevin Douglas, Dame Jean Conan Doyle, Sir John Drummond, Most Reverend Joseph Duffy, Professor Paul Dukes, Professor Tom Dunne, Jim Dunnigan, Kathleen Lady Dunpark, Jim Eadie, Ms Brigid Teresa Dudley Edwards, Ms Mary Dudley Edwards, Dr Michael Edwards, Professor Robert and Mrs Sheila Dudley Edwards, Dr Ruth Dudley Edwards, Professor Marianne Elliott, Rt Reverend Monsignor John Tracy Ellis, Professor Richard Ellmann, Gwynvor Evans, Dr Winifred Ewing, Jim Fairlie, Dr William Ferguson, Professor Kenneth J Fielding, SE Allen Figgis, Dr Helen Finnie, Professor Thomas Flanagan, Michael Foot, Professor RF Foster, Professor Alastair Fowler, Philip French, Christopher Fyfe, Douglas Gageby, Michael Gallagher, Professor Tom Gallagher, Llew Gardner, Professor Norman and Mrs Dorothy Gash, Mrs Rosemary Gentleman, Professor Anthony A Goodman, Professor Susan-Mary Grant, Professor ERR Green, Dr Geoffrey Green, Richard Lancelyn Green, Ms Deirdre Grieve, Dorian Grieve, Michael Grieve, John Tudor Gwynn, James Halliday, Professor John D Hargreaves, Noel Hartnett, Sir Rupert Hart-Davis, Professor Christopher Harvie, Reverend Professor Adrian Hastings, Ms Anne Havard, Professor Denys Hay, Professor Michael Heale, Professor Waldo H Heinrichs, Dr Patrick Henchy, Hamish Henderson, President Chaim Herzog, President Michael D Higgins, Dr Fabian Hilfrich, Merlin Holland, Richard Holloway, Professor Andrew Hook, Dr Tom Hubbard, Dr John Hutchinson, Professor Alvin Jackson, Professor Rhodri Jeffreys-Jones, Jack Johnston, Professor Hugh Kearney, Denis Kennedy, Mrs May Kennedy, Michael Kennedy, Professor Kevin Kenny, Professor Dermot Keogh, Revernd Fergus Kerr, Professor Declan Kiberd, Professor VG Kiernan, Laura Kuenssberg, Professor Emmet Larkin, Professor Maurice Larkin, Professor Owen Lattimore, Professor Nigel Leask, Professor JJ Lee, Ms Elizabeth Balbirnie Lee, Fergus Linehan senior, Magnus Linklater, Dr Jennifer Litster, Captain Denis Little, Mrs Maureen Little, Michael Little, Ms Catherine Lockerbie, Professor Edna Longley, Dr Michael Longley, Professor Walter D Love, Professor Michael Lynch, Professor Patrick Lynch, Professor FSL Lyons, Willie Lyttel, President Mary McAleese, Kenny MacAskill, Revd Herbert McCabe, Professor Lawrence J

McCaffrey, Norman MacCaig, Jack McConnell, Professor Sir Neil MacCormick, Hugh MacDiarmid, Reverend Alex MacDonald, Ms Margo McDonald, Professor RB McDowell, Dr Duncan Maclaren, Dr Leslie Macfarlane, Dr Christopher McGimpsey Dr Ian McGowan, Dr Catherine McGowan, Dr Michael McGrath, Tom and Professor Thomas McGrath, Dr Robert MacIntyre, Professor Richard Mackenney, Dr Duncan MacLaren, Dr James Maclean, Dolvan Maclennan Micheal MacLiammóir, Alf Mac Lochlainn, Archbishop Malcolm McMahon, Professor James F McMillan, Ms Joyce McMillan, Sean Mac Réamoinn, Ken Maginnis, Professor James Maguire, Professor Aubrey Manning, Allan Massie, Dr Robin Marsh, Professor Peter and Ms Liselotte Marshall, Dr John McInnes, Mitch Miller, Professor FX Martin, Professor Robert Mason, Jamie Maxwell, Stephen Maxwell, Brian Meek, Bill Meek, Professor Rosalind Mitchison, Professor TW Moody, Dr Kenneth Morgan, Roger Mullin, Professor John A Murphy, Tom Nairn, Sandy Neilson, Dr Colin Nicolson, Professor Kevin B Nowlan, Professor Conor and Ms Maire Cruise O'Brien, Cardinal Keith Patrick O'Brien, Leon O Broin, Reverend Thomas O'Callaghan, Basil O'Connell, Professor Maurice O'Connell, Sean O Faolain, Aindreas O Gallchoir, Tadhg O Murchadha, Professor Thomas P O'Neill, Dr Helen O'Shea, Mr John Osmond, John, Mary and Patrick O'Sullivan, Professor Gearoid O Tuathaigh, Professor Peter Parish, Professor Lynn Parsons, Drs Sara and Paul Parvis, Professor Lindsay Paterson, Mark Peel, Basil Peterson, Henry L Philip, Dr Nicholas Phillipson, Professor A Finn Pollard, Professor Kenneth Wiggins Porter, Dr Leila Prescott, Professor David Quinn, Reverend Professor Oliver Rafferty, Pat John Rafferty, Sir George Reid, Professor Alen Riach Dr Douglas Cameron Riach, Principal Duncan Rice, Reverend Professor John Richardson, James Robertson, President Mary Robinson, Professor WW Robson, Professor Johnny Rodger, Rabbi David Rosen, Rabbi Michael Rosen, Dr Michael Rosie, Very Reverend Anthony Ross, Desmond Ryan, Dr Reza Sabri-Tabrizi, Ms Moira Salmond, Dr Roger Savage, Brendan Scott, Ms Melanie Scott, Dr John Joseph Shanley, Dr Owen Sheehy-Skeffington, Tommy Sheppard, Professor George ('Sam') Shepperson, Robert Shirley, Jim Sillars, Sean Skeffington, Professor Christopher Smout,

Professor David Sorensen, Martin Spencer, Professor David Spring, Bridget Stevens, Professor ATQ Stewart, Douglas E Stewart, Miss Pat Storey, Mrs Pat Strong, Ms Nicola Sturgeon, John Swinney, James Thin, Dafydd Elis Thomas, Ms Elizabeth and George Thomas, Mark Thomson and the cast of his Royal Lyceum Theatre production of *Iliad*, Ms Elizabeth and George Thomas, Dr David Thornley, Professor Charles Townshend, Professor John Tricamo, David Trimble, Denis Tuohy, Moya Tuohy, Dr Rosemary Tyzack, Professor Norman Vance, Gore Vidal, Mrs Elizabeth and James Wall, Eileen and Francis Wall, Mrs Maureen Wall, Michael O'Neill Walshe, Ms Agnes Watson, Terence de Vere White, Revd Dr Iain Whyte, Dr Jonathan Wild, Dr David Williams, T Michael Williams, Ms Leslie L Williams, Dr Phil Williams, Professor William HA Williams, Gordon Wilson, Cardinal Thomas Winning, William Wolfe, Ian S Wood, Richard Wood, Professor C Vann Woodward, Professor Michael Worton, Allen Wright, Cameron Wyllie. Many are dead now, but all are most benevolently alive for me.

The National Library of Scotland has been invaluable as always and the personal courtesy and wisdom of all its staff are unrivalled, and I am most grateful to Jawad Rafiq for guidance in Islamic studies. The National Library of Ireland guided my student footsteps; the National Library of Wales and University College Aberystwyth were generous hosts and guides; the British Library, the Library of Congress, the Libraries of Harvard, Yale, South Carolina, and above all Johns Hopkins Universities gave me endless aid, as did those of Aberdeen, Glasgow, Trinity and University College Dublin, and above all of my own Edinburgh University, its resources, colleagues and students.

Gavin MacDougall of Luath Press I came to know in our grief for the loss of Stephen Maxwell and preparation of his work for publication (under the guidance of Stephen's son Jamie) so that this book has been work for a valued colleague and friend as well as homage to another. Alice Latchford as a classicist provided admirable inspiration as my Luath editor in the early stages. Frances Tappin edited this book for Luath in its later and final stages despite Covid-19 and its global effects. She is a first-class graduate of our University, in

Philosophy, and she has shown herself a first-class publishing editor at the outset of her career. Her patience, thoughtfulness, wisdom, understanding, industry, vigilance – these only begin the summation of her quality and promise of a great future. No author can have more reason for gratitude than this one.

I am deeply grateful to Michael Longley for permission to reprint 'Cease-fire', and for the wisdom and beauty of all his poetic invocation of the classics. My debts to the late Conor Cruise O'Brien are gigantic, and this book mounts them up still further, including the inspiration and quotation from his *God Land*, countless other great works in which he has taught us all so much, and his personal guidance, wisdom and affection for half a century. I have to think his literary executor and our friend Michael Williams whose constructive hard questioning constantly kept my ideas on nationalism on their toes. I have to thank all the Grieve family for so much, and specifically to Deirdre and Dorian Grieve for permission to quote from Hugh MacDiarmid.

And had it not been for the endless patience and technological skills of our beloved next-door neighbours Dominic Koe and Heather Stewart, this book would never have been accomplished.

Also, many thanks to Rachael Murray for ultimate supervision.

University of Edinburgh
ODE

Index

JAMES, Saint, disciple of Jesus and
author of Epistle 204
JAMES I, King of Scots, prisoner in
England, poet, later killed in
Scotland 226
JAMES II, King of Scots, ruthless
authoritarian killed by exploding
cannon 226
JAMES IV, King of Scots, self-styled
Emperor killed in battle of
Flodden 69, 226
JAMES V, King of Scots, husband
of two successive French
wives 231, 236
JAMES VI AND I, King of Great
Britain 11, 14, 17,
31-32, 68, 69, 88,
116, 117, 119, 133,
148, 152, 162, 182, 207,
217-246
JAMES VII AND II, King of
Great Britain ousted for his
Catholicism 36, 78, 148,
172, 248
'JAMES III AND VIII, King of Great
Britain', its unsuccessful
invader 78
JAY, John, Chief Justice, USA 45
JEFFERSON, Thomas, drafted
Declaration of Independence, 3rd
President USA 61, 196
JENKINS, Robert, Captain, wounded
by Spanish officials with loss of
ear 32
JENKYNS, Richard, encyclopaedic
analyst of Virgil, 207
JEREMIAH, Old Testament
prophet 146, 149
JESUS CHRIST 28, 40, 71,
78, 95, 96, 111-112,
125-126, 132, 136, 138,
141, 144-145, 149, 157,

162, 182, 205, 256, 257,
259, 263-264, 267, 292
JOAN/JEANNE D'ARC, Saint,
early French nationalist and
martyr 19, 60, 123, 126,
223, 245
JOEL, Son of Samuel 160
JOHN the Baptist, Saint, forerunner
and kinsman of Jesus 132,
144, 162, 259
JOHN the Evangelist, Saint, disciple
particularly beloved of
Jesus 162, 202
JOHN XXII, Pope, French cleric,
resident at Avignon, impressive
administrator 83, 141, 265,
284
JOHN XXIII, Saint, Pope, reformer of
Roman Catholic Church 83,
141, 265
JOHN, King of England, youngest son
of Henry II, lost Normandy to
France 43, 158
JOHN PAUL II, Saint, Pope, Polish
survivor of Nazi and Communist
rule 83, 148
JOHN of Gaunt, son of Edward
III, ancestor of Lancastrian
kings 69, 219, 223
JOHN, Don, of Austria (i.e. Don Juan
of Spain) 224-225
JOHNSON, Boris, Prime
Minister 10, 11, 13,
21, 24, 33-34, 50,
85, 87, 97, 98, 106,
166, 178
JOHNSON, Lyndon Baines, 36th
President, USA 156, 269
JOHNSTONE, Tom, Secretary of State
for Scotland, pioneer Socialist
polemicist 273

SANDERS, Bernie, US Senator, Presidential candidate 100
SARWAR, Anas, Scottish Labour leader 114
SASSOON, Siegfried 136
SAUL, King of Israel 150, 152
SCHUMACHER, Ernst Friedrich, philosopher 21
SCOTT, Sir Walter 43, 61, 73-74, 132, 142, 168, 271, 274, 276-278
SCOTT-MONCREIFF, George 138
SELKIRK, Alexander, pre-Crusoe 31
SELLAR, William Carruthers 59, 71
SEWARD, William H., Governor, Senator, Secretary of State USA 51
SEYMOUR, Thomas, Admiral, Lord 248
SHAKESPEARE, Hamnet 224
SHAKESPEARE, William 11, 13, 16-17, 22, 60, 71-72, 96, 143, 176, 182, 185, 218, 246, 247
SHAPIRO, James, historian of Shakespeare 227
SHAW, Revd Francis, S.J. 266-267
SHAW, George Bernard 224, 252, 262-264
SHELLEY, Percy Bysshe 277
SHEPPARD, Oliver, sculptor 265
SHIRLEY, Robert, economist 109
SIMPSON, James Young the younger 138
SIWARD, Earl (Jarl) of Northumbria, initially vassal to King Cnut 221, 229
SIWARD the younger 229
SMITH, Anthony D., historian 19
SMITH, John 118

SMITH, Sydney Goodsir 147, 272
SMYLLIE, Robert Maire 251, 252
SOCRATES 143, 205
SOLOMON 222, 245
SOMERSET, Edward Seymour 5th Duke, Lord Protector 245
SOPHOCLES 180
SOUTHAMPTON, Henry Wriothesley 3rd Earl 245
SPARK, Muriel 73
SQUIRE, John Collings 125
STALIN, Josef 44
STANLEY — see DERBY
STARMER, Sir Keir 10, 29
STEVENSON, Robert Louis 73, 270, 271
STEWART, Donald, Provost of Stornoway, SNP President, and legislator 92
STEWART, Rory 98
STONE, Harlan Fiske, Chief Justice USA 50
STORRAR, Revd William 165
STOWE, Harriet Beecher 56
STUART, Esme, 1st Duke of Lennox 232
STURGEON. Nicola 85, 97
SWIFT, Jonathan 138

TACITUS, P. Cornelius 24, 212-213
TALIESIN 22
TARQUINIUS SUPERBUS, dethroned Roman King 208
TAYLOR, Ann 136
TAYLOR, Jane 136
TAYLOR, Alan John Percivale 40
TAYLOR, Zachary, President USA 51
TENNYSON, Alfred 1st Lord 42, 194-199, 202

Luath Press Limited

committed to publishing well written books worth reading

LUATH PRESS takes its name from Robert Burns, whose little collie Luath (*Gael.*, swift or nimble) tripped up Jean Armour at a wedding and gave him the chance to speak to the woman who was to be his wife and the abiding love of his life. Burns called one of the 'Twa Dogs' Luath after Cuchullin's hunting dog in Ossian's *Fingal*. Luath Press was established in 1981 in the heart of Burns country, and is now based a few steps up the road from Burns' first lodgings on Edinburgh's Royal Mile. Luath offers you distinctive writing with a hint of unexpected pleasures.

Most bookshops in the UK, the US, Canada, Australia, New Zealand and parts of Europe, either carry our books in stock or can order them for you. To order direct from us, please send a £sterling cheque, postal order, international money order or your credit card details (number, address of cardholder and expiry date) to us at the address below. Please add post and packing as follows: UK – £1.00 per delivery address; overseas surface mail – £2.50 per delivery address; overseas airmail – £3.50 for the first book to each delivery address, plus £1.00 for each additional book by airmail to the same address. If your order is a gift, we will happily enclose your card or message at no extra charge.

Luath Press Limited
543/2 Castlehill
The Royal Mile
Edinburgh EH1 2ND
Scotland
Telephone: +44 (0)131 225 4326 (24 hours)
email: sales@luath. co.uk
Website: www. luath.co.uk